EEG METHODS FOR THE PSYCHOLOGICAL SCIENCES

CHERYL L DICKTER AND PAUL D KIEFFABER

Los Angeles | London | New Delhi
Singapore | Washington DC

Los Angeles | London | New Delhi
Singapore | Washington DC

Learning Matters
An imprint of SAGE Publications Ltd
1 Oliver's Yard
55 City Road
London EC1Y 1SP

SAGE Publications Inc.
2455 Teller Road
Thousand Oaks, California 91320
SAGE Publications India Pvt Ltd

B 1/I 1 Mohan Cooperative Industrial Area
Mathura Road
New Delhi 110 044

SAGE Publications Asia-Pacific Pte Ltd
3 Church Street
#10-04 Samsung Hub
Singapore 049483

Editor: Michael Carmichael
Editorial assistant: Keri Dickens
Production editor: Imogen Roome
Copyeditor: Elaine Leek
Proofreader: Mary Dalton
Indexer: Adam Pozner
Marketing manager: Alison Borg
Cover design: Wendy Scott
Typeset by: C&M Digitals (P) Ltd, Chennai, India
Printed in India at Replika Press Pvt Ltd

Library of Congress Control Number: 2013937182

British Library Cataloguing in Publication data

A catalogue record for this book is available from
the British Library

ISBN 978-1-4462-4923-9
ISBN 978-1-4462-8300-4 (pbk)

TABLE OF CONTENTS

ABOUT THE AUTHORS

Cheryl L. Dickter is an Assistant Professor in the Department of Psychology and a Faculty Affiliate of the Neuroscience Program at the College of William and Mary in Williamsburg, VA, USA. She received her Ph.D. in Social Psychology from the University of North Carolina in 2006. Her research uses a social cognitive neuroscience approach to examine how individuals perceive members of different social groups, and how these perceptions differ based on contextual information such as stereotypes. Dr. Dickter also examines how the cognitive processes involved in the processing of drug-related stimuli are affected by exposure, craving, and motivation. Her research has been funded by the National Science Foundation and the National Institutes of Health.

Paul D. Kieffaber is an Assistant Professor in the Department of Psychology and a Faculty Affiliate of the Neuroscience Program and the Department of Applied Science at the College of William and Mary in Williamsburg, VA, USA. He received a dual-degree Ph.D. in Psychology and Cognitive Science from Indiana University-Bloomington in 2006. Dr. Kieffaber's research is focused on the psychophysiology of attention and cognitive control. His research aims to develop models of the component cognitive processes inherent to constructs like attention, task-set, and cognitive control and to improve our understanding about the mechanisms of cognitive dysfunction in psychopathology.

PREFACE

Neuroscience methods have become integrated with nearly all domains of psychological inquiry over the past several decades. Once thought to be an archaic technology likely to fade into the shadow of techniques like functional magnetic resonance imaging, electroencephalography (EEG) as a research tool in social and personality psychology has instead seen dramatic increases in application. This trend is likely due to both rapid advances in desktop computing, making possible highly sophisticated analysis of the information-rich EEG signals, and to the affordability and accessibility of EEG by comparison with other brain imaging technologies. Our foremost goal in authoring this book was to provide an introduction to the technology and techniques of EEG in the context of social neuroscience research that would appeal to both individuals wishing to broaden their research aims to include EEG measures and to individuals already using EEG, but wishing to develop a better understanding of the technology and methods. This book provides an introduction to the theory, technology, and techniques of EEG data analysis with a focus on providing practical skills required to engage this popular technology.

Beginning with a brief history of EEG and an important background in the neural basis and electric principles involved in recording EEG, readers will be introduced to many practical considerations of EEG recordings and guidelines for the configuration of an EEG laboratory including hardware and software considerations. This book will also provide readers with practical skills required to perform conventional analyses with EEG data in the context of contemporary social neuroscience research. Analyses covered include event-related potentials, spectral asymmetry, and time-frequency analysis. For each type of analysis, we provide a conceptual background, a review of the application of that method to contemporary research within the fields of social and personality psychology, and a guided analysis including step-by-step instruction for performing the analysis in EEGlab. Sample datasets are provided for each of the analyses on a companion website (www.sagepub.co.uk/dickter). Finally, we end with a review of several additional research areas within social and personality psychology to provide a demonstration of how EEG measures have been used to answer important research questions, and provide suggestions for future directions for using EEG methods to study additional social and personality psychological issues.

This book will likely be particularly appealing to new investigators setting up an EEG laboratory, especially those in the social and personality psychology fields. In addition, researchers who already use EEG techniques in their laboratory will find this book useful as an instruction manual to help new research assistants with background and instructional information. This book will also serve well as a text-book in a graduate or an upper-division undergraduate course in any area of behavioral neuroscience such as social neuroscience or cognitive neuroscience, as it provides a solid introduction to EEG and its techniques while also supplying datasets with step-by-step instructions in which students will be able to obtain practical experience with EEG data analysis using free, easily accessible software. Finally, this book is a good reference text for graduate students, post-doctoral students, and faculty studying social and personality psychology who currently employ EEG techniques.

1

INTRODUCTION TO SOCIAL NEUROSCIENCE

Social and personality psychologists have historically excelled as behavioral scientists, tackling difficult questions about the complexities of human social behavior. The tools of social and personality psychologists have traditionally been questionnaires, behavioral paradigms, and observational skills. Within the last two decades, however, research in social and personality psychology has become increasingly imbued with neuroscience methods. The field of social neuroscience has emerged as a popular subfield in its own right, including specialized societies, journals, conferences, and textbooks. Indeed, there has been an explosion of interest in the field over the past few decades as neuroscience methods have become increasingly available and accessible to social and personality psychologists trying to address questions about the biological underpinnings of human social behavior.

WHAT IS SOCIAL NEUROSCIENCE?

The term social neuroscience was first used by John Cacioppo and Gary Berntson in a 1992 publication in *American Psychologist*, in which they wrote about the place of social psychological research and theory in the 'decade of the brain'. In fact, because of this landmark publication and years of significant contributions to the literature, John Cacioppo and Gary Berntson are often regarded as the fathers of social neuroscience. Put simply, the term 'social neuroscience' refers to a field that is broadly defined by its aim of developing an understanding about how information relevant to our social interactions is processed by the brain. Social neuroscience is a highly interdisciplinary field, attracting anthropologists, economists, neuroscientists, philosophers, psychiatrists, psychologists, and sociologists, each of whom bring a unique perspective to bear on questions about human social information processing. At the heart of the field is a dedication to understanding how biological systems affect social processes and behavior. More specifically, the goal of the field is to understand the cellular, genetic, hormonal, and neural mechanisms that determine the nature of social behavior and the cognitive processes that are engaged in the course of social interaction.

ORY OF SOCIAL NEUROSCIENCE

rest in understanding how the brain and social behavior are related began long
ore social or personality psychology were defined as fields. Indeed, Erasistratos, a
Greek doctor in the 3rd century BC, in trying to find the cause of a boy's erratic heart
rate, measured the boy's heart beat in the presence of his attractive stepmother.
Erasistratos concluded that infatuation, not an illness, was causing the variability in
heart rate. Many centuries later, individuals interested in identifying the strength of
personality traits such as conscientiousness and skills such as language used phrenology diagrams to locate bumps on the skull that supposedly corresponded to such
traits and skills. Although work by phrenologists like Franz Joseph Gall has long been
discredited (though phrenology services were ruled to be subject to a 6% sales tax in
Michigan as recently as December 2007), the idea behind phrenology was not a bad
one. That is, although specific functions of the brain are not related to the location of
bumps on the skull, the notion that they may be localized in the brain has been a
major impetus for cognitive neuroscience research over the past few decades.

The most notable early observation of functional specialization in the brain
comes from the story of Phineas Gage and his fateful accident in 1848. While working with explosives and an iron tamping bar to prepare a road for an impending
railroad track, the blasting powder exploded, sending the 3-foot iron rod into the
side of Gage's face and through his brain. Though the rod completely passed
through Gage's brain, he survived the incident, but not without changes to his personality and social behavior. That Gage's social behavior became intolerable to
those who knew him but that his other cognitive abilities such as speech remained
intact provided important evidence to support the idea of functional specialization
in the brain. A great deal of evidence for this kind of functional specialization has
accumulated over the last several decades, but there is also a general consensus
among neuroscientists that many different areas of the brain likely work together
to make complex behavior and mental processes possible.

As mentioned above, psychologists have been successful in using behavioral and
self-report measures to assess social phenomena. At the same time, researchers have
been aware of the drawbacks of relying on such methods to investigate certain social
processes that cannot be assessed by behavioral measures, and have tried a variety
of methods to evaluate these underlying processes. For example, researchers studying racial prejudice against Blacks in the United States in the mid-20th century began
to worry that White participants in their studies were not answering questions hon-
estly regarding their attitudes about Blacks. That is, they worried that self-report
methods were susceptible to self-presentation biases that arose from an increase in
egalitarian racial attitudes and a general stigma against those with racist beliefs. To
examine more subtle measures of racial bias, Rankin and Campbell (1955) conspicu-
ously measured galvanic skin response – a measure of anxiety – and found that White
participants had greater skin conductance when interacting with a Black compared
to a White experimenter. To more directly examine the effects of social desirability in
the measurement of racial attitudes, Sigall and Page (1971) used a bogus pipeline
procedure in which participants who were told that the electrodes on their arms
were connected to a (fake) lie detector machine admitted to more racially biased

attitudes than participants who simply provided their racial attitudes. The findings from this line of research suggest that relying on self-reported measures of racial prejudice, which have demonstrated steady declines in negative racial attitudes over the past 70 years (e.g., Devine & Elliot, 1995), may not accurately portray the true state of affairs in Whites' racial attitudes. For psychologists interested in studying phenomena such as prejudice, a neuroscience measure that permits the characterization of processes that are unknown to participants or considered undesirable may therefore be appealing. The field of racial prejudice is just one area in which researchers may desire to assess phenomena that are subject to social biases; we will describe several other areas of research throughout this book that have and can benefit from the use of neuroscience measures.

The development of new and exciting measurement techniques has played a role in the use of physiological measures throughout the years. One of the first tools developed to measure a physiological event was the capillary electrometer, which was developed in the 1870s and used mercury to measure electrical activity with electrodes. It was used by Waller in 1887 to record the electrical activity of the human heart. Social psychologists today use heart rate to study threat and challenge responses (e.g., Blascovich & Tomaka, 1996). Human electroencephalography (EEG) was popularized in 1929 by Berger to measure electrical activity in the brain using electrodes at the front and the back of the head. Through the years, social and personality psychologists have used developing physiological techniques to better understand social processes such as using electrodes placed on the face to measure muscle movements in the face to study emotional processes (e.g., Cacioppo & Petty, 1981). Modern social psychologists use EEG to examine a host of social processes, such as person perception (see Chapter 5), emotional responses (see Chapter 6), and empathy (see Chapter 7).

In the 1970s and 1980s, the development of new brain imaging methods like computerized axial tomography (CAT) and positron emission tomography (PET) permitted some of the first structural and functional imaging of the brain with good spatial resolution in three dimensions. Only as recently as the early 1990s was functional magnetic resonance imaging (fMRI) introduced to the neuroscience community. Since its introduction, fMRI has been the most popular method for brain imaging due to the fact that it is relatively non-invasive. The explosion of research using fMRI over the past several decades has contributed significantly to the rapid development of our understanding about the localization of function in the brain and has arguably helped shape consensus regarding the critical role of neuroscience in social and personality psychology.

This consensus has been expressed, in part, by the promotion of neuroscience techniques. For example, both the *Journal of Personality and Social Psychology* – one of the leading journals in the field of personality and social psychology – and *Neuropsychologia* included special sections on social neuroscience in 2003. The journal *NeuroImage* followed suit in the next year. In March of 2006 the first journal dedicated to the field, *Social Neuroscience*, was launched, followed quickly by *Social Cognitive and Affective Neuroscience* in June of the same year. In 2010 *Social Cognition* emphasized publications describing how social psychological theory has been advanced by findings in neuroscience, including articles by a number of pioneers in the field of social neuroscience, including David Amodio, Bruce Bartholow, John Cacioppo, William Cunningham, Tiffany Ito, and Jeffrey Sherman. Today social neuroscience research permeates all of the leading journals in the fields of social and personality psychology as well as many general psychological journals.

WHY ADD NEUROSCIENCE METHODS TO SOCIAL AND PERSONALITY PSYCHOLOGY?

Two common fallacies regarding social neuroscience research are (1) that the aim of social neuroscience is to localize (i.e., 'map') psychological processes regarding social and personality variables to specific areas in the brain and (2) that investigators using neuroscience methods are simply rehashing earlier research using behavioral and self-report methods. Although each of these research approaches has its time and place, applying neuroscience techniques to social and personality research questions can add much more to the field than these limited directions.

One way that the use of neuroscience methods can aid in studying substantive questions related to social and personality psychology is by providing unobtrusive measures of an individual's response to a stimulus that he/she may be unable or unwilling to report (for a review, see Guglielmi, 1999). Although researchers have begun using implicit measures such as reaction time paradigms to examine less explicit attitudes or biases, these measures also have their drawbacks. For example, although often discussed as reflecting cognitive processes, reaction time data actually reflect the outcome of a cognitive operation rather than the operation itself. That is, reaction time data confound concept activation with response output processes (Ito, Thompson, & Cacioppo, 2004), and thus cannot indicate the level at which the cognitive process occurs. It is often desirable and perhaps necessary to expand existing behavioral research on a topic to a methodology that allows the examination of multiple components of the cognitive process. Neuroscience measures can provide a multifaceted picture of the neural activity associated with a given cognitive process.

Another benefit that neuroscience measures can offer social and personality psychologists is the identification of the time-course of specific cognitive processing that occurs as a result of social events. That is, the use of neuroscience methods such as EEG allows for the precise measurement of rapid changes in neural activity related to observable stimuli, making it possible to assess the timing of task-relevant cognitive operations and to separate component processes in the stream of information processing (Stern, Ray, & Quigley, 2001). Measures that are temporally accurate are important in studying many phenomena that social and personality psychologists are interested in studying. For example, researchers have used event-related potentials to investigate when the processing of facial expressions occurs. EEG studies demonstrated that faces depicting emotions affect neural processing between 120 and 180 ms following exposure to human faces (see Eimer & Holmes, 2007). These findings have helped inform models of emotional processing and elucidate the time-course of this processing.

Utilizing neuroscience methods can also allow for an examination of the effects of social events and stimuli on neural processing, making it possible to understand how social phenomena affect the brain. Eisenberger, Lieberman, and Williams (2003), for example, used fMRI data to demonstrate that the processing of social pain caused by social rejection is processed in similar brain regions that are activated during the experience of physical pain. Using EEG measures, Crowley, Wu, McCarty, David, Bailey, and Mayes (2009) also demonstrated that the perceived distress experienced by participants following social rejection was correlated with neural responses in the late positive potential after this event. Studies such as these can help provide insight into the neural basis of social cognitive perceptual processes, and help inform theory in social and personality psychology. Some of the major research areas that have been explored with the use of neuroscience methods are described in more detail in later chapters of this book.

There are several imaging technologies that social and personality psychologists use to investigate the neural processes involved in social behavior. The strengths and weaknesses of each measure (e.g., fMRI, PET, EEG) are well documented and thus will not be reviewed extensively here. Social and personality psychologists trying to decide which method is best for them should weigh the benefits and drawbacks of each method for their particular research question in deciding which technology to use. Generally speaking, when trying to identify where in the brain neural activity is occurring resulting from a specific behavior or trait, imaging technologies such as fMRI are better than EEG because with EEG measurement, the minuscule bioelectric voltages produced by post-synaptic potentials are both attenuated and dispersed by the obstacles through which they pass, making it difficult to pinpoint from where they originate. On the other hand, if your goal is to examine the time-course of an unfolding cognitive event or behavior, using EEG would be the better option because of its ability to measure voltage dynamics over time. For example, it is common to record EEG at a rate of 1000 samples/second, permitting a unique characterization of the scalp-recorded voltages every millisecond. This distinguishes EEG from other imaging methods like PET and fMRI that provide temporal resolution on the order of seconds. Importantly, this means that EEG can be effectively used to characterize sensory, perceptual, and cognitive processes as they unfold. Another, more practical advantage of EEG over other imaging methods is the cost. While technologies such as PET and fMRI require millions of dollars in equipment and personnel, an EEG laboratory can be established for well under $50,000 and is generally associated with very low maintenance and operational costs. Because the focus of this book is on EEG, below we briefly review the history and the basic principles of this methodology.

ORIGINS OF ELECTROENCEPHALOGRAPHY

It was just over a century ago that biologists discovered the bioelectric nature of nerve impulses. In 1870, Gustav Fritsch and Eduard Hitzig published a landmark paper entitled 'On the Electrical Excitability of the Cerebrum' (Fritsch & Hitzig, 1870), demonstrating that electrical stimulation of the cerebral cortex could produce limb movements contralateral to the hemisphere of stimulation. In addition to being the first clear experimental demonstration of the involvement of the cerebral cortex in motor function, their research provided the first evidence that the cortex was electrically excitable. Shortly thereafter, Richard Caton (1875) described the first observations of electrical impulses recorded directly from the surface of the cerebral cortex in living, animal subjects. A review of some of these early experiments can be found in Brazier (1963).

In 1929, a German psychiatrist named Hans Berger published his work demonstrating the first recordings of the human electroencephalogram (EEG), opening the door to a new era of neuroscience. At a time when the field was consumed by questions about morphology and cerebral localization, Berger's research prompted a shift to questions about the dynamics of neural activity as reflected in the electrical patterns of the brain. In addition to coining the term 'electroencephalogram', Berger is best known for his observation of rhythmic oscillations in the range of 10–30 Hz, which he likened to the 'rhythm A' component of oscillations that had been previously described in recordings of peripheral action currents in the elbow joint (Hoffman & Strughold, 1927). Berger was also the first to demonstrate that this oscillatory activity, later known as the 'Berger rhythm' or Alpha band (8–13 Hz), was related to the mental state of the individual. For example, he described the so-called alpha blockade or suppression of alpha rhythms that occurs when an individual opens his/her eyes.

As remarkable as the impact of Berger's early research is the primitive nature of the technology with which it was carried out. At the time, electrophysiological activity, including EEG, was recorded by photographing the deflections of the light beam of a galvanometer. Recording these deflections at regular intervals provided a means by which to reconstruct an EEG trace. Galvanometers were soon replaced by cathode-ray oscilloscopes, which displayed voltage as a function of time such that a single photographic record now contained a brief but continuous series of voltages. In the 1940s, two technological leaps for EEG were the development of 'pen writers', which made possible the recording of an immediate and permanent record of the continuous voltage dynamics without the need for photography, and the differential amplifier – a technology still in use today.

Developing alongside these technological advances was recognition of EEG's vast potential as a non-invasive measure of brain activity that could be used to address questions about the nature of sensory, cognitive, and motor functions. For example, Pauline Davis (Davis, 1939) provided one of the first demonstrations of a sensory-evoked potential in the scalp-recorded EEG, presenting participants with acoustic tones while recording from a single EEG channel. Davis observed what she referred to as an 'on-effect', a polyphasic wave immediately subsequent to the onset of an acoustic stimulus. Davis' early research also revealed that 'on-effects' could be observed prior to the onset of the acoustic stimuli after a number of repetitions in a predictable sequence of stimuli. These 'anticipatory' effects may thus constitute one of the first examples of an evoked-potential measure of endogenous cognitive brain activity.

EEG Basics

EEG is a measure of electrical potentials thought to be produced by post-synaptic potentials in the brain. EEG is recorded from sensors (electrodes) placed on the scalp. There are many ways that EEG recordings can be used to address research questions in psychology. One of the most common methods is known as the event-related potential (ERP) technique. The essence of the ERP technique (explained in more detail in Chapter 5) is that brief segments of ongoing brain activity (i.e., EEG) are measured repeatedly immediately following the presentation of some experimentally relevant stimuli (e.g., images, tones, etc.). Because the EEG segments are all taken with respect to the onset of a stimulus, averaging the segments together yields a measure of the EEG voltages that are consistently related to the sensory, perceptual, and decision-making processes that followed the stimulus. Although sometimes used interchangeably, the terms EEG and ERP are used to denote ongoing and event-related brain activity respectively. While the ERP technique is generally concerned with the amplitude of voltages at a specific point in time, other approaches to EEG analysis, including quantitative EEG (qEEG) and event-related oscillation (ERO) techniques, aim to characterize the voltage dynamics over time. The term qEEG is often used to describe the measurement of oscillatory activity in ongoing EEG and, similar to ERP, ERO describes measures of the average oscillatory activity time-locked to experimentally relevant events. EEG and its derivatives (e.g., ERPs, qEEG, and EROs) have been used to address questions in many research contexts relevant to social and personality psychology, several of which will be covered in subsequent chapters of this book.

CONCLUSION

As you can see, social and personality psychologists stand to gain many benefits from utilizing neuroscience measures in their research. Although there are several different neuroscience measures, each with its own strengths and weaknesses, the focus of this book is to describe the use of EEG data in investigating research questions that are typical of social and personality research.

REFERENCES

Berger, H. (1929). Über das Elektrenkephalogramm des Menschen. *European Archives of Psychiatry and Clinical Neuroscience*, *87*(1), 527–570. doi:10.1007/BF01797193.

Blascovich, J., & Tomaka, J. (1996). The biopsychosocial model of arousal regulation. *Advances in Experimental Social Psychology*, *28*, 1–51.

Brazier, M. A. B. (1963). The history of the electrical activity of the brain as a method for localizing sensory function. *Medical History*, *7*(3), 199–211.

Cacioppo, J. T., & Petty, R. E. (1981). Electromyograms as measures of extent and affectivity of information processing. *American Psychologist*, *36*(5), 441–456.

Caton, R. (1875). The electric currents of the brain. *British Medical Journal*, *2*(1), 278.

Crowley, M. J., Wu, J., McCarty, E. R., David, D. H., Bailey, C. A., & Mayes, L. C. (2009). Exclusion and micro-rejection: Event-related potential response predicts mitigated distress. *NeuroReport*, *20*(17), 1518–1522.

Davis, P. A. (1939). Effects of acoustic stimuli on the waking human brain. *Journal of Neurophysiology*, *2*(6), 494 –499.

Devine, P. G., & Elliot, A. J. (1995). Are racial stereotypes really fading? The Princeton trilogy revisited. *Personality and Social Psychology Bulletin, 21*, 1139–1150.

Eimer, M., & Holmes, A. (2007). Event-related brain potential correlates of emotional face processing. *Neuropsychologia, 45*(1), 15–31.

Eisenberger, N. I., Lieberman, M. D., & Williams, K. D. (2003). Does rejection hurt? An fMRI study of social exclusion. *Science, 302*(5643), 290–292.

Fritsch, G. T., & Hitzig, E. (1870). On the electrical excitability of the cerebrum (1870). In G. von Bonin, *Some papers on the cerebral cortex* (pp. 73–96). Springfield, IL: Charles C. Thomas.

Guglielmi, R. S. (1999). Psychophysiological assessment of prejudice: Past research, current status, and future directions. *Personality and Social Psychology Review, 3*(2), 123–157.

Hoffman, P., & Strughold, H. (1927). Ein Beitrag zur Frage der Oszillationsfrequenz der willkurlichen Innervation. *Zsch. Biol., 85*, 599–603.

Ito, T. A., Thompson, E., & Cacioppo, J. T. (2004). Tracking the timecourse of social perception: The effects of racial cues on event-related brain potentials. *Personality and Social Psychology Bulletin, 30*(10), 1267–1280.

Rankin, R. E., & Campbell, D. T. (1955). Galvanic skin response to Negro and white experimenters. *Journal of Abnormal and Social Psychology, 51*(1), 30–33.

Sigall, H., & Page, R. (1971). Current stereotypes: A little fading, a little faking. *Journal of Personality and Social Psychology, 18*(2), 247.

Stern, R. M., Ray, W. J., & Quigley, K. S. (2001). *Psychophysiological recording*. Oxford: Oxford University Press.

2

FROM CORTEX TO COMPUTER: THE PRINCIPLES OF RECORDING EEG

THE NEURAL BASIS OF EEG

Electrical Potentials in the Brain

When scalp-recorded EEG was first described, there was considerable skepticism in the scientific community regarding its validity. Many simply refused to believe that the small electrical potentials generated by neural activity could be recorded at such great (relatively speaking) distances and through barriers such as the meningeal layers, skull, and scalp. Today the physics and physiology that give rise to scalp-recorded EEG are more widely accepted and better understood.

The first step toward understanding the neural origins of EEG is to clarify the difference between electrical current and electrical potential. Electrical current is the *flow* of electric charge, meaning that current (typically measured in amperes) is a measure of the amount of charge moving across a surface in a given time. Electrical currents can be generated in a number of ways. For example, the electrical current that powered your coffeemaker this morning can be attributed to the flow of electrons in the conductive wiring of your home. The electrical currents used by your brain as you read this book, however, are caused by the movement of charged atoms and molecules called ions.

Electrical potential is a form of potential energy and can be thought of as the potential for current to flow. Electrical potential is usually measured in volts (V) and is directly related to the *difference* in charge between two points. One example of how electrical potentials are generated in the brain is the resting membrane potential of neurons. The resting membrane potential is a direct result of the unequal concentration of ions between the inside and outside of the cell, resulting in a difference in charge across those two points. For example, the combination of high concentrations of sodium (Na^+) and chloride (CL^-) ions outside the cell and high concentrations of potassium (K^+) and other anions (negatively charged particles) inside leads to a net difference of charge across the cell membrane measuring approximately 75 millivolts (mV) or 0.075 V. While the resting membrane potential of neurons serves as a good example of how voltages can be generated in the brain, it has no direct relationship to EEG recorded at the scalp. Thus, we now consider two other important sources of voltage in the brain – action potentials and post-synaptic potentials.

Action Potentials

The action potential is the primary means of cell-to-cell communication in the brain and consists of a sequence of transient perturbations of the resting membrane potential. The action potential is characterized by a sudden increase in the permeability of the cell membrane leading to a brief positive 'spike' in the voltage recorded at a given point on the cell. This change in voltage, lasting only about one millisecond, causes a perturbation of the resting membrane potential at neighboring points on the axon, meaning that the action potential will have a consistent trajectory, usually propagating from the cell body to the axon terminals where it triggers the release of neurotransmitters to subsequent neurons.

Post-synaptic Potentials

Neurotransmitters released as the result of an action potential bind to receptor sites on the dendrites of a post-synaptic neuron. Post-synaptic potentials are a consequence of this binding of neurotransmitters with their post-synaptic receptors. Like the action potential, post-synaptic potentials are the result of changes in the permeability of the cell membrane, leading to changes in the concentration of ions (voltage) across the membrane at the receptors location. Unlike the action potential, however, post-synaptic potentials can be either depolarizing (positive change in the resting membrane potential) or hyperpolarizing (negative change in the resting membrane potential). Because action potentials are triggered by positive changes in the resting membrane potential, depolarizing post-synaptic potentials are referred to as excitatory post-synaptic potentials (EPSPs) and, because they decrease the likelihood of an action potential, hyperpolarizing post-synaptic potentials are referred to as inhibitory post-synaptic potentials (IPSPs). Another important characteristic of EPSPs and IPSPs that distinguishes them from action potentials is their time-course. Whereas the action potential is resolved in about one millisecond, EPSPs and IPSPs can span tens to hundreds of milliseconds.

Potentials Measured at the Scalp

You may have noticed that all of the bioelectric potentials just described refer to voltage measured across the cell membrane. While it is certainly possible to record these voltages in vivo using implantable microelectrodes, we must now consider how these minuscule voltages can be recorded at a distance and through a variety of biological tissues including other brain cells, blood, cerebrospinal fluid, skull, and scalp – a process known as 'volume conduction'.

The Electric Field and Electric Dipoles

The first concept important to developing an understanding about how the voltages generated by neuronal activity can be recorded as far away as the scalp is that of the electric field. The electric field is a space surrounding an ion in which

A

B

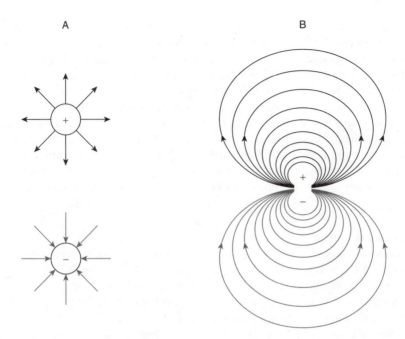

Figure 2.1   (A) Illustration of force exerted by a point charge. (B) Illustration of the forces exerted by an electrical dipole.

force is exerted on other ions. For example, the electrical field produced by a single positively charged ion (e.g., Na^+) exerts a small positive (i.e., repelling) force on neighboring ions with positive charge and a negative (i.e., attracting) force on neighboring ions with a negative charge (see Figure 2.1). The strength of the electric field is related to the magnitude of charge at the source and decreases with the square of the distance between the two ions. Of course, the electric field produced by any one ion is infinitesimal as far away as the scalp, but because the voltage generated by a group of ions is equal to the sum of the voltages of each of the individual charges, large numbers of ions can produce aggregate electric fields strong enough to be measured at a distance.

A second important concept is that of the 'dipole'. When charges of opposite sign are separated in a conductive medium, the combination of their respective electrical fields forms an electrical dipole as depicted in Figure 2.1. Like the electrical potential generated by a point charge, the potential generated by a dipole decreases as a function of distance. However, the voltage generated by a dipole is positive at one end, negative at the other, and decreases to zero as the position of measurement moves from the poles to the perpendicular axis where the positive and negative charges cancel.

Neurophysiologically, dipoles are thought to occur as the result of postsynaptic potentials (EPSPs and IPSPs). For example, an EPSP results in the depolarization of the membrane potential at the dendrite of the post-synaptic cell due to the influx of positively charged sodium (Na^+) ions. This movement of positive charge into the cell leaves behind a region of extracellular space that is now negatively charged with respect to the extracellular space at the opposite end of the post-synaptic neuron. Likewise, an IPSP results in a hyperpolarization of the resting membrane potential. Whether due to the influx of negatively charged ions (Cl⁻) or the efflux of positively charged ions (K⁺), the result is a region of extracellular space near the synapse that is positively charged with respect to the extracellular space at the opposite end of the post-synaptic neuron. In other words, both EPSPs and IPSPs result in a separation of charge in the extracellular space (a conductive medium) inducing an electric dipole with an electrical potential that is theoretically similar to that pictured in Figure 2.1. Again, the voltage produced by a dipole created by the activity at a single synapse is infinitesimally small; however, the synchronous activity of a population of thousands or hundreds of thousands of synapses will summate to produce electrical potentials measureable at the scalp.

Volume Conduction

The summation of electrical potentials occurs as a direct result of 'volume conduction' – a term used to describe the measurement of electrical potentials (or magnetic fields) through biological tissues. It is the propagation of electrical fields through tissue that allows neighboring potentials to sum together. Unlike magnetic fields, however, the volume conduction of electrical fields is impeded to various degrees by tissues with varying conductive properties. For example, tissues with high resistance (e.g., the skull) will tend to attenuate and spread electrical potentials. This distortion of the electrical potential by the tissues through which it must pass is what makes localization of EEG/ERP sources such a challenging problem.

That said, without volume conduction and the summation of electrical potentials there would simply be no measureable EEG signal. However, the additive property of electric fields also imposes a number of constraints on the nature of the brain activity that will be 'visible' to sensors placed at the surface of the scalp. Factors such as cell geometry, dipole orientation, and spatial and temporal contiguity of neural activity all play important roles in determining how brain activity will be expressed as voltages at the scalp.

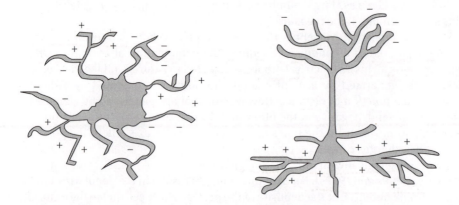

Figure 2.2   (*Left*) Stellate neuron with radial processes. (*Right*) Pyramidal cell with triangular cell body and large apical dendrite extending upward.

Consider, for example, the geometry of stellate and pyramidal neurons (see Figure 2.2). Because of its radial configuration of dendrites, activity at a number of synapses in the stellate neuron will produce small electric dipoles at a variety of orientations, meaning that the positive end of one dipole may be adjacent to the negative end of another. The result is a net cancellation of voltage. The pyramidal cell, by contrast, is characterized by one large apical dendrite and a large number of basal dendrites. With this geometry, activity at a number of synapses (in the apical dendrites for example) produces dipoles with similar orientations and net positive and negative charges at opposite ends of the neuron. When a large number of small dipoles, such as those generated by activity in a pyramidal cell, are summed together, the resulting electrical potential can be described as a single, larger dipole referred to as an 'equivalent current dipole' (ECD). The ECD has an orientation equal to the average of the orientations of the smaller dipoles. It is the electrical potential from these ECDs that is thought to give rise to the EEG signal.

The geometry of the pyramidal cell alone, however, does not ensure that an ECD will be measureable at the scalp because the orientation of the ECD itself will be determined by the orientation of the pyramidal cell. Recall that the voltage produced by a dipole is largest in amplitude at the two poles and decreases to zero at the axis perpendicular to the poles (see Figure 2.1B). Thus, pyramidal cells (and their ECDs) oriented perpendicular to the surface of the scalp will tend to produce strong positive or negative voltages at sites near the region of cortical neural activity. In contrast, pyramidal cells with an orientation that is parallel with the scalp will produce zero (or at least very small) voltages at sensors placed near the region of activity. Fortunately, the pyramidal cells of the cortex tend to possess an orientation that is perpendicular to the surface of the brain, with their apical dendrites occupying the outermost layers of cortex and their cell bodies and basal dendrites

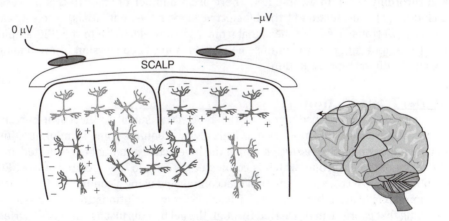

Figure 2.3 Illustration of the propagation of electrical potential to the scalp. Active pyramidal neurons are indicated in black. Note that only the ECD generated by those pyramidal cells oriented perpendicular to the scalp are sensed by the surface electrodes. Because the electrical potential is equal to zero on the perpendicular axis of an ECD, pyramidal neurons oriented parallel to the scalp will not be sensed by nearby electrodes.

occupying deeper layers of cortex. Unfortunately, however, the situation is complicated by the folding of cortical tissue that makes up the sulci and gyri of the brain. This folding of the cortical layers of the brain means that two neighboring populations of pyramidal cells may elicit ECDs of very different orientations causing some cancellation of the voltage observed at the scalp (see Figure 2.3).

The extent to which summation of voltage can occur also depends critically on the spatial and temporal contiguity of neural activity. Spatial contiguity is required because the voltage generated by an ECD decays with distance. Temporal contiguity is required because the voltages due to action potentials and post-synaptic potentials are all discrete, time-limited events. Summation of action potentials requires near simultaneity of neural activity because the time-course of an individual action potential is only about one millisecond. Post-synaptic potentials, however, possess a much more protracted time-course, lasting between tens and hundreds of milliseconds. This property of post-synaptic potentials greatly facilitates voltage summation given that it can be achieved under conditions of slight asynchrony in the activity of individual neurons.

Combined with their geometry and orientation, the fact that pyramidal cells are the most numerous cells in the mammalian cortex gives rise to the contemporary notion that much of the EEG signal reflects the sum of the activities in populations of cortical pyramidal neurons.

PRINCIPLES OF RECORDING EEG

In addition to understanding the principles of volume conduction, including how voltages are induced by post-synaptic potentials and summed at the scalp, it is important to understand the technological principles of measuring those voltages and recording them on a computer. There are a number of steps in this process, including (1) transduction of the bioelectric signals (i.e., potentials) to electrical current, (2) transmission of the signal from a sensing electrode to the EEG amplifier, (3) amplification of the minuscule signals, and (4) conversion of the analog signal to a digital representation.

Signal Transduction

The conversion or 'transduction' of the bioelectric signal to electrical current occurs at the surface of the electrode. This always requires some form of junction between the conductive tissues in which the bioelectric potential is generated and the metal of the electrode, which is connected directly to the circuitry of the EEG amplifier. In most cases, this junction is accomplished using a conductive fluid such as commercially available EEG gels.[1] These electrolyte solutions contain free ions, meaning that charge can be carried through the gel by ions just as charge is carried in biological tissues. Thus, the gel used to make EEG recordings can be considered

---

[1]Capacitive or 'dry' electrodes, which make direct contact with the scalp, are currently available but tend to have recording characteristics inferior to gel-based electrode systems and are not yet widely used.

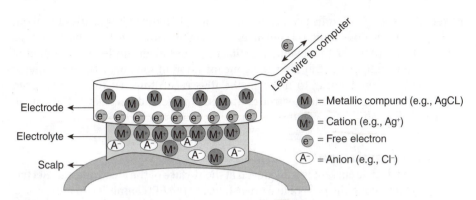

Figure 2.4   Illustration of the distribution of charge in an electrode and electrolyte gel.

an extension of the conductive biological tissues (e.g., brain, CSF, meninges, skull, and scalp) through which the electrical potential must pass before reaching the surface of the electrode. Interaction with the electrolyte gel involves the exchange of charge (electrons) between the gel and the electrode. More specifically, at the electrode's surface, the primary mechanism of signal transduction is redox (oxidation–reduction) reactions involving the exchange of electrons between the gel and the metal of the electrode. Consider, for example, the case of an electrode made of silver chloride (AgCl) in contact with an electrolyte gel. In this case, the movement of an electron from the wire to the electrode-electrolyte junction will result in oxidization of AgCl liberating Cl^- from the electrode to the electrolyte. The reverse process may also occur when Cl^- is reduced as it bonds with the solid silver (Ag) of the electrode, producing AgCl and liberating a free electron to the wire.

Electrode Characteristics
The quality of recorded EEG signals depends, in part, on the electrical characteristics of the electrodes, which is largely determined by the type of metal used. Common metals used to make electrodes for EEG recordings are aluminum, copper, silver, silver–silver chloride, and gold. Each of these metals has different electrical characteristics determined by the way in which they interact with the electrolyte gel.

When the rates of oxidation and reduction reactions at the electrolyte–electrode border are equal, the electrode is said to be 'non-polarizable' and the potential difference between the electrode and the electrolyte gel (absent any additional current) is zero. However, none of the currently available electrodes are truly non-polarizable, meaning that there is some disparity between the rates of oxidation and reduction. This disparity leads to the accumulation of charges of opposite sign on each side of the electrolyte–electrode junction. The voltage produced by this difference in charge between the electrode and electrolyte gel is referred to as the 'electrode potential' or 'half-cell potential' (see Figure 2.4). Large half-cell potentials can be problematic because they can introduce so-called 'DC offset' to the recordings, shifting the mean of the recorded voltage by a constant amplitude in the amount of the half-cell potential. While it may be possible to subtract the DC offset off-line, large DC offset can cause 'clipping' when the voltages are shifted out of range of the analog-to-digital converter. Electrodes with large half-cell potentials can also be more prone to movement artifact because even subtle displacement of the electrode and/or gel can alter the concentration of ions near the electrolyte–electrode junction, leading to noise in the EEG recordings. Of the metals listed above, silver–silver chloride electrodes are often preferred because of their small half-cell potentials.

Signal Transmission

Once the bioelectric current is transduced at the surface of the electrode, the electric current travels along the path of least resistance to the EEG amplifier. In most cases, this transmission of the EEG signal occurs along conductive wiring leading from the sensing electrodes to the circuitry of the amplifier. Lead wiring is typically constructed of a highly conductive material like copper and is typically both insulated and shielded. Insulation of lead wires typically takes the form of a protective jacket surrounding the wire. These insulating jackets have very high resistance to the flow of electric charge, simply preventing the transmission of charge in one lead wire from influencing the signal in neighboring leads. The shielding of lead wires reduces the extent to which electrical noise in the environment (discussed below) interferes with the transmission of the EEG signal. Shielding can be accomplished in a number of ways but often takes the form of a metallic tape or foil surrounding the insulating jacket. The importance of protecting lead wires from electrical noise cannot be understated. This is because virtually all of the electrical noise in EEG recordings is introduced in the lead wires between the electrodes and the amplifier.

Sources of Noise During Transduction/Transmission

There are many potential sources of noise in EEG recordings in addition to the half-cell potential. Importantly, *all* noise (with the exception of instrumental noise) is introduced to the EEG signal during signal transduction and/or transmission. In the context of EEG and/or ERP research, the term 'artifact' is often used to refer to noise in the recordings, which can be any voltages that are not related to the neural process currently under consideration. Three general classes of such artifact are (1) mechanical and instrumental, (2) environmental, and (3) physiological.

Mechanical and Instrumental Artifacts

Perturbation of the half-cell potential by displacement of the electrolyte gel is just one example of mechanical artifact. Artifacts can also be introduced to ongoing EEG recordings by electromagnetic induction. Electromagnetic induction is the process by which current is generated by the movement of a conductive material through a magnetic field. Thus, because the wires conveying current from an individual's scalp to the EEG recording equipment are necessarily highly conductive, their movement can lead to the induction of large (by comparison with the EEG signal of interest) electrical artifacts. Even a static charge carried by an experimenter's favorite wool sweater as she/he walks around the room can induce electrical artifact in the wiring between an electrode and the recording equipment.

One form of instrumental noise is the artifact that is superimposed on the EEG signal by the amplifier itself. Instrumental noise is introduced by all biopotential amplifiers and is due to the electrical currents that power the various components of the device. Reduction of this type of electrical noise can only be accomplished through careful design of the amplifier circuitry. Another form of instrumental noise is 'quantization noise'. Quantization noise occurs during the process of converting analog voltages to digital values that can be stored in a computer. Quantization noise is moderated by factors such as the resolution of the analog-to-digital converter (ADC) and the desired measurement range. Details regarding the resolution and range of the ADC and how they produce quantization noise will be discussed in the Analog to Digital Conversion section below.

Environmental Artifacts

Environmental artifacts, like amplifier noise, are produced by the operation of electrical devices. Unlike amplifier noise, however, many environmental artifacts can be mitigated by either removing the device from the recording area, or by electromagnetic isolation. All electronic devices emit some level of electromagnetic interference (EMI). Although FCC regulations minimize the EMI emitted by devices so that it is typically very low, it can produce measureable effects in very sensitive instruments such as an EEG amplifier. Perhaps the most common sources of environmental noise in EEG recordings are computer monitors and ambient lighting. Some methods for minimizing environmental artifact are discussed in Chapter 3.

Physiological Artifacts

Other sources of potential artifact in EEG recordings are physiological in nature. Unlike instrumental and environmental artifacts, which tend to be constant throughout a recording and impact all of the EEG channels similarly, physiological artifacts arising from the activity of the heart (electrocardiogram or ECG), localized changes in conductivity at the scalp ('skin potentials'), muscle contraction (electromyogram or EMG), and eye movements are transient events and are unevenly distributed over the scalp.

ECG artifacts can appear in EEG recordings as a result of the electrical field produced by a pulsating heart or as a result of 'pulse artifact'. An active heart itself produces a large electrical field that is propagated to the scalp via volume conduction in the same way as the electrical fields produced by brain activity. Because the heart is situated on the left side of the body in most people, artifacts generated in this way tend to have a larger impact on EEG recordings taken over the left hemisphere. ECG can also be expressed as pulse artifact when an electrode is positioned over a pulsating blood vessel. In this case, the pulsating movement of the blood vessel will cause subtle movements of the electrode, inducing (by electromagnetic induction) current in the conductive wiring leading from the electrode to the EEG recording equipment. Although nothing can be done to prevent the former ECG artifact, careful placement of electrodes can minimize the presence of pulse artifact.

Skin potentials are an artifact typically characterized by slow (low frequency), large amplitude changes in electrical potential at the scalp. These changes in potential reflect changes in the resistance (impedance) at the electrode–electrolyte junction that are due to the secretion of sweat from eccrine glands present in virtually all skin. Artifact due to skin potential can be reduced by carefully preparing the electrode site, minimizing resistance prior to recording, and by making recordings in a cool, low-humidity environment.

EMG artifact is produced by the electrical fields associated with the contraction of muscles and is typically characterized by fast (high frequency), large amplitude changes in electrical potential at the scalp. Depending on the offending muscle group, some EMG artifacts can be localized to only a few electrodes while others are widely distributed. For example, subtle contractions of the temporalis muscles of the head commonly produce EMG artifact in small groups of electrodes just behind the temple and over the ears. Contractions of the large group of muscles responsible for moving the jaw and face can produce more widespread artifact. Thus, ensuring that research participants refrain from talking, chewing gum, or making facial expressions during the recording session can reduce many such artifacts. Other logistical considerations include the participant's posture and/or the nature of any motor responses to be made by the participant during a recording session.

EOG artifacts are produced by changes in the orientation of the electrical fields of the eyes. These electrical fields are the result of electrical dipoles created by a separation of charge between the front (cornea) and back of the eyeball. Movement of the eyes as an individual scans the environment (or the screen of a computer monitor) alters the orientation of those dipoles, leading to changes in the electrical potential at the scalp. Because of their proximity to the eyes, electrodes over anterior scalp sites are most susceptible to the large artifact generated by these eye movements. One common approach to limiting eye movement during an experimental session is to ask research participants to maintain their gaze on a fixation point (e.g., crosshairs) usually at the center of the monitor.

Perhaps the most nefarious of EOG artifacts is that due to blinking. A common misconception among those new to EEG research is that blink-related EOG artifact is due to the closing and opening of the eyelid. However, blink-related EOG artifact is actually generated by rapid downward and inward movement of the eyeballs that occurs during blinking. Because humans blink at a rate of about once every 5 seconds, contamination of some of the EEG signal of interest is inevitable. Methods for addressing blink-related EOG artifact include avoidance, compensation, and removal techniques. Blink-related artifact can be avoided by simply asking participants to refrain from blinking during a prescribed interval of interest. While this technique can be effective for limiting observable artifact, it can increase task complexity, requiring research participants to exert cognitive control over the otherwise obligatory blink response. Another approach to dealing with blink-related artifact is to simply anticipate that some proportion of experimental trials will be contaminated by blinks and to compensate for this by increasing the number of total trials so that one can retain an adequate number of blink-free trials for subsequent averaging. This is an attractive solution because it does not place any additional demands on research participants. In practice, however, compensatory techniques may not be practical as the number of contaminated trials will vary from individual to individual and experimental procedures may become excessively long.

The last and most common technique for dealing with blink-related artifact is to use a mathematical algorithm to remove the artifact from recorded data. These so-called 'correction' procedures attempt to estimate the blink-related artifact in each channel of the data and then subtract that artifact, leaving behind a best guess as to what the EEG signal would have looked like if there had not been a blink in the first place. There are a number of popular blink-correction algorithms, including regression-based procedures, principal components analysis (PCA), and independent components analysis (ICA). Some of these procedures will be discussed in greater detail in Chapter 4. Blink-correction procedures are popular because they are relatively easy to implement and they permit the recovery of trials originally contaminated by blink artifact, meaning that experimental procedures can be run in less time and need not take into account individual differences in blink rate. However, these techniques should be approached with some caution given that they constitute a transformation of the original data.

Amplification

The minute voltages transduced at the scalp, combined with any of the above-mentioned voltage artifact that is picked up during signal transmission, must be amplified to accommodate the sensitivity of the display or recording equipment. Before computers, this amplification magnified the signal so as to drive the deflection of pens. Today, this amplification brings the signal within range of an analog-to-digital converter (ADC), a device that converts the continuous (analog) input voltage into a discrete numerical representation (digital) that is proportional to the input voltage. The magnitude of the amplification can be as little as 100 and as much as 100,000 times the original input signal. The amplification factor will vary from manufacturer to manufacturer and is typically described as the 'gain' of the amplifier, a number that represents the ratio of the amplitude of the input to the amplitude of the output. Because EEG signals are very small, high gain is required in amplifiers optimized for EEG recordings.

Common Mode Rejection

Because the small EEG signals of interest are contaminated by large environmental artifact such as line-noise, a simple 1-stage amplification of the voltages measured at the input of each electrode to the amplifier would result in larger EEG signals embedded in astronomical levels of noise. Thus, a critical stage of the amplification process is what is known as differential amplification. Differential amplification is, just as you might expect, the amplification of the voltage difference between two channels. All modern EEG systems are differential amplifiers, requiring at least three (yes three!) input channels for each output channel. It will be convenient to characterize differential amplification in terms of a simple difference in voltage between one active channel and one reference; however, recall that voltage is a measure of electrical potential, which by definition reflects a *difference* in charge between two points. Thus, the voltage in any given channel really reflects a difference between that channel and some other point. In virtually all EEG amplifiers, this point against which each of the individual channels is compared in order to measure voltage is the same for all channels and is called the 'common' or 'ground' channel.

The concept of differential amplification is elegantly simple. Take one 'active' signal containing EEG+noise, subtract a second 'reference' signal containing just noise, and amplify the difference containing only the EEG signal of interest. Of course, the arithmetic only works when the noise is common to the two channels from which the difference is derived. Thus, this process of differential amplification is often referred to as 'common mode rejection' as it serves to reject that component of the signal that is common to active and reference channels.

Common mode rejection is the first and best line of defense against large ambient artifact such as line-noise and can also help to reduce instrumental noise produced by the electronics of the amplifier. This is because ambient EM artifacts like line-noise are theoretically identical in all of the lead wires leading to the amplifier. Of course, even if the noise impacting a pair of leads is identical, differences in the capacity of the leads and/or the amplifier to similarly conduct that noise will lead to subtle measurement differences. Unfortunately, any differences in measurement of common part of the signal will be amplified along with the EEG signal of interest. The extent to which an EEG amplifier is capable of accurately amplifying the differential signal of interest and rejecting the common-mode signal (noise common to the two channels) is typically measured using the common-mode rejection ratio (CMRR), a ratio of the differential gain to the common-mode gain. For example, if a potential of 1 V were applied to only the active channel and the output of the differential amplifier changes by 1 V then the system can be said to have a differential gain of 1. However, if a 1 V potential is applied simultaneously to both the active and common channels and the output voltage of the amplifier changes by 0.00001 V, this value would indicate a common-mode gain of 0.0001 and reflects inaccuracies in the common-mode rejection. In this case, the CMRR is 1/0.00001 = 100,000. In other words, amplification of the signal difference is 100,000 times the amplification of the signal common to both channels. It is very important that EEG amplifiers have a high CMRR given that biopotentials measured at the scalp are so small relative to ambient EM noise. The CMRR is often expressed as a ratio of the power of the differential to the common-mode gain and is measured in decibels (e.g., $20*\log_{10}(1/0.00001) = 100$ dB). A CMRR of at least 100 dB is desirable for most EEG recordings.

Analog to Digital Conversion

Once the common-mode noise is removed by differential amplification, the remaining signal must be represented in some form amenable to storage, visualization and/or analysis. In the case of modern EEG recording equipment, the ADC represents the analog, time-varying voltages using binary code that is stored on a computer. Because the numeric values stored in a computer are in binary form, the resolution of the ADC is expressed in bits and is a function of the number of unique values available to the ADC, which is always a power of two. For example, a 3-bit ADC is capable of representing voltages as any one of eight (2^3) discrete values (see Figure 2.5). The process of converting the infinite number of unique voltages arriving to the ADC into a smaller number of discrete values is referred to as quantization. Because quantization involves the assignment of continuous voltages to the nearest discrete value, the process inherently introduces (hopefully

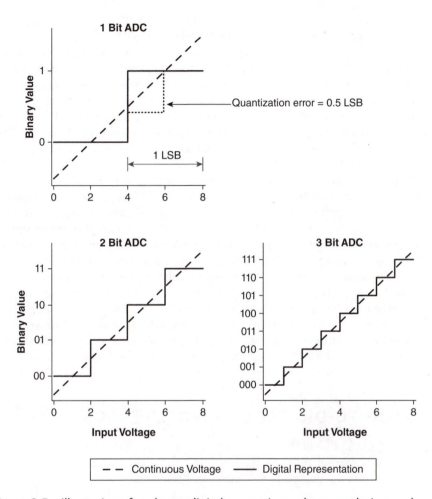

Figure 2.5 Illustration of analog to digital conversion, voltage resolution, and quantization error.

small) errors of measurement. Quantization error, differential non-linearity error, and integral non-linearity error are three of the many ways to quantify measurement error in an ADC – each of which is informative about the true voltage resolution of an ADC.

Voltage Resolution of the ADC

Whereas the quantization resolution of an ADC can simply be described as the number of discrete values available for quantization, the *voltage* resolution of an ADC refers to the size of the range of continuous voltages that will be assigned to the same quantization level and is thus a function of both the ADC's quantization resolution and its 'dynamic range'. The dynamic range of an ADC refers to the full scale over which voltages will be quantified. For example, if the dynamic range of a 3-bit ADC is 8 V, then the voltage resolution of the ADC will be 1 V because there are eight discrete values available to be distributed over the 8 V range (see Figure 2.5). Although a smaller dynamic range can improve voltage resolution of small signals like EEG and ERPs, a dynamic range that is too small will lead to *saturation* of the ADC wherein measured voltages exceed the maximum or minimum quantization value available. Saturation, also called 'clipping', is analogous to reaching the maximum deflection mechanically possible with the older pen-recording EEG devices. Selection of an appropriate dynamic range is thus very important in order to maintain both sufficient resolution of low amplitude voltage dynamics and avoid data loss due to saturation.

Most modern EEG amplifiers are equipped with at least a 16-bit ADC, which provides good quantization resolution with 65,536 (2^{16}) discrete values available. This means, for example, that with a dynamic range of 1200 μV (e.g., ± 600 μV) a 16-bit ADC achieves a voltage resolution of about 18 nV (0.018 μV). Of course, a great deal more resolution can be achieved by moving to 18- and 24-bit ADCs given that the quantization resolution increases by a power of two for each additional bit. However, because little is gained by improving voltage resolution beyond 18 nV, the additional quantization resolution with 18- and 24-bit ADCs is often used to increase the amplifier's dynamic range. Demand for 24-bit ADCs is on the rise given their promise for good voltage resolution and huge dynamic range. However, there are a number of factors that influence the performance of an ADC and it is often the case that error in the ADC limits the resolution that is otherwise theoretically achievable.

ANALOG-TO-DIGITAL CONVERTER ERROR

While a full discussion of the factors that contribute to ADC measurement error is well beyond the scope of this book, there are several factors that are important to understand from the perspective of a user and consumer of EEG technology.

Quantization Error

Quantization error is a measure of the difference between the value of the analog voltage that arrives at the input to the ADC and its quantized digital value. Quantization error is a form of instrumental noise that is present any time a continuous signal is converted to digital units by an ADC and is a result of the fact that each digital value corresponds to a *range* of voltages. Figure 2.5 provides a simple illustration of quantization error for an ideal ADC. Whereas the analog voltage in Figure 2.5 can have any of an infinite number of values in the range between 0 μV and 4 μV, there are only four available quantization levels, each separated by 1 μV. In other words, 1 μV is the minimum change in voltage that is required to reach the next quantization level, a value that is referred to as the least significant bit (LSB) voltage and is equal to the voltage resolution of the ADC described above. The job of the ADC is to assign each voltage from the continuous signal to that quantization level that is closest to the actual amplitude. The error that occurs during that assignment is quantization error and, as is illustrated in Figure 2.5, is limited to the range ±½ LSB.

Differential and Integral Non-linearity Error

In the case of an ideal ADC, the voltage resolution (e.g., 1 LSB) is determined by the number of bits used to quantize the input voltage and the dynamic range over which voltages are represented. However, an ideal ADC is virtually impossible to achieve in practice and, much to the consternation of its users, an n-bit ADC may not exhibit n-bit accuracy. In order to determine the practical voltage resolution of an ADC, one must take into consideration its differential non-linearity (DNL) and integral non-linearity (INL) characteristics.

The DNL, also called differential linearity error (DLE), refers to the difference between the actual width of the range of input voltages that are assigned to a given quantization level and the ideal width of one LSB. DNL can be visualized by plotting the transfer function (the staircase-like function that relates input voltage to output codes) of the system. Figure 2.6 illustrates DNL error, which is typically expressed in terms of LSB units. For example, an ideal 2-bit ADC (2^2 = 4 quantization codes) used to digitize voltages in the range of 0 V to 8 V will have a resolution (LSB) of 2 V. In other words, the width between quantization code-to-code transition points will be 2 V under ideal circumstances. If, however, the width between transition points is not constant across the dynamic range (0–8 V), then the DNL error can be quantified as the deviation from 2 V (LSB).

INL, also called integral linearity error (ILE), is defined as the integral of the DNL errors, so the size and distribution of DNL errors will determine the integral linearity of a system. Figure 2.6 illustrates the measurement of INL error. When the ADC is ideal, the transfer function is perfectly superimposed on a straight line,

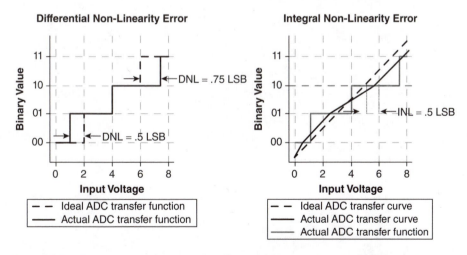

Figure 2.6 Depiction of the measurement of differential and integral non-linearity error.

called the transfer curve, drawn through the midpoint of each step (see Figure 2.6). Drawing a 'line' through the midpoints of the actual transfer function of the system will reveal the presence of nonlinearity. The maximum deviation of this actual transfer curve from the ideal transfer curve is the measure of INL and is usually expressed in terms of LSBs. ADCs are sometimes described as being 'n-bits linear'. For example, an ADC with 18 bits of resolution and an INL of 4 LSBs would be described as being '16-bits linear'. This is because 1 LSB in an ideal 16-bit ADC covers the same input voltage rage as 4 LSBs in an ideal 18-bit ACD. In other words, the actual voltage resolution realized by an 18-bit ADC with an INL of 4 LSBs is really no better than that of an ideal 16-bit ADC (provided the same dynamic range and INL of 0 LSB).

3

THE EEG LABORATORY

Configuring an EEG laboratory is much easier today than it was even just 10 or 15 years ago. Increasingly, manufacturers of EEG amplifiers offer their systems complete with electrode caps, computers, monitors, data acquisition software, stimulus presentation software, response devices, and other technologies that facilitate research with EEG. With so many 'plug and play' systems on the market, it is important to understand each of the components of these systems and how they work together to help you make informed decisions about which components and configurations are best suited to your specific research needs. Here we review several important technical and practical considerations regarding the setup and operation of an EEG laboratory; however, the interested reader should also refer to Curtin, Lozano, and Allen (2007) and Chapter 8 of Luck (2005).

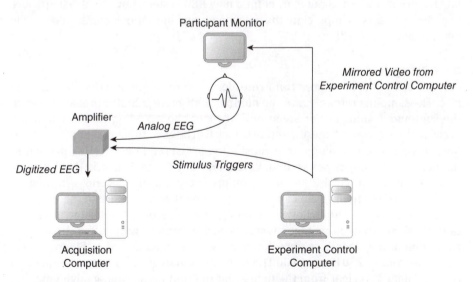

Figure 3.1   The primary components of an EEG recording system.

Figure 3.1 depicts the essential physical components of a modern EEG labora-tory. The first component, the EEG amplifier, magnifies the minuscule voltages gen-erated by the brain and transduces those voltages into digital values that can be stored on an acquisition computer. Because the vast majority of research using EEG techniques is concerned with measuring the neural response to discrete experi-mental events, a second computer is often needed for the control of experimental protocols. Additionally, this experiment control computer is often equipped with a second monitor for the participant that is distal to the experimenter and other noise-producing equipment. In addition to presenting stimuli to the participant, the experiment control computer usually has some way of communicating with the EEG amplifier (or the acquisition computer) in order to mark the occurrence of experimentally significant events such as a stimulus appearing on the monitor. This communication is essential to anyone desiring to measure ERPs due to the fact that computing an ERP depends on time-locking the EEG signal to a series of events. Although nearly all EEG laboratories conform to this basic configuration (illus-trated in Figure 3.1), there are a number of qualities of both hardware and software components that merit further consideration.

HARDWARE CONSIDERATIONS

The most important piece of hardware in an EEG laboratory is the amplifier. There are a number of commercially available amplifiers marketed specifically to those conducting neuroscience research with EEG. Shopping for an EEG amplifier can be a daunting process for newcomers in particular, because it can be difficult to evalu-ate the varied hardware specifications. Becoming familiar with some of the most important specifications of EEG amplifiers will not only help with the decision-making process when in the market for a new EEG system, but can also help more experienced users to appreciate the advantages and limitations of the data she/he may already be recording.

Sampling Rate

Perhaps one of the most important considerations of an amplifier is the sampling rate. The sampling rate refers to the number of discrete samples that are taken of the continuous voltages per some unit of time. The sampling rate is important because, once recorded, these discrete values will be used to represent the continu-ous voltages. The sampling rate is most often measured in hertz (Hz), defined as the number of samples per second. Values typically range from 250 Hz (1 sample every 4 milliseconds) to 2000 Hz (1 sample every 0.5 milliseconds) in modern amplifiers. The sampling rate can also be thought of as a measure of the temporal resolution of the amplifier. Lower sampling rates inherently confer lower resolu-tion of the continuous voltages whereas high sampling rates offer the highest resolution of the signal's temporal dynamics. This is illustrated in Figure 3.2 for sampling rates of 250 Hz and 1000 Hz over the course of 50 ms with a segment of real EEG data. It is clear from the figure that the continuous voltage dynamics are well characterized using discrete samples taken at a rate of 1000 Hz (panel B of Figure 3.2) whereas some of the temporal dynamics are lost when the continuous

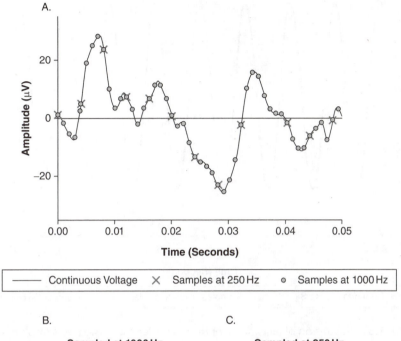

A.

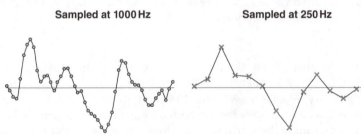

Figure 3.2 (A) 50 ms of continuous voltage (straight black line) with discrete samples at 250 Hz and 1000 Hz sampling rates overlaid. (B) Observed waveform resulting from the 1000 Hz sampling rate. (C) Observed waveform resulting from the 250 Hz sampling rate.

signal is sampled at 250 Hz (panel C of Figure 3.2). In particular, because there is a 4 ms window between each consecutive sample, high-frequency voltage fluctuations occurring within that window will not be visible in the digitized recordings made by the amplifier.

The problems associated with low sampling rates are not only limited to missing subtle features of the continuous voltage dynamics. When the sampling rate is too low relative to the frequency of the signal being measured, non-existent signals can be inadvertently introduced to the recordings. This is called *aliasing* error. Figure 3.3 illustrates aliasing error for a simple sinusoidal waveform of 8 Hz. In this example, samples of the continuous waveform taken at a rate of only 10 Hz (10/second) produce an artificial oscillation of 2 Hz. In order to avoid aliasing error

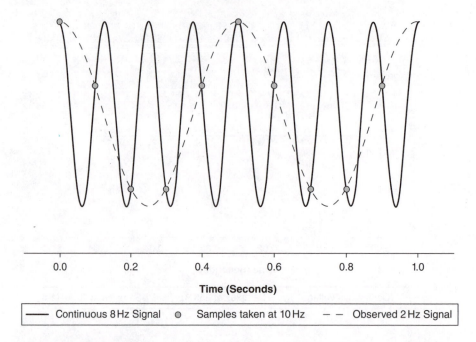

Figure 3.3   Illustration of aliasing error due to under-sampling (i.e., sampling at rates lower than the Nyquist frequency).

such as this, one must sample at a rate that is high enough to be able to accurately reconstruct the highest frequencies in the original signal. This rate is determined by sampling theory (Shannon & Weaver, 1949). Sampling theory states that a continuous signal can be accurately reconstructed from its samples provided the highest frequency present in the signal is lower than half of the sampling rate. In other words, the highest frequency that can be accurately reconstructed from a digitized continuous signal is one half of the sampling rate. Thus, according to sampling theory, an amplifier must sample at a rate of at least 16 Hz in order to accurately reconstruct the 8 Hz sinusoid in Figure 3.3. This value of half the sampling rate is also sometimes referred to as the Nyquist frequency.

Though sampling theory necessitates a sampling rate of twice the highest frequency, it is often advisable to select rates that are 3–4 times the highest observable frequency in order to protect against aliasing error. Ideally, one would always use the highest sampling rate possible as doing so permits the most accurate representation of the original signal dynamics. However, there are some costs to sampling at high rates. One logistical cost of a high sampling rate is that considerable disk space is required to store the recorded data. With 128 channels of EEG, a 30-minute recording session can easily generate files of a gigabyte or more. Although there has been a huge increase in hard-drive capacity over the past decade, manipulating and processing data files of this size can be problematic. The sampling rate can be adjusted in many commercially available EEG amplifiers so the selection of a sampling rate may be driven by research goals. If the goal of the research is to characterize ERP components, signals that are typically less than 20 Hz, then a sampling rate of 250 Hz should be more than adequate. However, if the goal is to characterize high-frequency oscillatory dynamics in the 30–100 Hz range, then sampling rates of 1000 or even 2000 Hz are desirable. The sampling rate is also limited, to some extent, by the number of channels being sampled. This particular limitation will be discussed in the section on ACD architecture below.

Filters

Electronic filters are devices or processes that aim to remove unwanted components from a signal. Here we will briefly discuss the use of filters in the hardware of an EEG amplifier. A more thorough discussion of the nature of filters and their use in the processing of EEG data can be found in Chapter 4. Filters are an essential part of the recording process in all EEG amplifiers. Although there is considerable variety in the way in which filters are implemented across manufacturers, the goal of each is the same: to remove noise from the recordings prior to amplification. On the one hand, filters that remove very high-frequency noise, known as 'low-pass' filters, help to remove ambient noise from the voltage signals passed to the ADC and also help to prevent aliasing. For example, ambient noise from cellular phones and Wi-Fi networks can exceed 900 MHz (900,000,000 Hz), far exceeding even the highest sample rates used by modern EEG amplifiers. In order to avoid aliasing error due to under-sampling of these high frequencies, low-pass filters are used to remove those frequencies that are above the Nyquist frequency. Low-pass filters are typically designed to attenuate frequencies ranging from one-half (e.g., 500 Hz for a sample rate of 2000 Hz) to one-fifth (200 Hz for a sample rate of 2000 Hz) of the Nyquist frequency.

Many amplifiers also remove low-frequency noise using 'high-pass' filters. Very low-frequency noise, such as that due to the half-cell potential, can be quite large in amplitude, causing 'saturation' or 'clipping' to occur when the voltage exceeds the dynamic range of the ADC. This kind of noise is sometimes referred to as 'DC offset' and is most commonly removed via high-pass filters. It is common for the high-pass filter used with EEG recordings to attenuate frequencies below around 0.01 Hz.

There are also filters that can attenuate frequencies within a very narrow band. These so-called 'Notch' filters are sometimes used to remove mains interference (e.g., 50/60 Hz) from the input signal. One critical point to make here is that *all* filters distort your data (see Chapter 5 of Luck, 2005), some more than others. Notch filters, for example, are notorious for introducing sometimes dramatic distortions of the original signal in frequency bands that are well outside the notch. Another important point is that when filters are implemented in the hardware of the amplifiers, there is no way to evaluate distortion by the filter against the original signal. For these reasons, it is generally desirable that the electronic filters of an amplifier be as conservative as possible so as to prevent (or at least reduce) clipping and avoid aliasing error. In some cases, recordings can be made without using a high-pass filter. These so-called DC recordings are usually only possible with 24-bit ADCs, due to their large dynamic range.

ADC Architecture

Another hardware consideration is the architecture of the ADC. Generally speaking, the ADC architecture determines how voltages are sampled from the input channels and converted to a digital representation at any given point in time. The two most popular architectures are *successive approximation register* (SAR) and *sigma–delta* ($\Sigma\Delta$) ADCs. A complete review of these ADC architectures is far beyond the scope of this book and there are many complex trade-offs when considering which architecture might be best suited to a specific research program. Our intention here is to provide a simplified introduction to these architectures and give just one example of the factors that are important to consider when comparing the two.

As the name implies, SAR ADCs convert analog signals into a discrete digital representation by making a series of successive guesses about the amplitude of the input voltage. SAR ADCs typically have an input *sample-and-hold* (SHA), which keeps the input signal constant during the brief conversion cycle. At each of a series of steps in the conversion, the input voltage is compared to a reference voltage. The first step, for example, might compare the input voltage to a reference voltage at the midpoint of the amplifier's dynamic range. The result of this comparison is stored in a successive approximation register (SAR). Then the next comparison is made, this time against a new reference voltage. Consider, for example, an input voltage of 75 µV to an amplifier with a dynamic range of 0 to 500 µV. For the first step of the conversion process, the 75 µV input is compared to a 250 µV reference voltage (half of the dynamic range). The result of the comparison is that the input is less than 250 µV so the SAR is updated to reflect the narrowed range of the input (e.g., 0–250 µV). The process is repeated, this time with a reference voltage of 125 µV and the SAR is updated again to reflect the narrowed range (0–125 µV). For the next step, the reference voltage is 62.5 µV and the comparator reports that the input is more than the reference, so the SAR is updated to reflect the narrowed range of 62.5–125 µV. These steps are repeated until the approximation converges to a solution within the resolution of the amplifier.

By comparison with SAR ADCs, $\Delta\Sigma$ ADCs (also known as a delta–sigma ADCs) are much more complex and can be implemented in a wide variety of ways. Briefly, $\Delta\Sigma$ ADCs oversample the input signal by a large factor. A digital filter known as a 'decimation filter' is then applied to the oversampled data, which filters unwanted noise and reduces (i.e., decimates) the output sampling rate. Application of the decimation filter introduces 'pipeline delay', which is an important consideration in multiplexed applications like EEG where the digitization must be performed in rapid succession over a large number of channels. Pipeline delay is due to the fact that the decimation filters require settling time – a measure of the time it takes for the system to yield a stable output within the desired resolution. When the input is multiplexed over a number of channels, the system must wait for the duration of the settling time before the output for a channel measurement is valid and it can move on to the next channel. There is no pipeline delay for a SAR type ADC, making them easier to use in multiplexed applications like EEG.

It must be reiterated here that pipeline delay is just one of many complex issues that bear on the comparison of ADC architectures and in many research contexts, such as the measurement of ERPs, differences between ADC architectures are likely negligible. That said, significant pipeline delay can be a factor worthy of consideration in some research contexts. One example is the measurement of phase coupling (discussed in Chapter 7) between electrodes – an increasingly popular way to investigate communication between distant neuronal populations. There is particular interest in phase coupling in the Gamma band, including frequencies between 30 and 100 Hz. Because the phase angle of a Gamma-band oscillation at 75 Hz changes by 1 degree about every 37 microseconds (0.037 milliseconds), a multiplexed input must be able to sample from the various channels at a very high rate (e.g., <37 µs) in order to achieve high resolution of the relative phases of the 75 Hz signal in two different electrodes. For reasons such as this, it is important to carefully evaluate the properties of ADC architecture with respect to anticipated research strategies.

Input Impedance

Electrical *impedance* is a measure of opposition to the passage of current through an AC circuit when a voltage is applied and is analogous to electrical *resistance* in DC circuits. The nature of the difference between impedance and resistance is not important here, so we will simply refer to impedance as the level of resistance to the flow of current. When the resistance is very low, only a small voltage is needed to drive the flow of current in a circuit. It is important to maintain very low impedance at the scalp–electrode junction so that the very small voltages produced by neural activity can drive current in the wires leading to the amplifier.

The input impedance of the amplifier similarly describes the resistance to current flow but at the input stage of the amplification process. For reasons beyond the scope of this book, it is important that the input impedance of the amplifier be higher than the impedance at the scalp–electrode junction. A high ratio of the amplifier's input impedance to the electrode impedance ensures more accurate measurement of the signal from the electrodes. When this ratio is small, there can be considerable loss of signal, leading to poor CMRR. Thus, the higher the input impedance, the better an amplifier can tolerate higher electrode impedances while maintaining good CMRR. This means that high-quality recordings can be made with very little scalp abrasion/preparation. Typical values of the input impedance are in the range of 200 megaohms (MΩ) to >4 gigaohms (GΩ). One caveat to keep in mind with high-input impedance amplifiers is that they can be more susceptible to ambient noise and movement artifact. This is easily mitigated by placing the subject in close proximity to the amplifier and using lead wires from the electrodes to the amplifier that are as short as possible, a good idea irrespective of the input impedance.

Peripherals

Another important consideration is the extent to which an amplifier is capable of hosting peripheral inputs. At the very least, an amplifier should have one peripheral input to receive time-locking event markers from the experiment control computer. These event markers, sometimes called 'triggers', are used to synchronize the presentation of experimental stimuli, marking the time at which a stimulus (or

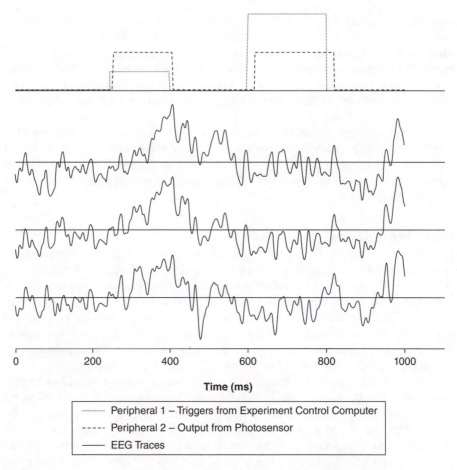

Figure 3.4 Illustration of the use of peripheral inputs for event synchronization. The top lines display the actual 'signal' sent to the parallel port with magnitude represented on the Y-axis. Note that some systems will automatically detect only the rising flank of the input signal to the parallel port, returning the magnitude of that rising flank as a 'trigger value' at a single instant.

response) occurred (see Figure 3.4). In most cases it is necessary to demarcate several different types of stimulus events so many commercial systems provide a digital input port with 8–12 bits of resolution (i.e., 256–4096 discrete values). Additional peripheral input ports can also be very useful. For example, additional ports might be used to record the voltage output by a photosensor mounted to the participant's computer monitor, a voice key recording participants' verbal responses, or a response device recording manual responses by a participant. An advantage of linking peripherals such as these directly to the digital input of the amplifier as opposed to routing the signals from those devices through a computer is that one can address (and even circumvent) any temporal imprecision in the synchronization of stimuli/responses with the triggers inserted by the experiment control computer to the data stream. The problem of temporal imprecision is illustrated in Figure 3.4 using a sample of data recorded in our laboratory. Notice that the dotted line, indicating a trigger from the experiment control computer, does not perfectly overlap with the dashed line, indicating the activation of a photosensor attached to the participant monitor. The use of a photosensor as a second peripheral input in this case thus permits correction for timing errors in the synchronization between the triggers marking the onset and offset of visual stimuli and the actual manifestation of the stimulus on the participants' computer monitor. The reasons for these kinds of timing errors are complex, but may be due to factors such as background computer processes running concurrently with your experiment, low-quality computer video hardware, or even inconsistencies in the software used for experiment control.

Number of Channels

Commercial EEG amplifiers are available with many possible configurations of channels. In most cases, the number of channels used for EEG research in the fields of social and personality psychology ranges between 24 and 128, though the exact number of available channels depends on the hardware design by the manufacturer. Many systems are extensible, meaning that two or more units may be 'chained' together to increase the total number of channels. The two factors most likely to determine the number of channels used by any given lab are cost and research goals. The cost of high-density EEG arrays is not only driven by the increased expense of an amplifier with many input channels, but also by the added expense of high-density EEG caps, the costs associated with cap repairs (which are more likely with a higher number of leads), and the need for more data storage capacity. There are also time costs associated with having many channels since each will take some time to prepare prior to recording.

There is a general trend in the literature toward recording from higher density channel arrays. While there are certainly some advantages to recording from many channels, high-density arrays may be excessive in some research contexts. This can be true, for example, in the context of research employing ERP techniques. Though it is often desirable to visualize the topographical distribution of an ERP component, requiring at least some coverage of the scalp, much of the research using ERPs ultimately relies on the measurement of ERP amplitude/latency in just one channel of EEG recordings. There are also research aims that may demand more channels. For example, most software for EEG analysis includes algorithms that attempt to estimate the locations of brain sources that gave rise to a recorded pattern of voltages on the scalp. The reliability of these 'source localization' algorithms depends on having as complete coverage of the head as is possible, requiring a large number of channels.

SOFTWARE CONSIDERATIONS

Software is critical to the operation of modern EEG laboratories. Data acquisition software is used to control the amplifier recording parameters and visualize recordings on-line. Stimulus presentation software is used to control the delivery of experimental protocols and record behavioral responses by the participant. Finally, data analysis software is used to reduce the vast amounts of recorded data to a small number of meaningful measurements relevant to the experimental hypothesis. Many commercial EEG systems include some or all of this software. While the look and feel of these software interfaces varies, there are several practical qualities of each that are worthy of consideration.

Data Acquisition

All modern amplifiers are controlled via software interfaces. Recording parameters such as the sampling rate, number of output channels, and gain factors can often be specified here. Of these, the capability to select a subset of output channels is the most likely to be modified with any regularity and is an option that can be useful when specific research aims obviate the need for a dense array of channels.

Before any data can be recorded, electrodes must be properly affixed to the scalp. As was discussed previously, impedance (used synonymously with resistance for our purposes) measures the quality of an electrode's connection with the scalp. Most laboratory protocols call for the adjustment of impedances to within about 5 kilohms (kΩ). There are impedance meters that can be used to make the impedance measurements prior to recording; however, it can be very time-consuming to individually test and adjust each electrode. Even when multiple channels can be input simultaneously to an impedance meter, special configuration is usually required. Thus, a very useful feature to look for in data acquisition software is an impedance testing function. Ideally, this function will make available the numerical value of the impedance at each electrode and also permit rapid visualization of the set of electrodes using a color-coding scheme to identify impedance levels falling within pre-specified bins (e.g., 0–5 kΩ, 6–10 kΩ, etc.).

To our knowledge, all data acquisition software offers some way of visualizing the EEG data on-line during a recording session. This is an important feature because it permits continuous evaluation of the quality of the recordings and can be used to identify recording problems if/when they occur. It is also important to be able to concurrently visualize the peripheral input or event triggers. One useful option with respect to the recording display is the capability to select subsets of channels for on-line inspection. This is particularly important when the total number of channels is large. For example, in order to visualize 128 channels in a single display, the scale of the visualization must be very small, making it difficult to discern the activities of any single channel. Better than simply selecting subsets of consecutive channels for display is the capability to select user-defined subsets for display. In our lab, for example, the primary display during experimental recordings consists of a subset of channels along the midline of the scalp.

Another important visualization option is display filtering. As was discussed earlier, filters are used to eliminate noise in the recordings by removing unwanted frequencies. Common settings for these hardware filters remove frequencies below ~0.01 Hz and above ~250 Hz. However, even with these filters in place, there will be some low-frequency drift and high-frequency noise within the dynamic range of the amplifier. Thus, it can be useful to apply filters more liberally to the data before it is displayed. For example, filtering out frequencies below ~0.5 Hz will greatly reduce any visible drift in the data and prevent adjacent EEG traces from overlapping in the display. Because these filters are only applied to the data that are displayed and do not affect the data that are written to file, there is no need to be concerned with potential distortions of the data that can be caused by liberal filtering.

Experiment Generation

Flexible and accurate experiment control is key to any EEG research program. There are a number of commercial and open-source software options available for the generation of psychological experiments. Most of these options claim to provide accurate control of experiment timing to within a millisecond. However, they vary considerably in flexibility and ease of use. Unfortunately, these two important properties of experiment control software – flexibility and ease of use – tend to be inversely related to one another. The reason for this is that programming an experimental protocol is actually quite complicated. In order to simplify the process, software writers must implement a number of assumptions about the most likely uses for their program, relieving users of the burden of having to understand the underlying program, but at the same time constraining them to work within the boundaries defined by those assumptions. Finding a good balance of flexibility and ease of use is important so that dynamic research needs can be addressed but implementation of those needs does not require mastery of a programming language. While a complete review of the available software is beyond the scope of this book, thorough reviews occasionally appear in the literature (e.g., Stahl, 2006).

Most commercial software is available through stand-alone packages, meaning that the software has no dependencies other than those that are already a part of the installation package. Some examples of commercial software commonly used in conjunction with EEG data acquisition are E-Prime, SuperLab, Presentation, MediaLab, and DirectRT. It can be quite difficult to draw direct comparisons between these options because each has a unique set of strengths and weaknesses across varied research contexts. Importantly, each has the capability to communicate with external devices including ports (e.g., parallel, serial, etc.) on the host computer. This communication is critical to EEG research, which requires that relevant experimental events (e.g., stimulus onset, response execution, etc.) be marked via triggers sent by the experiment control software to the EEG amplifier. The well-developed graphical user interfaces (GUIs) of E-Prime and SuperLab appear to make them two of the most popular choices. Each of these offers drag-and-drop type interfaces wherein simple experiments can be generated almost entirely using only the computer mouse to select when and how events should occur in sequence. Arguably the best way to evaluate which software is right for an individual is to request trial versions of the programs being considered and use each to generate an experiment that is representative of the kind of protocol most likely to be used in the context of his/her research.

In addition to software packages that are commercially available, there are an increasing number of open-source software options that are free. Most open-source software is available as an add-on or a plug-in to a host programming environment that must be installed separately. One popular example of open-source experiment generation software is Psychtoolbox (http://psychtoolbox.org/HomePage). Because Psychtoolbox is written in Matlab, its use requires that the user already have a licensed installation of Matlab. Thus, while Psychtoolbox is freely available, there is an indirect, prerequisite cost of obtaining Matlab. One completely free alternative to Psychtoolbox is PsychoPy (http://www.psychopy.org/). An advantage of PsychoPy is that it is written in the Python programming language, itself a free alternative to Matlab. The Appendix to this book provides instructions for generating a simple experiment using PsychoPy to orient readers to this software. Open-source software offers the most flexibility because the user has complete access to and control over all aspects of the underlying program. This flexibility, however, comes at the cost of ease of use. For example, use of Psychtoolbox for even simple experiments requires a good deal of familiarity with the Matlab programming language. One exception to this is PsychoPy, which offers the full flexibility of Matlab/Psychtoolbox but also includes a user-friendly GUI with drag-and-drop features, allowing simple experiments to be generated without any knowledge of the Python programming language.

Data Analysis

The final category of software one must consider is a data analysis package. Similar to the experiment generation software, there are both commercial and open-source options available. Three of the most commonly used, commercial options for data analysis are EMSE, Analyzer, and SCAN (now integrated with the Curry neuroimaging suite). These software packages range in price from ~$5000 to ~$12,000 for the initial license. Open-source options include EEGlab (Delorme & Makeig, 2004), FieldTrip (Oostenveld, Fries, Maris, & Schoffelen, 2011), and Brainstorm (Tadel, Baillet, Mosher, Pantazis, & Leahy, 2011), but as was the case with Psychtoolbox, each of these requires a pre-existing installation of Matlab.

The trade-off between ease of use and flexibility is also similarly applicable to and perhaps more evident in data analysis software. Each of the commercial software packages listed above offers point-and-click analysis options in a Windows-type environment, requiring no knowledge of any particular programming language. This ease of use, however, confines users to the analytic options implemented by the writers of the software. Concern with this confinement is abated by the wide variety of options available in each of the aforementioned programs; however, differences between software packages can sometimes make it difficult to replicate a published analytic strategy when using a program that is different from that used to perform the original analysis. Software developers have attempted to improve the flexibility of their programs by providing a scripting interface and/or integration with third-party software such as Matlab. Purchasing software with one or both of these capabilities will make available to the user any analysis imaginable, but requires that the user learn to do some programming in order to implement the analysis (again, the flexibility/ease of use trade-off). This is a non-issue with open-source options because the existing program can be changed on-demand or new programs can be written to address any limitations encountered.

Whether selecting commercial or open-source software, there are several considerations that may help to guide the decision-making process:

Analysis options: More important than simply counting the number of data analysis options available is the subset of options pertaining to an individual's research needs. For example, if a majority of an individual's research program entails the measurement of ERPs, select software with the best selection of analyses in the time-domain.

Visualization options: As we will see in the guided analyses in subsequent chapters of this book, visualization of the data is central to quality control and interpretation of experimental effects, and will even guide the decision-making process for measuring ERPs. Thus, it is important that a number of options exist for visualizing the data.

Statistics: Most of the programs currently available offer some integrated statistical testing both within and across subjects.

Dataset history: In our experience, a very useful feature of data analysis software is the capability to perform automatic record-keeping regarding a given dataset's history. This feature can save many hours of re-processing in the event that questions arise about the analysis pipeline through which a particular dataset was passed.

Batch processing: Another time-saving feature is the ability to replicate a set of data processing routines across multiple files in a study. In addition to time saved, this kind of batch processing reduces idiosyncrasies and errors in data management.

Study management: Another convenient feature is the capability to manage a group of datasets simultaneously, facilitating analyses that require group-based averaging or group-level statistical analyses.

Publication quality graphics: The software should provide some means for both generating and exporting high-quality graphical representations of the data, including time-domain plots of waveforms, topographical maps, and both frequency and time-frequency domain transforms.

File export: Finally, options should be available for exporting processed data to text files that are easily opened by third-party software. This is especially important when software has limited support for the generation of publication quality graphics given that those graphics must be generated outside the data analysis software.

ELECTRODES/MONTAGE

Another important consideration in the configuration of an EEG laboratory is the selection of electrodes, or leads, as they are sometimes called. Electrodes vary in shape and size and can be made of a variety of conductive materials. The importance of selecting electrodes consisting of materials that are maximally conductive and have a low half-cell potential was discussed in Chapter 2. Here we consider more practical aspects of electrodes and their configuration.

Electrodes/Caps

The majority of contemporary EEG recordings are made using electrodes that are sewn into a fabric cap. Because the fabric caps can make it difficult (if not impossible) to lift the electrodes in order to prepare the scalp and apply the electrolyte gel, cap-based electrodes are usually disk-shaped with a small hole in the center that permits site preparation and delivery of the electrolyte directly beneath the sensor. One difference between some of the various electrodes on the market is the size of this access hole. When the hole is small, one will be able to insert a blunt-tip syringe for electrolyte gel delivery, but may find it difficult to manipulate the hair beneath the electrode in an effort to distribute the gel and/or improve conductivity by reducing the impedance. Small access holes can also make it difficult to ascertain exactly how much electrolyte has been delivered to the site. This can be a problem because excess gel can spread in the vicinity of neighboring electrodes. When the electrolyte gel beneath two adjacent electrodes overlaps, a 'salt bridge' is formed between the two sensors. When a salt bridge is present, the two overlapping electrodes convey identical voltages to the amplifier, essentially functioning as one large electrode, rather than two small ones. Larger holes can alleviate some of these problems, making it easier to prepare the underlying scalp, visualize the gel delivery, and manipulate hair during the impedance adjustment process. However, larger holes also mean that there will be less conductive surface area on the sensor itself. Thus, it is important to find sensors that offer improved scalp access, but do not forfeit too much surface area.

There are also a variety of EEG caps to choose from. The biggest limitation of EEG caps is that the electrodes tend to be situated farther from the scalp than if those sites were prepared and electrodes positioned independently using an adhesive or electrode paste. As a result, more electrolyte gel is needed to fill the gaps and recordings are more susceptible to artifact due to displacement of the electrodes. These inconveniences, however, are outweighed by the drastic time savings of using a cap by comparison with individual electrode placement. When selecting a cap for research purposes, it can be tempting to select a cap providing the snuggest fit to the scalp. In principle, this would alleviate some of the above-mentioned concerns. In practice, however, caps that are too snug can lead to serious discomfort for subjects after just a few minutes of use. This can be problematic because even some of the simplest ERP tasks commonly exceed 30 minutes in duration and others can last more than an hour (not including setup time!). The ability to provide research participants with a comfortable experience can be especially important when working with special populations (e.g., children, older adults, etc.).

Electrode Positioning

Electrode caps can be configured in a number of ways. In the late 1950s a standardized positioning system was developed in order to ensure consistency of electrode placement across laboratories. This system, known as the 10–20 system, has since become the most common and widely accepted electrode positioning system in the field. The 10–20 system originally designated 21 distinct sites defined by the underlying cortical region and inter-electrode distance and identified using letter–number pairs. The letters F, T, C, P, and O are used to designate electrodes placed over frontal, temporal, central, parietal, and occipital cortices, respectively ('C' is an exception to this rule given that there is no 'central' lobe). The numbers used in the 10–20 system designate both the cerebral hemisphere (e.g., left or right) and the lateral extent of the placement. Even numbers are used to identify electrodes placed over the right hemisphere and odd numbers are used for the left. The magnitude of the number indicates the lateral extent of the placement within that hemisphere such that smaller numbers indicate closer proximity to the midline of the two hemispheres. For example, the labels F2, F4, F6, and F8 designate a group of electrodes over the frontal cortex of the right hemisphere beginning in close proximity to the midline and moving laterally. Technically speaking, the number 0 indicates placement on the midline between the two hemispheres, however, the letter z (for 'zero') is used by convention. For example, electrode Cz is positioned on the midline over the vertex of the scalp.

More than just a general nomenclature, the 10–20 system specifies a coordinate system that determines the exact placement of electrodes. This specific positioning is defined by the geometry of an individual's head, which is determined by measuring the contours between fiducial (i.e., reference) points on the head. The distance between the nasion (where the nose meets the forehead) and inion (bony protrusion marking the lowest point on the skull from the back of the neck) is used to determine placement on the horizontal axis and the distance between the left and right pre-aricular points (immediately anterior to the ear) is used to determine placement on the lateral axis. Once these total distances have been determined, electrodes are positioned at intervals such that the inter-electrode distance is either 10% or 20% of the total distance – hence the name '10–20' system (see Figure 3.5). Over time, extensions to the original 10–20 system were developed to accommodate more electrodes. The 10–10 and 10–5 systems, for example, make use of the spaces between the original 10–20 locations and can be used to designate as many as 74 and 345 positions respectively. Other positioning systems (e.g., equidistant positioning) are sometimes used, but even these alternatives typically include several positions that correspond directly with commonly used electrodes from the 10–20/10–5 systems.

Electrode caps are often additionally outfitted with a number of 'drop' leads – electrodes not sewn into the fabric of the cap. In most cases, these electrodes are used to record ocular artifact and are thus positioned around the eyes. The horizontal electro-oculogram is typically recorded using electrodes placed at the left (LO1) and right (LO2) canthus of each eye. Vertical electro-oculogram is typically recorded from electrodes placed just above (SO1/SO2) and below (IO1/IO2) the superior and inferior orbits of the eye respectively. Historically, these electrodes were included for the purpose of identifying and later correcting for ocular artifacts such as blinks and saccadic eye movements. Many still use them for this purpose, but some electrode caps are beginning to

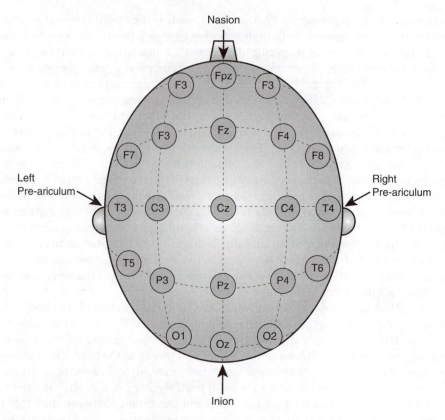

Figure 3.5   Standard 10/20 electrode positioning.

be sold without any of these drop leads (save the reference). One reason this might be the case is that recently popularized techniques for artifact correction (e.g., independent components analysis) do not rely on the presence of peri-ocular channels to estimate the noise components.

In addition to peri-ocular channels, the reference and common (i.e., ground) channels are sometimes configured as drop leads from the cap in order to facilitate careful positioning. In the case of the common channel, its placement on the scalp is almost completely a matter of personal preference. Typical positions for the common channel are near the vertex of the scalp (e.g., next to Cz; no drop lead required) or the middle of the forehead, but its location has almost no bearing on the quality of the differential measurements made between active and reference channels. To see why this is so, consider the voltages measured at electrodes Cz and Reference. Each of these voltages actually reflects the difference between each channel and the common channel (e.g., Cz-Common and Reference-Common). Thus, when the Reference is subtracted from Cz in the process of differential amplification, the measurement can be expressed as (Cz-Common)−(Ref-Common) = Cz-Ref. In other words, the content of the Common channel is negated during subtraction of the Reference voltage.

Placement of the Reference channel is another matter entirely. While there is some variability in the selection of reference site, the position of the Reference channel will have a significant impact on the nature of the recordings made. The electrode montage section below describes the configuration of the reference in EEG recordings.

Electrode Montage

The 'referential montage' in which each channel is referenced to a single designated reference electrode is the most commonly used montage in behavioral neuroscience. Placement of the reference electrode in the referential montage is an important consideration when recording EEG because it is the site relative to which the brain potentials in all other active channels are measured (Hagemann, Naumann, & Thayer, 2001). The ideal placement of the reference electrode is therefore a site that is completely 'neutral' with respect to brain activity. Common sites for the reference electrode include the earlobe, the mastoid process (a bony protrusion of the skull just behind the ear), and the nose-tip. When only one earlobe or mastoid is used (e.g., on the right side of the head) as a reference, the EEG amplitude tends to be reduced in those channels that are closest to the reference (e.g., active channels in the right hemisphere) due to the fact that some small amount of brain activity is inadvertently recorded by the reference. Thus, 'linked' mastoids or earlobes are commonly used in order to address this potential asymmetry. The linking of reference electrodes can be either physical (e.g., two wires soldered together) or algebraic (e.g., Reference = [Reference$_{RIGHT}$ + Reference$_{LEFT}$]/2). Using the nose-tip is sometimes preferred because of its midline position (less chance of asymmetry) and distal proximity to brain potentials. However, having an electrode taped to the tip of the nose can be a distraction for some participants and, though distal, is not immune to influence by large brain potentials near the anterior pole of the brain. Regardless of its placement, it is critical that care be taken to ensure good signal quality in the reference channel. Poor placement or a failure to reduce impedance in the reference channel can lead to the introduction of noise into every one of the active channels from which it is subtracted!

Two other montages are the 'average reference' and 'bipolar' montages. Just as the name implies, the reference 'signal' in an average reference montage is calculated by taking the average of all electrodes (Dien, 1998). In principle, the average reference montage approximates an ideal reference because the sum of the positive and negative voltages recorded over the surface of a sphere (e.g., the head) containing electromagnetic dipoles (e.g., brain potentials) will be zero. However, this is true only when measurements are taken at evenly distributed sites over the entire surface of the sphere. Thus, it can be difficult to approximate the true average reference because EEG recordings are usually limited to only about 2/3 of the 'sphere's' surface and are sometimes unevenly distributed over that surface. The 'bipolar montage' is unique because the active channels do not share a reference point. In the bipolar montage, each active channel is referenced to one of its neighboring active channels. The bipolar montage is very sensitive to localized potential differences and is thus used quite frequently in clinical applications to identify the focus of pathological brain activity.

Because all EEG data are stored digitally, any montage can be generated algebraically from any other montage. Given that the selection of a reference site can have a strong influence on the nature of EEG recordings, it is important to consider how the montage used modulates the outcome of an EEG study. Another important consideration with respect to the EEG montage is comparability/reliability across laboratories. For this reason it is often recommended that a reference be selected for a particular study so that it is most similar to prior research in that area.

MISCELLANEOUS TIPS FOR THE EEG LABORATORY

Managing Environmental Noise

The root cause of environmental noise, whether emitted by monitors or lighting, is what is known as 'mains-interference'. Mains-interference, also called 'line-noise', occurs as the result of the alternating current (AC) used to deliver power to nearly all electrical outlets found in homes and businesses. In contrast with direct current (DC) wherein a constant voltage is maintained in the electrical power lines, AC uses sinusoidal voltages with a frequency of 60 Hz (50 Hz in Europe and Asia). The dynamic electromagnetic fields produced by AC-powered devices induce unwanted current in the conductive wires leading from the electrodes to the EEG amplifier. Sixty Hz mains-interference is particularly problematic because mains voltage is typically at least 110 V, which far exceeds the 5–20 μV (0.000005 to 0.000020 V) signals of interest in most ERP research. Given the ubiquity and necessity of electronic devices in modern research, it is important to consider several factors that may mitigate the presence of mains-interference in EEG recordings.

Without question, the best way to reduce mains-interference is to remove it completely. Turning off any non-essential electronic devices will also go a long way toward reducing noise in the environment. Of course, some electronic devices are required for the experimental procedure. To the extent that it is possible, moving these devices away from the participant can greatly reduce the impact of emitted EMI. Other powered devices may not be under the experimenter's direct control. For example, elevators and HVAC units are notorious generators of large amplitude EMI. When moving the entire lab is not possible, it may be desirable to identify a location within the lab where EMI is at its least pernicious. This can be done using an EMI meter. There are inexpensive (~$40) meters available that are designed for the explicit purpose of measuring mains-interference (i.e., 60 Hz EMI).

Other necessary evils such as computer monitors and ambient lighting can be selected so as to minimize the amplitude of mains-interference. LCD monitors, for example, emit less EMI than do older CRT monitors. Fluorescent lighting produces more EMI than incandescent lighting. There are also DC-powered options available in the case of both monitors and lighting. Replacing as many AC-powered devices with DC-powered devices as possible is arguably one of the best ways to eliminate mains-interference, but this can also be an expensive undertaking.

Another approach to reducing EMI is electromagnetic isolation. Isolating, or shielding, your recordings from stray EMI can be accomplished using enclosures made from conductive materials like copper. When the source of ambient EMI is small, such as a computer monitor, it can be effective to simply isolate the device. For example, small chambers, sometimes called Faraday cages, for shielding recordings against EMI emitted by a monitor can be easily constructed using metallic mesh and a sheet of EMI-shielded glass for one of the four sides of the cage (see Luck, 2005: ch. 3). In other cases it may be desirable to isolate the participant (and surrounding area) from ambient EMI. In this case, larger chambers are commercially available, or can be constructed using an up-scaled version of the same basic design just described. However, factors such as the volume of the shielded space and the conductive properties and thickness of the metal used must be considered given that each can impact the effectiveness of the shielding.

Optimizing Computers

Whether a computer is included with the purchase of an EEG system or purchased separately, it is important to take steps to optimize each computer's performance for the task to which it is assigned. Realizing that computer processors are serial in nature, one of the first and simplest ways to improve performance is to prevent unnecessary programs from running on the computer during data collection. This is important because each running program occupies some of the computer's RAM and consumes cycles on the processor. When many programs are running simultaneously, the operating system must perpetually switch between them, making it difficult in some cases for those programs that demand a high level of resources to function smoothly. Because most software used in the EEG laboratory is only PC-compatible, we will address only common issues and solutions pertaining to the Windows operating system (OS).

Computers purchased from the large commercial vendors are notoriously loaded with a myriad of Internet chat software, animated sidebars, auto-update programs, and other goodies, each of which consumes valuable resources on the host computer. In many cases, this software can be removed from the computer by conventional means. One of the first places to look for these applications is in the Startup folder, since programs listed here will be executed automatically each time the computer is booted. Some programs, such as Internet browsers and email applications, may be needed periodically. In these cases, it is important to make sure that the software is closed (i.e., not running) during the recording session. In other cases, it is not possible to remove a program completely, but it can usually be disabled. This is true for both screensaver and power-management applications. It may even be beneficial to disable unnecessary hardware devices. For example, disabling audio (at least on the acquisition computer) and networking devices can be a very effective way of preventing both unwanted network traffic on the computer and untimely use of related applications by research assistants during a recording session.

Another step that can be taken to improve the computer's performance is to disable some of the many 'services' that are loaded with the Windows OS. A Windows service is a small program that runs continuously without any user interaction. Some of these services are critical to the functioning of the Windows OS, but many others can be disabled without affecting performance as it relates to data acquisition or experiment control. To access control over these services in Windows 7, click the Start button then right-click Computer and select Services and Applications. A list of all services (running and idle) will be made available. Use the description of the service to determine whether it is needed.[1]

Another route to optimization is to compile the components and build the computers yourself. While this can seem daunting to someone who hasn't done it before, assembling a computer is actually quite simple, takes only about three hours (including software installation), and can be done for a fraction of the price. Two advantages of this route are (1) that options for selecting high-performance hardware are much less restricted, and (2) that complete control can be exercised over the software that is installed. The additional freedom to select from a variety of high-performance hardware is especially useful for tailoring computers to their dedicated tasks. For example, experiment control computers will benefit most from high-end video and audio cards. A good video card may also be important for the acquisition computer given the need to display data on-line, but high-end audio is likely unnecessary. The essential components of a system include: (1) computer case and power supply (these are often packaged together), (2) motherboard with integrated network interface and CPU (these are often packaged together), (3) RAM, (4) video card, (5) audio card, (6) CD/DVD drive (often needed for software installation), (7) a monitor, and (8) a copy of the Windows operating system.

Using a Pneumatic Gel Dispenser

As was mentioned previously regarding electrode design, it can be difficult to know with certainty how much electrolyte gel has been delivered to an electrode site even with larger apertures in center of the electrodes. This can be especially problematic for inexperienced users because too much gel can easily create salt bridges between sensors. Using too much gel also means higher costs per experimental subject, more clean-up at the end of the experiment, and potentially unhappy subjects when they discover the mess left behind.

One way that this issue can be addressed in the laboratory is to use a pneumatic dispenser to deliver the electrolyte gel. Construction of these dispensers is really quite simple and can be accomplished for around $200. The two components that are needed are (1) an air compressor and (2) a fluid-dispensing controller. For most applications, only a small air compressor is needed with a capacity of 1–2 gallons. The simplest way to ensure compatibility between the compressor and the dispensing controller is to be sure the compressor houses a 'quick connect' coupler, which makes it very easy to attach a variety of hoses and utilities.

---

[1]Windows XP includes a feature called 'Hardware Profiles' that allows users to select a specific configuration of services and applications when the computer is booted. Unfortunately, this feature was removed from Vista and 7.

There is also a variety of fluid dispensing controllers available. The most important feature of the dispensing controller for present purposes is that it have a 'timed-shot' feature, meaning that each depression of the dispenser switch releases pressure to the syringe for a specified duration. Another nice feature is the so-called 'suck-back' feature, which applies negative pressure to the syringe at the end of each timed shot in order to prevent excess gel leakage from the tip of the syringe between shots.

Assembly of the dispenser is as simple as connecting a hose between the compressor and the controller and then plugging each into a nearby electrical outlet. Because each of these units is potentially an additional source of mains interference in the recordings, it is important to be sure they are both unplugged following electrode preparation. Our own experience with the pneumatic gel dispenser has been that it drastically reduces the amount of electrolyte gel used with each participant, reduces electrode preparation time, and also facilitates the training of research assistants because much less time is spent learning the art of electrode preparation.

Working with Human Participants

Working with human research participants comes with a unique set of challenges, as social and personality psychologists are well aware. Here we aim to highlight a few miscellaneous tips that can improve both data quality and the experience of the participants in the EEG laboratory. The most common complaints by research participants are discomfort during the electrode preparation process and the time needed to prepare high-density arrays. Extra time and discomfort during the preparation process is usually attributable to the process of reducing high impedances between the scalp and the conductive surface of the electrodes, which is often due to the presence of hair oils, conditioning, and/or styling products. Whenever possible, it is a good idea to ask participants to wash their hair the night before EEG recordings are to be made and to refrain from applying conditioner and/or styling products the day of the experiment.

Another procedure that has proven very effective in our lab is to ask participants to brush their hair/scalp upon arriving to the laboratory. Using a very stiff-bristled brush for just a few minutes can quickly remove excess oil and hair products. Additionally, as the bristles of the brush scrape against the surface of the scalp, they help to remove part of the stratum corneum layer of the epidermis – a layer of dead skin cells that are perpetually shed. This is important because dry, dead skin cells are very poor conductors and thus contribute to higher impedances. There are also preparations available that contain mild abrasives for reducing the resistance at the skin, however, these can be difficult to apply when the participant is wearing an electrode cap. We do recommend using an electrode preparation gel on the areas of the face where the peri-ocular, reference, and common electrodes will be attached prior to electrode attachment – these will improve the impedance of these electrodes considerably. One important point to remember when preparing participants for EEG recording is that electrode impedances will 'settle' as the skin becomes hydrated by the electrolyte gel. Thus, a strategy that will speed up the electrolyte application process is to dispense the gel to the electrode site and then immediately move on to the next electrode. By the time this process is completed, the impedance at electrodes at the beginning of the sequence will have had time to settle and a judgment can be made about whether further adjustment is necessary. If the impedance at an electrode is not as low as desired, research assistants can use a blunt needle to gently abrade the scalp at the problematic electrode by rubbing it back and forth on the scalp to remove dead skin cells. If impedance is still not acceptable, more electrolyte gel can be inserted, although care should be taken not to inject too much, given the risk of creating a bridge between electrodes.

Dealing with participant fatigue can also present a challenge. Due to the repetitive nature of most research protocols and the fact that participants are often seated in a dimly lit room (in order to reduce distractions from the monitor) it is quite common for participants to become fatigued during an experiment. Providing a number of opportunities for breaks during an experimental procedure can help to maintain alertness. Some researchers even play music during the recording session or provide caffeinated beverages. While arguments can be made against each of these potential remedies to the problem of fatigue, it is important to consider that any variability introduced to the data (e.g., effects of caffeine, attention periodically oriented to music, etc.) is likely preferable to making recordings from participants during the early stages of sleep.

Another practical consideration when working with human participants is the recording environment, which should be cool and dry. Recall that the secretion of sweat from eccrine glands can induce low-frequency, large amplitude changes in the electrical potential at the scalp. These artifacts can be reduced by taking care to ensure that both temperature and humidity levels are maintained at low levels in the recording location. Cool, dry conditions in the recording environment will not only lead to improvements in signal quality, but may even improve statistical power in tests of ERP component amplitudes (Kappenman & Luck, 2010).

REFERENCES

Curtin, J. J., Lozano, D. L., & Allen, J. J. B. (2007). The Psychophysiology Laboratory. In J. A. Coan & J. J. B. Allen (Eds), *The handbook of emotion elicitation and assessment* (pp. 398–425). New York, NY: Oxford University Press.

Delorme, A., & Makeig, S. (2004). EEGLAB: An open source toolbox for analysis of single-trial EEG dynamics including independent component analysis. *Journal of Neuroscience Methods, 134*, 9–21.

Dien, J. (1998). Issues in the application of the average reference: Review, critiques, and recommendations. *Behavior Research Methods, 30*(1), 34–43.

Hagemann, D., Naumann, E., & Thayer, J. (2001). The quest for the EEG reference revisited: A glance from brain asymmetry research. *Psychophysiology, 38*(5), 847–857.

Kappenman, E. S., & Luck, S. J. (2010). The effects of electrode impedance on data quality and statistical significance in ERP recordings. *Psychophysiology*, *47*(5), 888–904.

Luck, S. J. (2005). An introduction to the event-related potential technique. Cambridge, MA: The MIT Press.

Oostenveld, R., Fries, P., Maris, E., & Schoffelen, J.-M. (2011). FieldTrip: open source software for advanced analysis of MEG, EEG, and invasive electrophysiological data. *Computational Intelligence and Neuroscience*, *2011*, 1:1–1:9.

Shannon, C. E., & Weaver, W. (1949). *The mathematical theory of communication*. Champaign, IL: University of Illinois Press.

Stahl, C. (2006). Software for generating psychological experiments. *Experimental Psychology*, *53*(3), 218–232.

Tadel, F., Baillet, S., Mosher, J. C., Pantazis, D., & Leahy, R. M. (2011). Brainstorm: A user-friendly application for MEG/EEG analysis. *Computational Intelligence and Neuroscience*, *2011*, 1–13.

4

GETTING STARTED WITH DATA ANALYSIS: DATA PRE-PROCESSING

OVERVIEW

This and the remaining chapters of this book combine exposition of topics related to the contemporary analysis of EEG data with guided analyses using EEGlab and ERPlab. Although EEGlab provides a graphic user interface (GUI), limiting the need for prior experience with Matlab and fluency in Matlab's native programming language, users new to EEGlab will find that some familiarity with Matlab will go a long way toward improving their experience. There are many good introductions to Matlab available, including several free resources on the Internet (e.g., http://en.wikibooks.org/wiki/MATLAB_Programming).

Before continuing, it is recommended that you download the tutorial data for this chapter and the two Matlab scripts, 'ERP_butterfly.m' and 'DK_PSD.m', from the companion site for this book at www.sagepub.co.uk/dickter. The data can be placed anywhere on your computer. The two Matlab scripts should be placed in the Matlab directory on your computer (e.g., C:\users\username\Documents\MATLAB).

Following the guided tutorials will also require you to download and install EEGlab (http://sccn.ucsd.edu/eeglab/) and ERPlab (http://erpinfo.org/erplab/), both of which are free, open-source software packages written in Matlab and designed specifically for the purpose of analyzing EEG and ERP data. Under perpetual development, there are many versions of EEGlab and ERPlab available. It is highly recommended that you download EEGlab version 12.0.2.0b or later and ERPlab version 3.0.2.1 or later. All of the analyses should be possible with computers even several years old, but it is recommended that they have at least a 2333 MHz processor and 2GB of RAM. All of the procedures described in this book were tested using Matlab version 2012a, EEGlab version 12.0.2.0b, and ERPlab version 3.0.2.1. All images depicting the EEGlab and/or ERPlab interfaces have been reproduced with permission.

INTRODUCTION TO EEGLAB

EEGlab is a free, open-source toolbox for Matlab with an interactive GUI. EEGlab contains functions for processing continuous and event-related EEG, MEG and other electrophysiological data, including independent component analysis (ICA), time/frequency analysis, artifact rejection, and event-related statistics. EEGlab is platform-independent (Windows, MAC, and Linux) and is also highly extensible. Users can write their own 'plug-ins' to implement analyses that aren't included with EEGlab, or use the many plug-ins written by other users (e.g., ERPlab). EEGlab also takes advantage of Matlab's powerful graphing capability, providing several useful modes of data visualization.

Once you have downloaded and installed EEGlab, it can be invoked by typing **eeglab** at the Matlab command prompt (i.e., >>). As EEGlab initializes, you will notice several corresponding changes in the Matlab window. First, the success/failure of the initialization process will be reported to the Command window as directories are added to Matlab's search path and installed EEGlab plug-ins are loaded. Second, the Workspace window will be populated with several default variables used by EEGlab. The most important of these is the variable titled 'EEG', which will ultimately contain the EEG data and all of its associated parameters. Once the initialization is complete, the EEGlab GUI will also appear. The GUI has a menu bar at the top and displays information about the currently loaded dataset in the bottom panel. In order to ensure smooth operation of the analyses described in this chapter as well as those in Chapters 5 and 6, rely on EEGlab's capability of having more than one dataset stored in the computer's RAM at any given time, it is important to ensure that this capability is enabled before continuing. Select 'File>Memory and other options' from the EEGlab GUI. When the 'Memory options' dialog appears, check that the very first option, 'If set, keep at most one dataset in memory. This allows processing hundreds of datasets within studies', is *not* selected and press 'OK'.

Select 'File>Load existing dataset' to load one of the tutorial datasets (the file named '1001raw.set' will be used for illustrations in this chapter and Chapter 5). Once the file has completed loading, the EEGlab GUI will be updated to reflect information specific to the loaded file. EEGlab uses the term 'frame' to describe samples or time-points. Thus, the 'Channels per frame' field refers to the number of channels at each time-point and the 'Frames per epoch' field refers to the number of time-points per epoch (or segment) of the recording. Before any processing of the data, there is only one 'Epoch', consisting of the continuous data from start to finish of the recording time. We will see in Chapter 5 that during segmentation the data will be divided into a larger number of short epochs. Other information, including the sampling rate, the presence/absence of 'Channel locations' describing the positions of the electrodes on the head, and the presence/absence of 'ICA weights' stored after running ICA are also displayed in the GUI (see Figure 4.1).

The information displayed in the GUI along with many more details of the dataset and the data themselves are stored in the EEG variable. EEG is what is known as a 'structure array' or simply a 'structure' type variable. Structures are very useful for collecting a group of related variables into one place. As such, the EEG structure

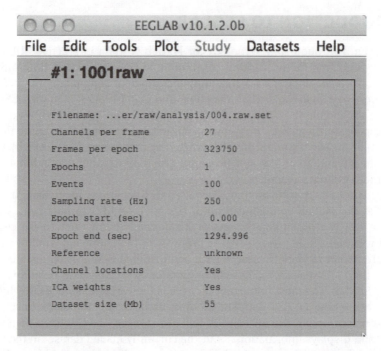

Figure 4.1 EEGlab GUI displaying information about currently loaded dataset.

is really a collection of other variables, all of which are relevant to the currently loaded dataset. To see the contents of the EEG structure, simply type **EEG** at the Matlab command prompt and press ENTER.

The different components of the EEG structure are called 'fields'. For example, the 'setname' field of EEG contains a text string used to identify the dataset. Individual fields can be referenced in Matlab by typing both the name of the structure and the name of the field separated by a period. For example, typing **EEG.data** at the command prompt references the 'data' field containing the channels × time array of raw voltages. Some fields of the EEG structure contain other structures. For example, the 'EEG.event' field contains a sub-structure that includes information regarding the triggers marking significant experimental events during the recording. Being a structure, the 'event' field is a collection of information about each of these events. Typing **EEG.event** at the command prompt will display a list of the fields belonging to the EEG.event structure. By default, EEGlab uses three fields to characterize each event, including its 'type' (usually a descriptor), 'code' (numeric code associated with event), and 'latency' (time at which event occurred during recording). Whereas EEG is a 1×1 structure array, EEG.event is a 1×N structure array where N is equal to the number of events. Information about individual events in the EEG.event structure can be accessed by providing Matlab with an index of the desired event number in parentheses. For example, typing **EEG.event(1)** will cause the type, code, and latency information about the first event to be displayed in the Command window.

QUALITY CONTROL

Quality control is the first and arguably most important step in the analysis of EEG data. The adage 'junk in – junk out' is especially true of EEG/ERP analyses, making it critical that the data from each participant in a research study receive careful review before being included in group-level analyses. Quality control procedures generally have several goals. One goal is to identify data segments with unacceptable levels of noise and/or artifacts so that they can be excluded. A second goal is to identify problems that may have occurred during the recording (e.g., bad channels). Finally, good quality control may help to identify cases in which a complete dataset should be excluded from the study. At the very least, quality control procedures ensure that an experimenter gets to know the data very well.

Fortunately, EEGlab has some simple tools for performing basic quality control. To begin reviewing the data, select 'Plot>Channel data(scroll)'. This will open the 'Scroll channel activities' window, an interactive figure in which one can view the voltage activity plotted as a function of time for all of the channels simultaneously. There are many parameters of the figure that can be changed dynamically. For example, we typically prefer to view the channel activities over a 15-second window as opposed to the default window of 5 seconds. Use 'Settings>Time range to display' from the menu bar inside the 'Scroll channel activities' window in order to change the default setting.

The buttons with angle brackets at the bottom of the 'Scroll channel activities' window can be used to browse the dataset. Single angle brackets will advance/ retreat the data displayed in one-second increments. Double angle brackets will advance/retreat the data displayed by one full display width (e.g., 15 seconds). Unfortunately, there are no established field standards when it comes to the identification and/or removal of artifacts from continuous recordings. Consequently, procedures and even tolerance of artifacts may vary considerably from laboratory to laboratory. Because quality control at this stage of the data processing is generally concerned with the most extreme artifacts, procedures in our lab to identify potential artifacts begin with the following two criteria: (1) individual data segments containing excessive amplitude (e.g., ±200 μV) in a large number of channels (e.g., >25%) and (2) individual channels containing excessive amplitudes over a large portion (e.g., >20%) of the recording. Segments of data containing large artifacts can be marked from within the 'Scroll channel activities' window. To mark a data segment for rejection, simply position the cursor near the beginning of the artifact-laden segment and click the left mouse button. Click again with the cursor positioned near the end of the segment to complete the markup, which will be highlighted in the figure window.

This procedure can be used to mark transient artifacts in the data, including EMG, movement artifact, clipping, and artifact not otherwise specified. Some examples of these types of artifacts are illustrated in Figure 4.2. It should be obvious that pervasive artifacts such as those due to line-noise (e.g., 50/60 Hz), EKG, and ocular artifacts are not appropriate targets of this procedure given that each would require the marking of many data segments, potentially leading to rejection of a majority of the recorded data. Still, it is equally important to deal with pervasive artifacts and

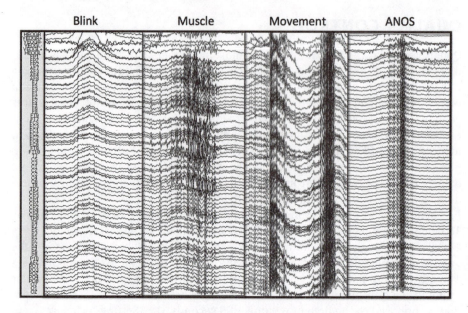

Figure 4.2   Illustration of several common EEG artifacts.

any such artifact should be noted during the review process. Fortunately, notes about a dataset can be stored within the EEG structure in EEGlab. To add notes regarding the currently loaded dataset, select 'Edit>Dataset info'. When the 'Edit dataset information – pop_editset()' dialog box appears, click the 'Enter comments' button.

Once the complete dataset has been reviewed and pervasive artifacts noted, the marked segments can be removed from the dataset by clicking the 'REJECT' button. Rejection of these artifacts from data constitutes an alteration of the original data file. Thus, an EEGlab dialog titled 'Dataset info – pop_newset()' will prompt you to make some decisions about how the modified data file should be saved. You will be making many changes throughout the analysis and nearly every change will be followed by this same dialog. Provide a name for the new dataset (with artifacts excluded) in the 'Name it' field. Select 'Overwrite it in memory' to replace the original dataset with the artifact rejected dataset. Note that this does *not* replace the data file stored on the hard drive of your computer. It only replaces the dataset currently stored in the Matlab workspace (the random access memory [RAM] of your computer). It is always a good idea to keep a copy of the original data file and to save additional copies of the modified dataset(s) at various stages of data processing. The frequency with which copies of the modified dataset are saved is a matter of personal preference. Making too many copies can lead to data management headaches and making too few can lead to regrets later on if a decision is made to re-process the data beginning at some intermediate stage of the analysis. We recommend saving the first additional copy of the data to disk following artifact rejection and ICA decomposition for ocular artifact correction.

ARTIFACT CORRECTION

Pervasive artifacts like line-noise, EKG/pulse, and ocular artifact cannot typically be removed from the data. There are, however, several techniques available to reduce the presence of these artifacts. These techniques constitute a family of computational artifact *correction* strategies that aim to isolate (in the mathematical sense) artifacts and subtract their estimated contribution to the recorded signal. Artifact correction is a very complex topic. The computational strategies employed range from very simple to very sophisticated and there is no single strategy that is optimal for all types of artifact. Given the complex nature of artifact correction and the varied approaches to dealing with different artifacts, the focus in this section will be limited to the most common artifact and just one popular correction method.

The one artifact that must be addressed in nearly all recordings of human EEG longer than a few seconds is that due to blinks and ocular movements. Recall that the physiology of the eyes is such that there is a separation of charge between the front and back of the eyeball, generating an electrical dipole. When the eyeballs move due to blinking or gaze shifts, displacement of this dipole propagates an electrical potential to the scalp electrodes that is typically much larger (e.g., ~75–200 µV) than the background EEG (see Figure 4.2).

Correcting for ocular artifact involves (1) estimation of the artifactual component of the recorded data and (2) subtraction of that component from the data for each electrode. A variety of methods for doing this have been proposed (and used) over the years. One of the earliest and most widely used methods involves simple least-squares regression. In general, regression-based techniques assume that the artifactual component of the data can be estimated by recording from peri-ocular electrodes and that subtraction of that signal can be guided by 'propagation factors', reflecting the proportion of the artifactual signal present in each scalp channel. There are a number of variants of this same basic method, each of which makes different claims about the best approach to estimating the propagation factors (Croft & Barry, 2000; Croft, Chandler, Barry, Cooper, & Clarke, 2005).

A more recently developed and increasingly popular method for the correction of ocular artifact uses independent components analysis (ICA), a blind source separation technique that aims to separate a set of independent signals from a set of mixed signals. In the context of EEG, the mixed signals include all of those recorded from the scalp and peri-ocular channels. These signals are 'mixed' because each is influenced by the voltages produced by a potentially large number of brain, ocular, and other voltage sources at any given time. Thus, the goal of ICA is to un-mix the various sources contributing to the collective voltage dynamics observed over the set of electrodes. When used for ocular artifact correction, the goal is to identify those sources (i.e., 'components') estimated by ICA that are thought to be related to ocular artifact and then subtract them from the data.

A thorough discussion of the costs and benefits of ocular artifact correction by comparison with prevention and/or rejection of ocular artifact can be found elsewhere (e.g., Luck, 2005, ch. 4). In general, experts in the field consider ICA to be superior to regression-based techniques (Hoffmann & Falkenstein, 2008).

In order to conduct ocular artifact correction using ICA in EEGlab, select 'Tools>Run ICA'. When the 'Run ICA decomposition' dialog appears, there will be the option to choose from among a number of ICA algorithms. Leave the settings at their default values, which will use the 'runica' option (an implementation of the 'infomax' algorithm) with the 'extended' option set to a value of 1 (click the 'Help' button for more information about these options). Click 'OK' to begin the ICA analysis. Information about the progress of the ICA decomposition will be printed to the Matlab command window. When the decomposition is completed (this may take some time), it is highly recommended that you save a new copy of the dataset using 'File>Save current dataset as'. Be sure to give the dataset a new name so as to not replace the original file.

In order to determine those components that best reflect the ocular artifact, it is usually necessary to inspect the topography and time-course of each of the ICA components. Although the procedures for identifying artifactual components vary from laboratory to laboratory, a common method is to first identify suspect components based on topographical distribution. Component topographies can be visualized in EEGlab by selecting 'Plot>Component maps>In 2-D' (see Figure 4.3). When the 'Plot component scalp maps in 2-D' dialog appears, add the text '‚'plotchans',[7:27]' to the 'Additional topoplot() options' field in order to prevent peri-ocular channels from being included in the topographical display and then click 'OK' to continue. Note that your results may look slightly different from those in Figure 4.3.

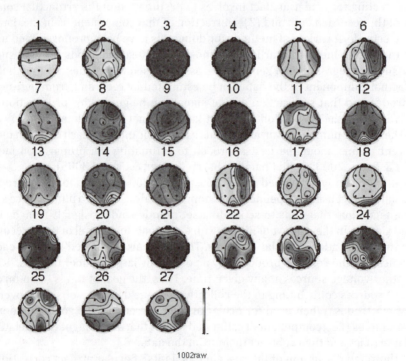

1002raw

Figure 4.3   Independent component topographies. The topographies of component numbers 1 and 5 are characteristic of ocular artifacts. Note that individual results may vary.

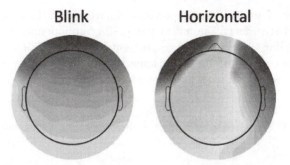

Figure 4.4   Topographies characteristic of blink-related artifact (left) and horizontal eye movement artifact (right).

Because ocular artifacts due to blinking and horizontal eye movements tend to possess distinctive scalp topographies, many components can be excluded based on visual inspection of the topographical maps alone. Arising due to the simultaneous downward movement of both eyes during blinks, blink-related artifact tends to introduce bilaterally symmetric voltages over anterior recording sites (see Figure 4.4). By contrast with blink-related artifact, horizontal movement of the eyes tends to introduce bilaterally asymmetric artifact with opposite polarity across the anterior recordings sites of each hemisphere (see Figure 4.4).

Considering the distinctive topography of artifacts related to blinks and horizontal eye movements, a small subset of the components can typically be selected for further evaluation. For example, considering the component topographies depicted in Figure 4.4, the first and fifth ICA components are likely candidates for further consideration. Once a subset of potential artifact components has been selected, it is typical to evaluate the time-course of these components against the best available measure of the true artifact. In many cases, this best available measure is the signal recorded from electrodes placed around the known source of the artifact, the eyes. The time-courses of these peri-ocular signals and those of the suspect components can be visualized separately in EEGlab. Use 'Plot>Channel data (scroll)' to visualize the original recordings from peri-ocular channels. Next, use 'Plot>Component activations (scroll)' to visualize the time-course(s) of the ICA components. Tiling these two windows on the computer screen and using the Settings menu to constrain the number of visible channels facilitates evaluation and comparison of the respective time-courses. Figure 4.5 illustrates this approach to evaluating ICA components. Notice that the time-courses of the first and fifth ICA components correspond with the blink-related artifact visible in the electro-oculogram (e.g., SO1/2 and IO1/2). This correspondence, combined with the topography of the first and fifth ICA components, indicates that they are good estimates of the artifactual signals due to blinking and lateral eye movements respectively and are thus good candidates for subtraction from the recordings (see Figure 4.5).

Once the artifactual ICA components have been identified, the recordings can be 'corrected' by subtracting those components from the data. Put simply, the subtraction of an ICA component is equivalent to reconstituting the original data from all of the independent sources (i.e., components) derived from the ICA solution *except* those identified as artifacts. The subtraction of ICA components can be performed in EEGlab by selecting 'Tools>Remove components' from the EEGlab menu. When the 'Remove components from data' dialog appears, enter the numbers that correspond with the components you wish to remove into the 'Component(s) to remove from

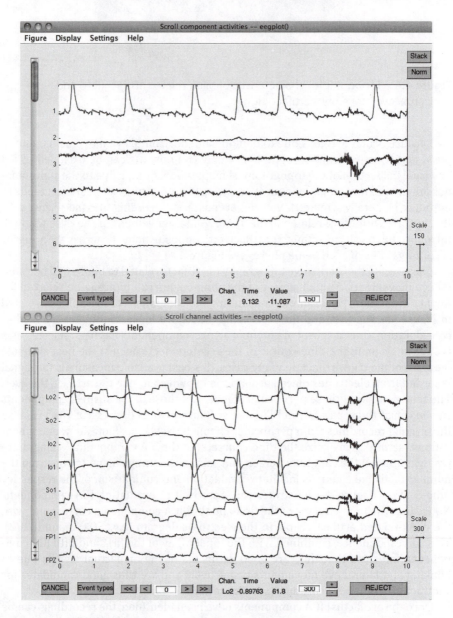

Figure 4.5   Illustration of the visualization of component time-courses (*top panel*) and blink-related artifact in peri-occular channels (*bottom panel*).

data' field and click 'OK'. When the 'Confirmation' dialog appears, you will have a chance to review the results of the artifact correction. Click the button labeled 'Plot single trials' to review the results. If the correction is successful, you will see that the corrected data no longer show any evidence of blinks or horizontal eye movements. When you are convinced that subtraction of the selected components yielded a satisfactory correction of the targeted artifact(s), close the review window and click the 'Accept' button in the 'Confirmation' dialog. After clicking 'Accept', you will be prompted by the 'Dataset info' dialog to save the artifact corrected data. Provide a name for the new dataset and click the box next to the 'Save it as file' field and provide a filename (this is the name of the file that will be saved to disk on your computer). Finally, click the button next to 'Overwrite it in memory' and press 'OK'. Save a copy of the artifact-corrected dataset using 'File>Save current dataset as'.

REFERENCES

Croft, R., & Barry, R. (2000). EOG correction: Which regression should we use? *Psychophysiology*, *37*(1), 123–125.

Croft, R. J., Chandler, J. S., Barry, R. J., Cooper, N. R., & Clarke, A. R. (2005). EOG correction: A comparison of four methods. *Psychophysiology*, *42*(1), 16–24.

Hoffmann, S., & Falkenstein, M. (2008). The correction of eye blink artefacts in the EEG: A comparison of two prominent methods. *PLoS One*, *3*(8), e3004.

Luck, S. J. (2005). An introduction to the event-related potential technique. Cambridge, MA: The MIT Press.

5

TIME-DOMAIN ANALYSIS

THE EVENT-RELATED POTENTIAL

The popularity of EEG as an instrument for cognitive neuroscience began in the mid-1960s with William Gray Walter's work describing the 'contingent negative variation' (CNV) (Walter, Cooper, Aldridge, McCallum, & Winter, 1964), a slow negative-going potential elicited by a stimulus *only* when that stimulus could be used to predict the onset of a target to which a motor response was required. In other words, the procedure for eliciting a CNV is what many psychologists refer to as a constant foreperiod reaction time experiment wherein a preparatory stimulus (S1) is followed by an imperative stimulus (S2) to which a motor response is made. Discovery of the CNV was quickly followed by the *Bereitschaftspotential* (German for 'readiness potential') (Kornhuber & Deecke, n.d.), also called the motor potential or readiness potential (RP), and the P300 (Sutton, Braren, Zubin, & John, 1965). Together, these discoveries are credited with seeding the explosion of EEG research over the last five decades aimed at improving our understanding about the physiological basis for psychological phenomena.

✱Critical to the success of these discoveries was the advent of computerized averaging of the recorded EEG (Galambos & Sheatz, n.d.), a method for extracting evoked potentials from the normally noisy background EEG activity. Prior to the introduction of signal averaging, measurement of the neural response to an eliciting stimulus was limited to those potentials large enough to be discriminated from noise in the continuous EEG recordings. These responses were called evoked potentials (EPs). However, signal averaging made it possible to visualize and measure much smaller potentials that were not easily discernable in the raw EEG recording. When EEG voltages are measured with respect to an eliciting stimulus and averaged over a number of repetitions of that (or a similar) stimulus, the result is typically referred to as an event-related potential (ERP), and is a measure of that part of the neural response that is consistently elicited by the stimulus. The importance of appreciating the process of signal averaging by which ERPs are obtained

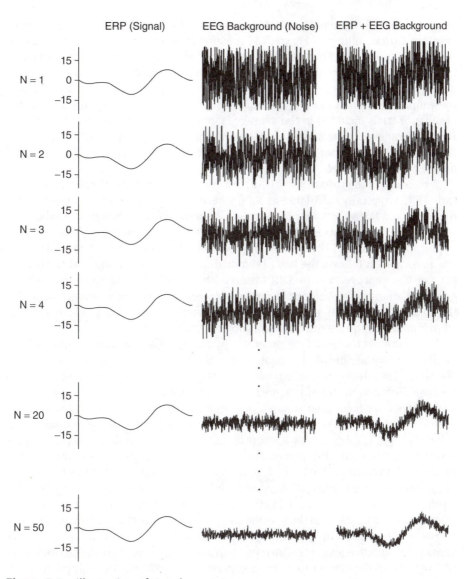

Figure 5.1   Illustration of signal averaging.

cannot be understated given that understanding the assumptions and limitations of signal averaging can both improve one's ability to interpret the existing literature and guide one's own research endeavors using ERPs.

There are two assumptions that are fundamental to the process of measuring ERPs: (1) the EP (i.e., 'signal') is invariant over trials; (2) the background EEG (i.e., 'noise') is random in each trial. Figure 5.1 illustrates how these two simple assumptions combine to yield a conventional ERP waveform across a number of trials for a case where a known ~20 μV signal occurs amidst ~50 μV of EEG background noise. The first thing to notice about Figure 5.1 is that resolution of the ERP signal of interest (first column of Figure 5.1) remains constant across the averaging process due to the fact that the amplitude of the EP at any given time point is assumed to be invariant across trials. Second, because the amplitude of the EEG background noise (second column of Figure 5.1) at any given time point is random across trials, the amplitude of the noise will be reduced (theoretically approaching zero) as the number of trials included in the average is increased. This noise reduction due to signal averaging can be seen to lead to a dramatic improvement in the ability to distinguish the ERP from background noise (third column of Figure 5.1) when the number of trials is large.

A measure of the capacity to distinguish signal from noise is the signal-to-noise ratio (SNR), typically calculated as S/N, where S is a measure of the amplitude of the signal and N is a measure of the amplitude of the noise. Although it may be obvious that the SNR increases with the number of trials, as depicted in Figure 5.1, it is important to note that the relationship between SNR and number of trials is not linear. Instead, it follows the law of diminishing returns, meaning that the magnitude of the improvement in SNR observed between one and four trials will be greater than the improvement observed between four and eight. In fact, provided the noise is Gaussian distributed, it can be shown that the SNR will only increase as a function of the square root of the number of trials.

Due to the fact that ERPs are generated by averaging across trials, their measurement is appropriate only in the context of evaluating a neural response that can be measured repeatedly and often over an extended period of time. Additionally, because ERPs are, by definition, measured with respect to the onset of an eliciting event (hence the term *event*-related potential), their use is limited to the study of cognitive and perceptual processes that can be time-locked to an exogenous stimulus. For example, ERPs are an appropriate instrument to study the cognitive processes associated with the presentation of single words (e.g., Bartholow, Fabiani, Gratton, & Bettencourt, 2001), but it would be inappropriate to use ERPs to measure the various cognitive events that unfold while reading a lengthy sentence. Careful forethought is therefore required in the design of an ERP experiment and much consideration must be given to the specific cognitive process(es) under investigation.

Because it is often the primary goal of ERP research to associate ERP components with cognitive processes, an equally important prerequisite to the conduct of ERP research is the development of an appreciation for the relationship(s) between the voltages of an ERP component and the latent electrical potentials generated by discrete cognitive processes in the brain. Generally speaking, the term 'component' is used in the context of an ERP analysis to denote a particular feature of an ERP waveform. In most cases, the feature(s) of interest is a transient modulation of amplitude appearing as a peak or trough in the waveform (top panel of Figure 5.2). As such, ERP components are typically identified by their polarity (i.e., peak or trough) and their temporal latency or duration. For example, the 'P50' component is a positive-going modulation of the ERP amplitude with a maximum voltage (i.e., peak) at about 50 ms following the onset of an auditory stimulus. Likewise, the 'N100' component is a negative-going modulation of ERP amplitude with a minimum voltage at about 100 ms. Alternatively, components are sometimes labeled

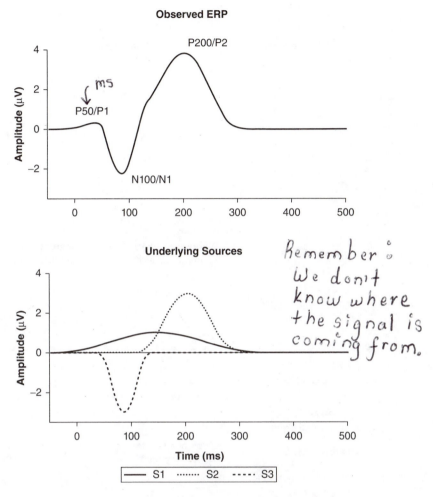

Figure 5.2 Illustration of how observed ERPs are produced by voltage summation.

according to the sequence in which they occur on an ERP waveform. For example, the N100 component may sometimes be referred to as the 'N1' because it is the first significant negative deflection of the waveform (see Figure 5.2).

Because discrete cognitive processes are believed to be the product of changes in the activity of localized populations of neurons in the brain, they are thought to be associated with the propagation of transient electrical potentials to the scalp. It can thus be tempting to draw the erroneous conclusion that the voltage peaks and troughs (i.e., components) in the ERP waveform necessarily correspond with the transient electrical potentials elicited by activity at specific brain sources. The error in this logic stems from the fact that the ERP voltage at any given time is, because of volume conduction, actually a sum of the activity of many underlying populations of neurons each generating its own electrical potential (see Figure 5.3). Because there is no way to know the location or even the number of sources of

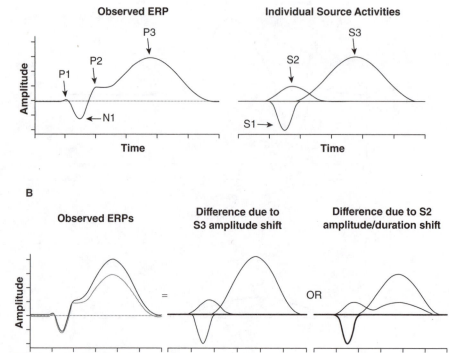

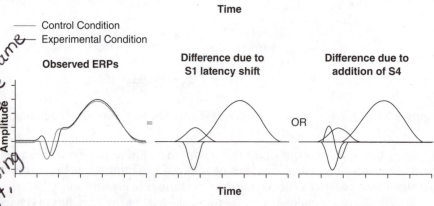

Handwritten margin note: *Problem! ERPs could overlap or shift the same. So might be difficult to actually say what is causing shift.*

Figure 5.3 (A) Illustration of a typical ERP waveform produced by the sum of the voltage activity of three sources. (B) Two possible modulations of the voltage sources that could produce the same increase in amplitude of the P3 component. (C) Two possible modulations of the voltage sources that could produce a latency shift in the N1 component.

electrical potential in the brain at any given time, it is impossible to link ERP voltages with localized potentials of brain sources. In fact, voltage peaks/troughs in an ERP waveform may even be artifacts of voltage summation at the scalp in some cases. For example, consider the electrical potential generated by source #1 (S1) in the bottom panel of Figure 5.2. Important characteristics including the peak amplitude and latency of the potential generated by S1 are almost completely obscured in the voltage trace of the ERP (top panel of Figure 5.2). Additionally, the P50 component appears to be an artifact of the temporal overlap of S1 and S3, indicating at best the onset of the S1 source activity.

This inherent difficulty of interpreting ERP voltages is sometimes referred to as the 'inverse problem'. An illustrative example of the inverse problem and, in particular, how it complicates the interpretation of experimental effects observed in ERP components is illustrated for a simulated ERP waveform in Figure 5.3. Panel A of Figure 5.3 illustrates an observed ERP waveform (left) and its constituent source activities (i.e., voltages). Panel B of Figure 5.3 illustrates two examples of commonly observed experimental effects. The top row of panel B illustrates a simple amplitude increase observed for the experimental condition (left). However, illustrated on the right of panel B are just two of the infinite number of possible changes in source activity that could yield the differences observed in the ERP. A similar example is shown on the bottom row of panel B for an apparent latency shift in the ERP waveform, which could be attributable to a latency change in the underlying source voltage, or the addition of a fourth latent source. In-depth discussion regarding the interpretation of ERP components and recommendations regarding the design of ERP experiments can be found elsewhere (Luck, 2005). Notwithstanding these limitations, many common components of the ERP have been well-characterized and successfully linked, via careful experimental design, to a number of specific cognitive processes.

In-depth descriptions of many specific ERP components can be found elsewhere (Luck & Kappenman, 2011), however, several useful distinctions can be applied to broad categories of components of the ERP waveform. ERP components are often classified as being either exogenous and endogenous components. Exogenous components are considered to reflect obligatory sensory/perceptual responses occurring very soon after (e.g., 1–200 ms) an eliciting stimulus. Though not immune to the internal (i.e., endogenous) state of the perceiver, these components are less susceptible to modulation by attention and task demands. The endogenous category of components, by contrast, generally occur ~200–1000 ms following a stimulus and are thought to be associated with high-level perceptual and cognitive processes related to stimulus evaluation and decision-making. Because most neuroscience research in social and personality psychology is concerned with the latter aspects of human cognition, it should come as no surprise that the majority of contemporary ERP research in this field concerns the endogenous components of the ERP.

Another important distinction between ERP components concerns the nature of the time-locking event. Components can be either stimulus-locked or response-locked. Stimulus-locked ERP components can be measured when the data are segmented with respect to the onset of a sensory (e.g., visual, auditory, somatosensory, etc.) event. Response-locked ERPs are generated in exactly the same way as stimulus-locked ERPs except that segmentation of the recorded data occurs with respect to a behavioural response. In the case of response-locked

ERPs, the time directly preceding or following the behavior can be the target of analyses. Because they reflect those cognitive processes that are associated with a response across trials, response-locked ERPs can be very useful, either alone or in combination with stimulus-locked ERPs, to address questions about decision-making processes relevant to task performance.

DOMAIN REVIEW: PERSON PERCEPTION

Most research in person perception has focused on the processing of faces. This research reveals that humans can very rapidly extrapolate information regarding age, race, emotion, behavioral intentions, and even personality traits (just to name a few) based only on a brief glance at an image of a face (for a review, see Macrae & Quadflieg, 2010). For example, research suggests that participants presented with an image of a face for as little as 100 ms will infer likeability, trustworthiness, and level of aggression and that these ratings correlate significantly with ratings given after longer exposures to the faces (Willis & Todorov, 2006). Additionally, individuals can accurately categorize novel faces by sex, race, or age quickly and automatically (Brewer, 1988; Fiske & Neuberg, 1990; Ito & Urland, 2003; Macrae & Bodenhausen, 2000). Understanding the nature of these rapid judgments is important because research suggests that they may lead perceivers to ascribe personality traits associated with the category (Brewer, 1988; Darley & Gross, 1983; Devine, 1989; Dovidio, Evans, & Tyler, 1986; Fiske & Neuberg, 1990) and even influence subsequent behavior (Bargh, Chen, & Burrows, 1996; Fazio, Jackson, Dunton, & Williams, 1995; Jussim, Palumbo, Smith, & Madon, 2000; Payne, 2001) toward the individual being perceived. For example, the activation of negative stereotypes may lead perceivers to take actions based on rapid inferences guided by the stereotypes.

Because activating social category information can have implications for later judgments and behavior, a great deal of research in the person perception literature has focused on understanding the processes and consequences of social categorization, as well as stereotype application and activation. Much theory focuses on the idea that social categorization influences most aspects of person perception, which further influences decision-making, memory, attention, and impression formation (Macrae & Quadflieg, 2010). Due to the automatic nature of many of these processes, it is not surprising that researchers have turned to EEG methods to examine how person perception unfolds in the brain.

One of the first ways in which an ERP was used to address the study of person perception was in the context of the P3 component. Because larger P3 amplitudes are often observed in response to novelty/expectancy and interpreted to reflect context updating in working memory, Osterhout, Bersick, and McLaughlin (1997) explored the possibility that the P3 component could be used to index an individual's response to unexpected social contexts. This research revealed that when presented with a sentence, the P3 amplitude was increased when the gender of the pronoun in the sentence violated an expectancy based on conventional stereotypes (e.g., 'Our aerobics instructor gave *himself* a break'). Interestingly, these responses were independent of self-reported ratings of how acceptable the sentences were, suggesting that the P3 may index implicit processing not otherwise observable in behavioral responses. Likewise, Bartholow et al. (2001) later replicated this effect and demonstrated that words that violated an experimentally determined expectancy were more likely to be later recalled than the expectancy-confirming words. This was interpreted to indicate that P3 amplitude may reflect the extent to which resources are dedicated to stimulus processing, with more resources facilitating memory encoding. Subsequent work demonstrated that these effects remain during passive viewing, when participants are not instructed to form impressions of targets (Van Duynslaeger, Van Overwalle, & Verstraeten, 2007). Taken together, these early studies helped to advance social psychologists' understanding about how social stereotypes may be reflected in brain activity. For a more extensive review about expectancy violations and the P3, see Bartholow and Dickter (2011).

In addition to using ERP methods to understand how the P3 is affected by person judgments, social neuroscientists have also used these ERP methods to examine how the social categorization process unfolds. Social categorization is thought to occur when we think of a person not as an individual, but as a member of a particular social group or groups. Theoretically, social categorization allows perceivers to minimize the amount of effort required to negotiate the social world by compartmentalizing social information (Bodenhausen, 1990; Fiske & Taylor, 1991). Research indicates that social categorization takes place very quickly and automatically (Devine, 1989), and can have harmful consequences because the schemas that are activated along with the social category often include negative stereotypes (Brewer, 1988; Darley & Gross, 1983; Fiske & Neuberg, 1990), which can have consequences for behavior (Bargh et al., 1996). Although most of the foundational research on social categorization was behavioral in nature, the implicit nature of social categorization and the lack of understanding of how exactly this process takes place led researchers to turn to ERPs to answer these lingering questions. Ito and Urland (2003) provided early ERP evidence that racial categorization occurs early in processing, with White participants showing differing N1 amplitudes to White compared to Black faces, demonstrating that racial categorization occurs as early as 120 ms after the presentation of a face. These researchers also found that P2 amplitude differed based not only on the race of the target faces, but also on the gender of the faces, suggesting that gender categorization occurs around 180 ms post-stimulus (Ito & Urland, 2003). These findings held regardless of whether participants were categorizing the targets along race or gender dimensions, suggesting that the early ERP components are sensitive to the implicit nature of social categorization. Furthermore, these patterns emerge whether participants are engaging in an explicit social categorization task or making more individuating decisions about the targets (e.g., deciding whether the target likes different kinds of vegetables) or deciding on the visual properties of a target-irrelevant stimulus (e.g., indicating whether a dot is present on the screen) (Ito & Urland, 2003). In addition, Kubota and Ito (2007) showed that blurred pictures of Black and White faces that had the same color and luminance as the faces typically used in these social categorization studies elicited completely different ERP waveforms and did not show race differences, clearly showing that the ERP effects reported above were the result of social categorization *per se* and not the physical properties associated with the faces.

Although Ito and Urland's (2003) finding that the N1 was sensitive to race has not always been replicated in subsequent work, their finding that White participants' P2 was larger to Black than White faces has been replicated extensively (Dickter & Bartholow, 2007; Ito, Thompson, & Cacioppo, 2004; Ito & Urland, 2005; Kubota & Ito, 2007; Walker, Silvert, Hewstone, & Nobre, 2008; Willadsen-Jensen & Ito, 2006, 2008). Although this effect was originally interpreted to reflect a threat response to the negative stereotypes to which Blacks are often ascribed, more recent work with non-White participants has shown that the P2 effect is larger to racial outgroup members than ingroup members, regardless of stereotype content (Dickter & Bartholow, 2007; Willadsen-Jensen & Ito, 2008). Researchers have also shown a consistent N2 racial ingroup effect such that a larger N2 amplitude is associated with the processing of racial ingroup relative to outgroup faces (Dickter & Bartholow, 2007; Ito et al., 2004; Ito & Urland, 2005; Kubota & Ito, 2007; Walker et al., 2008; Willadsen-Jensen & Ito, 2006, 2008). Because the N2 is associated with the processing of infrequent stimuli and is thought to monitor response conflict (see review above), Dickter and Bartholow (2010) sought to examine how stimulus frequency, group membership, and response conflict would affect N2 amplitude. Using a flanker task, they demonstrated that N2 amplitude to racial outgroup faces was unaffected by stimulus frequency or response conflict. However, the N2 to racial ingroup target faces was largest on high conflict trials (i.e., in which both Black and White faces were presented simultaneously) when participants were led to expect low conflict trials (i.e., in which all faces of the same race were presented). These findings suggest that attention to racial outgroup members is narrower than that to racial ingroup members such that information about compatibility and expectations does not affect the processing of racial outgroup faces during this stage of social categorization. For more detailed reviews, see Ito and Bartholow (2009) and Bartholow and Dickter (2011).

Although less work has investigated the behavioral implications of processing differences in ERP components to various social groups, researchers have established that differentiation in these early attentional components to certain social groups can predict behavioral measures of implicit prejudice. Ito and Urland (2005), for example, demonstrated that White participants' greater N2 amplitude to White faces compared to Black faces was associated with a larger implicit association between Blacks and violence. In addition, research using a shooter paradigm, in which participants must decide whether to shoot or refrain from shooting armed and unarmed Black and White individuals (Correll, Park, Judd, & Wittenbrink, 2002), revealed that larger P2s to Blacks and larger N2s to Whites were associated with increased racial bias on the shooter task, such that participants demonstrating these early ERP attentional biases were faster to shoot armed Blacks than Whites (Correll, Urland, & Ito, 2006). Furthermore, Dickter and Bartholow (2007) found that for both Black and White participants, a larger N2 amplitude to racial ingroup relative to racial outgroup targets was associated with a faster response on a social categorization task to ingroup relative to outgroup targets. Taken together, these studies suggest that differences in neural activation to targets of different racial groups predict the implicit associations activated by social categorization, although more research is needed to examine the underlying mechanisms involved in this relationship.

GUIDED ANALYSIS: ERP ANALYSIS WITH EEGLAB AND ERPLAB

The following guided analysis is based on research conducted by Cheryl Dickter and Ivo Gyurovski (2012). The central aim of their paper was to determine whether early attention to Black and White male faces would be affected by stereotypic expectancies. That is, as reviewed above, previous work demonstrated that early ERP components such as N1, P2, and N2 are modulated by attention to faces of varying races (e.g., Dickter & Bartholow, 2007; Ito & Urland, 2003, 2005; Willadsen-Jensen & Ito, 2006, 2008). Research also demonstrated that violations of stereotypic expectations lead to modulations of P3 amplitude such that the amplitude is higher for violations of expectation (e.g., Bartholow et al., 2001; Osterhout et al., 1997). The purpose of the Dickter and Gyurovski (2012) study was to examine whether stereotypic expectancies would also modulate earlier components of the ERP such as the N1, P2, and N2 components. This research is illustrative of how one of the greatest strengths of the ERP technique, its temporal sensitivity, can be used to develop and refine theoretical models in the social sciences about how perceptual processes influence the evaluation of group membership. For example, early attention allocated to group members who engage in counter-stereotypic behaviors may lead to more extreme evaluations compared with the evaluation of individuals who behave in a way that is consistent with stereotypic expectancies (e.g., Bettencourt et al., 1997).

Dickter and Gyurovski (2012) developed an impression-formation procedure with the aim of influencing participants' expectations regarding a subsequent target. The target in this case was an individual face of a White or Black male. Impressions were formed by having participants read sentences describing individuals engaging in behaviors that were either positive or negative in valence and consistent with stereotypes associated with either Black or White Americans. Target stimuli consisted of headshot photographs of Black and White males with neutral facial expressions and direct eye gaze. The faces were similar in attractiveness, stereotypicality, and age (Eberhardt, Davies, Purdie-Vaughns, & Johnson, 2006). Each trial consisted of a fixation cross which appeared for 500 ms, followed by the impression-formation sentence (which remained on the screen until participants indicated by button press that they had finished reading), followed by the target face, which remained on the screen for 500 ms. Participants were asked to indicate whether the target could be the person described in the preceding sentence by pressing one of two keys on the keyboard (counterbalanced between participants). The intertrial interval (ITI) varied randomly between 2000 and 4000 ms. Following a practice block of 10 trials, the experiment included five blocks of 16 trials each. Thus, the study design can be described as a 2 (Target Race: Black, White) × 2 (Stereotype Race: Black, White) × 2 (Stereotype Valence: Positive, Negative) repeated measures factorial design.

EEG recordings were made with a DBPA-1 Sensorium Bioamplifier (Sensorium Inc., Charlotte, VT) with an analog high-pass filter of 0.01 Hz and a low-pass filter of 500 Hz. The EEG was recorded from 74 Ag-AgCl sintered electrodes in an electrode cap, placed using the expanded International 10–20 electrode placement system. All electrodes were referenced to the tip of the nose and the ground electrode was placed in the middle of the forehead, slightly above the eyebrows. Eye movement and blinking were recorded from bipolar electrodes placed on the lateral canthi and peri-occular electrodes on the superior and inferior orbits, aligned with the pupils. Before data collection was initiated, all impedances were adjusted to within 0–20 kilohms.

Although Dickter and Gyurovski (2012) reported their findings for several ERP components, the guided analysis in this chapter will, in the interest of parsimony, focus only on the N2 component. As reviewed earlier in this chapter, the N2 is an ERP component commonly associated with the allocation of attentional resources. For example, when measured in White participants, the N2 tends to be larger when elicited by White faces compared to Black faces. Thus, the researchers expected to find an overall effect of target race, but they additionally expected that target race would interact with the valence and race of the information presented during the stereotype formation procedure.

The remainder of this chapter will illustrate the methods for generating and measuring ERP components with a tutorial-style analysis of the N2 component using the data ($N = 23$) from Dickter and Gyurovski (2012). Although generally straightforward, the process of conventional ERP analysis typically requires a number of steps. The number of steps may vary as a function of the options available in different software packages, or as a function of research goals. While the following guided analysis is by no means the only approach, our aim is to demonstrate the steps that make up a work-flow representative of a typical ERP analysis.

Introduction to ERPlab

As described in Chapter 4, ERPlab (http://erpinfo.org/erplab/) is a free, open-source software package that is written in Matlab and designed specifically for the purpose of analyzing ERP data. ERPlab has been designed as a plug-in to EEGlab, adding many useful analysis and visualization tools and meaning that many of its functions interact directly with the EEG data structure used by EEGlab. ERPlab is also integrated with the EEGlab GUI, making it easy to use for those who are less familiar with Matlab. The guided analysis that follows demonstrates the use of EEGlab and ERPlab to conduct an ERP data analysis beginning with the pre-processed, continuous data generated in Chapter 4. To install ERPlab, download the software from http://erpinfo.org/erplab/ and save it to the 'plugins' directory of EEGlab. Like EEGlab, ERPlab is under perpetual development. It is highly recommended that you download Version 3.0.2.1 or later. Once installed, the 'ERPLAB' menu option will be added to the menu bar inside the EEGlab GUI the next time EEGlab is started.

Loading the Data

Before beginning the ERP analysis tutorial that follows you will need to load one of the datasets created in Chapter 4 (e.g., 1001_clean_oar.set). If it is not already open, invoke EEGlab by typing **eeglab** at the Matlab command prompt and press ENTER.

Load the data file

- File>Load existing dataset

    o Navigate to one of the artifact-corrected datasets created in Chapter 4 and click 'Open'.

The EEGlab GUI will be populated with information about the file once it has completed loading. Notice that, prior to segmentation, the data are still considered by EEGlab to consist of a single epoch (Value of *Epochs* field = 1). Once the data have been segmented around each of the events (triggers), there will be as many epochs as there are events in the analysis.

Segmentation and Baseline Correction

Segmentation of the continuous data involves the extraction of a subset of the original, continuous data. In ERPlab this is accomplished by first using a *binlist* to assign condition labels to specific triggers or groups of triggers in the recorded data file. This assignment of condition labels will later be used to select only those segments of the data that are relevant to the current analysis.

ERPlab uses a 'bin descriptor file' (BDF), which defines the *bins* and can be created in any text editor. Each bin represents a container for those trials that meet the criteria specified in the BDF. The criteria for each bin are specified using three lines in the BDF. The first line gives the bin number. The second line is an identifying label for the bin. The third line gives the criteria that determine which triggers will be assigned to that bin.

There were eight conditions in the study by Dickter and Gyurovski (2012) so it will be necessary to identify eight distinct bins in the BDF. These conditions and their associated trigger codes (visible in the recorded data) are provided in Table 5.1.

bin 1
Black Positive Prime – Black Target
.{10}
bin 2
Black Negative Prime – Black Target
.{20}
...
bin 8
White Negative Prime – White Target
.{80}

The BDF file can be generated using any text editor. It is not necessary (at this point) to fully understand the syntax of the BDF since one is provided for you on the companion website (www.sagepub.co.uk/dickter). However, it is worth pointing

Table 5.1   Trigger Codes used by Dickter & Gyurovski (2012)

Trigger Code	Prime Race	Prime Valence	Target Race
10	Black	Positive	Black
20	Black	Negative	Black
30	White	Positive	Black
40	White	Negative	Black
50	Black	Positive	White
60	Black	Negative	White
70	White	Positive	White
80	White	Negative	White

out that the syntax of the BDF is extremely powerful, permitting the definition of bins with complex criteria including the specification of antecedent and subsequent conditions. Follow the steps below to apply the bin criteria specified in the file, 'Chapter5_BDF.txt' to the current file.

Prepare the EEG structure for compatibility with ERPlab

- ERPLAB>Eventlist>Create EEG EVENTLIST

   o When the dialog titled 'Create Basic Eventlist GUI' appears, click 'CREATE'.

   o An overwrite warning dialog may appear to warn you that information in the EEG structure will be changed. Click 'Overwrite them' to continue.

   o If the dialog titled 'Dataset info – pop_newset()' appears, click the 'Overwrite it in memory' box and then click 'OK'.

Assign events to bins in accordance with the criteria specified in the BDF file

- ERPLAB>Assign Bins (BINLISTER)

   o When the dialog titled 'BINLISTER GUI' appears, click the 'Browse' button under the heading 'Load Bin Descriptor File from'. Select the 'Chapter5_BDF.txt' file downloaded with the tutorial data and click 'Run'.

   o When the 'Dataset info – pop_newset()' dialog appears, select 'Overwrite it in memory' and click 'OK'.

Save the modified file

- File>Save current dataset as

  o Choose a filename that reflects the application of the BDF, such as '1038_oar_BDF.set'.

Extract segments of data with respect to the events/bins

- ERPLAB>Extract Bin-based Epochs

  o When the 'EXTRACT BINEPOCHS GUI' dialog appears, the user is asked to indicate the period of time around each event that should be extracted from the continuous data. Use the interval from −200 to 1000. Negative values for the lower boundary of the time window indicate that each extracted segment should begin prior to the event. In this case, each segment of the data will begin 200 ms before the target event and end 1000 ms after the event.

  o The parameters for baseline correction will also be specified in the 'EXTRACT BINEPOCHS GUI' dialog. Select the 'Pre' option to remove the average of the entire pre-stimulus (−200 ms to 0 ms) interval from each of the segments and then click 'RUN'.

  o When the 'Dataset info – pop_newset()' dialog appears, select 'Overwrite it in memory' and click 'OK'.

When this process has been completed, the fields of the EEGlab GUI will be re-populated to describe the segmented dataset. Notice that the 'Epochs' field now indicates the number of individual data segments that were extracted from the continuous recording.

Filtering

Used in many scientific disciplines, digital filters are mathematical operations applied to a discrete-time signal in order to enhance or attenuate certain aspects of the signal. In contrast with analog filters, which are implemented in an electronic circuit and operate on continuous-time signals, digital filters are typically used to attenuate unwanted frequencies in the recorded EEG. One of the most common motivations for filtering EEG is that when the signals of interest occupy a known frequency range, attenuation of extraneous frequencies (e.g., high-frequency EMG and low-frequency skin potentials) through filtering can improve the signal-to-noise ratio (Cook & Miller, 1992). Digital filters are often preferred over analog filters such as those used by the amplifier at the time the data are recorded because one can retain a copy of the original data, making it possible to evaluate a variety of filters and/or filter parameters and select those which yield the least distortion of the EEG signal of interest (Picton et al., 2000). This is important because anyone who uses filters in the course of data processing should be aware that *all* filters introduce some distortion of their data.

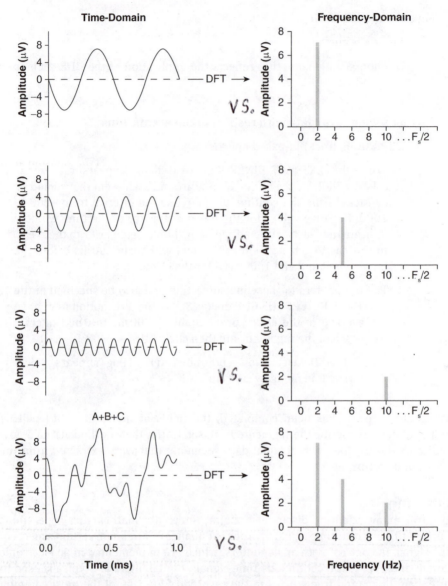

Figure 5.4   Illustration of the relationship between time- and frequency-domain representations.

The fundamentals of digital filtering will be described in the paragraphs that follow. However, readers are strongly encouraged to review other sources, which provide a more formal introduction to filtering (and the distortions it causes) in the context of EEG research (e.g., Cook & Miller, 1992; Luck, 2005). The first step to understanding filters and how they are used is to develop a basic understanding about the 'frequency-domain' representation of a discrete-time series. When signal amplitude is represented as a function of time, the data are said to be represented in the 'time-domain'. However, signal amplitude can also be represented as a function of frequency, called the 'frequency-domain' representation. The frequency-domain representation derives from Fourier theory (named after Joseph Fourier, 1768–1830), which states that any stationary[1] time-domain signal can be represented as the sum of a set of frequency components – sinusoidal waveforms, each with its own frequency, amplitude, and phase. In the context of EEG, the frequency of each sinusoid is usually expressed in cycles per second (Hz) and the amplitude in microvolts (µV). The phase of each sinusoid is usually expressed in radians or degrees and is a quantity that reflects the position in the cycle of the sinusoid at the first point of the signal. The Fourier Transform is a mathematical function that can be used to convert a signal from a time-domain to a frequency-domain representation. Because EEG data are sampled at discrete time intervals, the Discrete Fourier Transform (DFT) is used instead, which returns as its output the frequency components in discrete values or 'bins'. Figure 5.4 illustrates the relationship between time- and frequency-domain representations.

Filters are often described in terms of their 'pass-band', indicating the part of the frequency spectrum that is 'passed' or transmitted through the filter. The remainder of the frequency spectrum outside the pass-band is often referred to as the 'stop-band'. The simplest and most common filters used with EEG data are 'high-pass' and 'low-pass' filters, which selectively pass high and low frequencies respectively. For example, a low-pass filter with a cutoff frequency of 20 Hz would be used to pass frequency components lower than 20 Hz and attenuate frequency components higher than 20 Hz. Other filters include 'band-pass', which attenuate frequencies both above and below a frequency range of interest, and 'band-stop' filters, which attenuate frequencies within a narrow frequency range (e.g., 60 Hz).

The effects a particular filter has on the frequency components of an input signal are characterized by what is known as the filter's frequency response, also known as the 'gain function' or 'transfer function' of the filter. For example, the gain function of a filter is given by the ratio of the output signal to the input signal as a function of frequency. Ideally, the gain function is equal to one (indicating no attenuation) over the pass-band of the filter and zero (indicating complete attenuation) for any frequencies outside the pass-band (top row of Figure 5.5). Ideal filters are impossible to achieve in practice, however, and there is typically a range of frequencies between the pass-band and stop-band, known as the 'transition-band', over which the gain function takes on intermediate values (bottom row of Figure 5.5). In fact, the cutoff frequency occupies this transition-band at the point where the gain (ratio of input to output) is equal to 0.5. This is why the cutoff frequency for a filter is often described as the 'half-amplitude' cutoff. In practice, the gain of a filter is usually expressed in decibels (dB), a logarithmic scale used to describe ratios. Thus, the cutoff frequency is the point at which the filter attenuates the power of the signal by $10\log_{10}(0.5) \approx -3$ dB and the amplitude of the signal by $20\log_{10}(0.5) \approx -6$ dB.

---

[1] A stationary signal is one where the DC component is equal to zero and frequency components are stable over time.

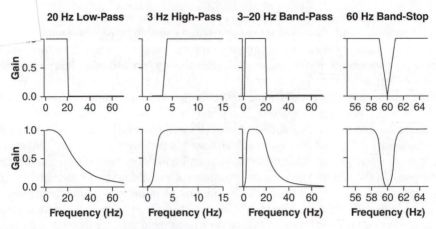

Figure 5.5 Idealized (*top row*) and realized (*bottom row*) gain functions for a variety of filters.

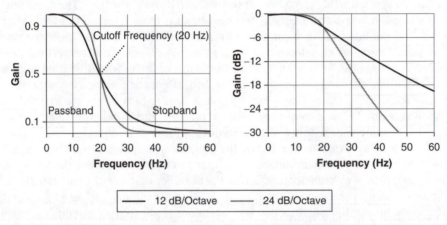

Figure 5.6 The relationship between the roll-off of a filter and the width of its transition band illustrated for both the gain function and the gain in dB units.

The slope of a filter's frequency response over the transition-band is referred to as the 'roll-off' of the filter and is typically measured in units of dB/octave, where 1 octave is a doubling of the frequency. The roll-off of a filter is a measure of its precision in the frequency domain. Filters with a steeper roll-off of 24 dB/octave, for example, possess a more narrow transition-band than filters with a roll-off of 12 dB/octave (see Figure 5.6), meaning that frequencies immediately surrounding the cutoff frequency are more precisely passed/attenuated. While it may be tempting to choose the filter that provides the highest precision in the frequency-domain, doing so comes with the cost of precision in the time-domain. In fact, filters with high roll-off can severely distort the time-domain representation of a signal. Thus, if the purpose of the filter is to isolate specific frequency components, it is better to

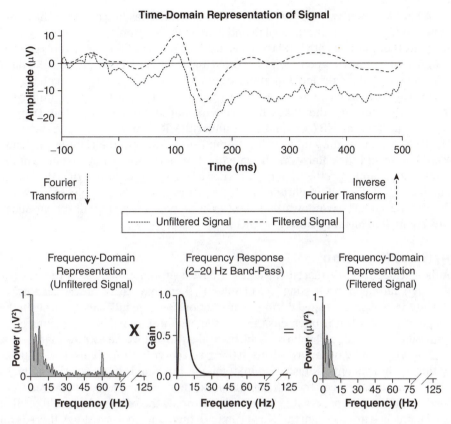

Figure 5.7   Illustration of the application of a band-pass filter to an ERP waveform.

choose filters with higher roll-off; however, when the purpose of the filter is to improve signal-to-noise ratio in the *time*-domain as is the case with the analysis of ERPs, it is desirable to select filters with lower roll-off so as to minimize temporal distortions.

Once a filter with the desired cutoff frequency and frequency response (including roll-off) has been selected, it can be applied to the data. The procedure for applying a chosen filter can be most easily described in the frequency-domain. The first step is to convert the original, unfiltered data from its time-domain to its frequency-domain representation using the DFT. Next, the gain function of the frequency response is calculated for the selected filter. The frequency-domain representation of the filtered signal is then calculated by taking the product of the unfiltered frequency-domain representation and the gain function. Finally, the frequency-domain representation of the filtered signal is converted to its time-domain representation using the inverse DTF. This process is illustrated for the application of a 2–20 Hz band-pass filter in Figure 5.7. Note that very low as well as very high frequency components of the unfiltered signal are visibly reduced in both frequency-domain and time-domain representations of the filtered signal.

All available software for processing EEG data includes functions for the application of filters. In fact, both EEGlab and ERPlab include tools for filtering data. In order to filter the data with ERPlab, select ERPLAB>Filter & Frequency Tools>Filters for EEG data. This will open a window titled 'Basic Filter GUI for epoched EEG data' with options for the design and application of a filter. Options for visualizing the filter properties are also available. Select the 'IIR Butterworth' option under the 'Filter Type' heading, the 'Filter frequency response' option under the 'Display' heading, and set the 'dB/oct' field to 12 under the 'Roll-off & filter order' heading. Next, enter a value of 20 into the 'Half-Amp (−6dB)' field to the right of the 'Low-Pass' button and click 'Refresh'. The gain function of the frequency response of the filter will be plotted in the upper left corner of the window. Notice that the gain is equal to 0.5 at the half-amplitude cutoff frequency of 20. Click 'Apply' to apply the filter to the data. The window titled 'Dataset info − pop_newset()' will appear. Select 'Overwrite it in memory' and click 'OK'.

Artifact Rejection

Although much of the artifact in the data will have been either removed or reduced (by filtering) during pre-processing (see Chapter 4), there may still be unwanted noise in the intervals of data selected during segmentation. Because ERPs are typically in the range of 1 to $20\,\mu V$, it is often desirable to remove those segments containing large amplitude (e.g., $\pm 100\,\mu V$) voltages, which are likely to distort the ERP average.

The most common approach to artifact rejection is to evaluate the voltages within each segment against a simple voltage threshold. If any of the voltages within a segment exceed the voltage threshold, then that segment is removed from further analyses. A conservative approach is to apply the voltage threshold to all of the channels within a segment. However, with high-density recordings there is an increased risk that one of the channels will contain a value exceeding the threshold and this can lead to the rejection of too many segments. A less conservative approach in the case of high-density recordings is to limit the threshold-based rejection of segments to a subset of the electrodes. This is most appropriate, and justifiable, when the data analysis is focused a priori on a specific ERP component with a known topographical distribution, but can lead to peculiarities when the voltages from all channels are visualized and one or more of the channels contains excessive artifacts. There are also a number of more computationally sophisticated ways of identifying artifact-laden segments of data. An attractive quality of many of these methods is that, rather than use an arbitrary threshold (e.g., $\pm 100\,\mu V$), they identify segments that are considered 'outliers' based on the distribution of some measure (e.g., mean voltage, kurtosis, etc.) of the data in the sample of all segments. The simple voltage threshold will be used to identify artifact segments for the purposes of this guided tutorial.

Detect segments containing artifacts with ERPlab

- ERPLAB>Artifact Detection in epoched data>Simple voltage threshold

    o When the 'Extreme Values' dialog appears, be sure the voltage limits are set to '−100 100'.

- ○ The first six channels are the peri-ocular channels, which are usually excluded from the voltage threshold procedure. Set the 'Channel(s)' field to '7:27' and click 'Accept'.

- ○ When the procedure is finished, two new windows will appear. The first window titled 'Extreme Values detection view' (see Figure 5.8), permits a review of the segments that have been marked for rejection. It is *highly* recommended to review all of the selections carefully. Click 'Cancel' to close the window.

- ○ The second window to appear, titled 'Dataset info – pop_newset()' is a prompt to let the user know that markers will be added to the file indicating which segments will be rejected from further analysis. Select 'Overwrite it in memory' and click 'OK'.

Save the new segmented dataset

- • File>Save current dataset as

  - ○ Name the file in such a way as to indicate the stage of the data analysis (e.g., '1001raw_ar_oac_epoch_filt').

Subject Averaging

Having removed potential artifacts, the next step is to compute the ERP from the sample of data segments. Generating the ERP is accomplished by computing the arithmetic mean over all segments separately for each time-point and channel.

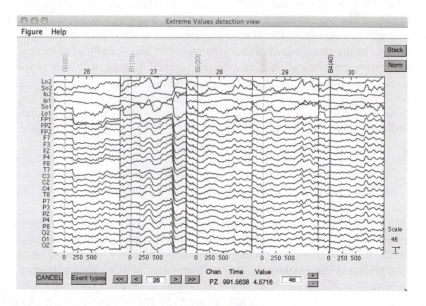

Figure 5.8   Review of rejected segments in ERPlab.

Computing subject averages with ERPlab

- ERPLAB>Compute Averaged ERPs

  o When the 'WEIGHTED AVERAGER GUI' dialog appears, be sure the number in the 'Dataset(s)' field corresponds with the EEGlab dataset you wish to average (default is the currently active dataset).

  o Select the option to 'Exclude epochs marked during artifact rejection' and click 'Run'.

  o When the 'Save Erpset GUI' appears, select 'Create a new erpset' and enter a name for the erpset in the corresponding field. You may optionally decide to save the erpset to disk at this time. Click 'OK' to continue.

The result of the averaging process is referred to as an 'erpset', and is stored in a new variable in the Matlab workspace named 'ERP'. You will not see any changes to the main EEGlab GUI after the new erpset has been created. To view details about the new erpset, simply type **ERP** at the Matlab command prompt and press ENTER.

Like the EEG variable used by EEGlab, ERP is a Matlab variable of the type *structure.* As such, it contains a number of subcomponents, each containing details of the computed ERP. Some of the fields of the ERP variable include the number of bins (nbin), the number of time-points in each ERP average (pnts), the ERP data itself (bindata), and the condition labels associated with each bin (bindescr). It is important to visualize the ERP for each participant. ERPlab includes a number of useful visualization tools. Some of these will be discussed in greater detail in the section on Component Characterization below.

At the very least, it is important to ascertain that there is some discernable signal remaining after the averaging process. Because the events in these data all correspond with the onset of a visual stimulus, one way to do this is to simply plot the ERPs at one of the channels at which you expect to see the signal of interest. For example, when presenting participants with visual stimuli, one can reasonably expect to observe an ERP over the occipital recording sites.

Plot the ERP for a single channel with ERPlab

- ERPLAB>Plot ERP Waveforms

  o When the 'ERP Plotting GUI' window appears, select channel Oz in the 'Channels to plot' field, leave all other default selections and click 'PLOT'.

The ERP at channel Oz is illustrated in Figure 5.9. Shown are the ERPs from each of the eight bins (conditions) with time (in milliseconds) on the X-axis and amplitude (μV) on the Y-axis. There are at least three noteworthy features of this waveform. First, the typical visual-evoked N1 ERP is clearly visible in each condition at about 180 ms post-stimulus. Second, voltage fluctuations associated with the ERPs in the post-stimulus period are considerably larger than any of the voltage fluctuations

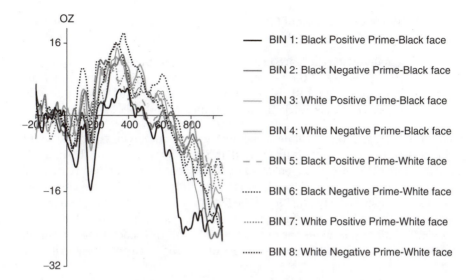

Figure 5.9   ERP for subject 1001 at electrode Oz.

visible during the pre-stimulus (baseline) period. Finally, experimental variance seen in the differences between conditions is also large relative to variance in the baseline. Keep in mind that there is considerable variability in the appearance of ERPs across subjects. If you haven't already done so, be sure to save the current ERPset using 'ERPLAB>Save current ERPset as'.

Grand Averaging

Once the pre-processing and erpset generation have been completed for all of the individual datasets, the ERPs from each subject and condition are averaged together to create a 'grand-average' ERP. Although the data submitted to statistical significance testing will be derived from individual subjects, the grand-average ERP is typically used for visualization of experimental effects and for determining the parameters that will be used to characterize the individual ERP components.

Generating a Grand Average with ERPlab
Select the files to be averaged

- ERPLAB>Average Across ERPsets (Grand Average)

  o When the 'Grand Averager GUI' opens, select the 'From ERPset files' option and click 'Add Erpset'. This will open a file browser that can be used to navigate to the directory containing the ERPset files created earlier (see Subject Averaging section of this chapter).

  o Select the 'Include standard deviation of data' option and click 'RUN' to generate the grand average.

- o When the 'Save list of ERPsets' dialog appears, click 'Save As' to save a text file record of the list of datasets included in the grand average.

- o Finally, when the 'Save Erpset GUI' window appears, select 'Create a new erpset' and then enter a suitable name for the grand average. Also select 'Save ERP as' and enter a similar name for the file that will be saved to disk. Click 'OK' to continue.

The grand-average ERPset will be saved both in the Matlab workspace (as an ERP structure) and on disk in the same way that ERPsets are saved for the individual subjects. Both the grand-averaged data and its associated information (e.g., sample rate, bin descriptions, channel locations, etc.) are stored in the ERP structure, which can now be visualized by typing **ERP** at the Matlab command line. Note that multiple erpsets may be loaded simultaneously. Individual erpsets can be selected from the 'ERPsets' menu in the menu bar of the main EEGlab GUI. Each time an erpset is selected in this way, the ERP variable is repopulated with the contents of that erpset.

Component Characterization

The grand-average ERPs can be used to visualize experimental effects and to define those parameters that will be used to measure components of the ERP waveforms. There are no field standards established to guide the identification and/or measurement of ERP components and the process may vary significantly from laboratory to laboratory. The following are some suggestions for conventional selection and measurement of ERPs that are consistent with published guidelines for the presentation of ERP results (Picton et al., 2000). The three properties that are most commonly used to define ERP components are: (1) polarity, (2), timing, and (3) topographical distribution. These characteristics of ERP components can be most easily visualized in an experiment-wise grand-average ERP (GA_{EW}; i.e., an average computed over all single subject grand-averages and all conditions).

Generating the GA_{EW} in ERPlab
Create an average across all conditions

- • ERPLAB>ERP Operations>ERP Bin Operations

  - o When the 'Bin Operation GUI' opens, create a new, ninth bin that is equal to the arithmetic mean of the existing bins 1–8 by typing the following equation into the equation editor field at the top left of the Bin Operation GUI:

  - o b9 = (b1+b2+b3+b4+b5+b6+b7+b8)/8 label GA_EW

  - o Select the 'Modify existing ERPset (recursive updating)' option under the 'Mode' heading and click 'RUN'.

Visualizing Component Properties in ERPlab

Once added to the grand-average ERPset, the GA_{EW} can be visualized in a number of ways. One way to visualize the GA_{EW} is to plot the ERPs for each channel of data in a topographic arrangement:

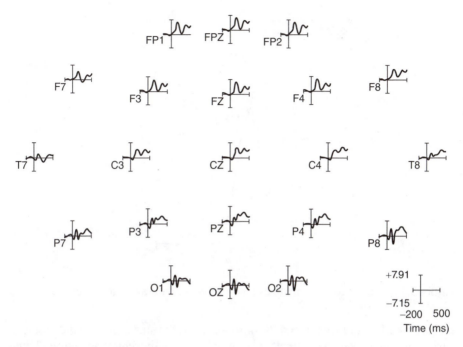

FP1   FPZ   FP2

F7   F3   FZ   F4   F8

T7   C3   CZ   C4   T8

P7   P3   PZ   P4   P8

O1   OZ   O2

+7.91

−7.15
−200   500
Time (ms)

Figure 5.10   Plotting a topographical arrangement of channels for the experiment-wise grand average.

Plot ERPs in topographic arrangement

- ERPLAB>Plot ERP Waveforms

  ○ This will bring up the same 'ERP Plotting GUI' used earlier. Enter '7:27' in the 'Channels to plot' field, indicating that the peri-ocular channels (1–6) should not be plotted. Enter '9' in the 'Bins to plot' field in order to plot only the GA_{EW}. Enter '−200 500' in the 'Time range' field in order to restrict the range of the plot. Finally, select the 'Topographic' option under the Style heading and click 'Plot' (see Figure 5.10). The result will be a new figure window with the ERP for each channel plotted at a 2-dimensional location corresponding with the position of that channel on the head. Note that clicking on any individual plot in this figure will open an exploded view of that channel in a new figure window, permitting a more detailed inspection.

Because the plots of individual channels are arranged topographically, it is possible to evaluate the polarity and timing of the ERP components as well as to estimate their topographical distribution. Looking at Figure 5.10, for example, one can see the early visual-evoked potentials most clearly over posterior scalp sites (bottom of figure). Clicking on channel OZ will open an individual plot of the ERP in that channel (see Figure 5.11). Components C1 (~50 ms), P1 (~100 ms), and N1 (~180

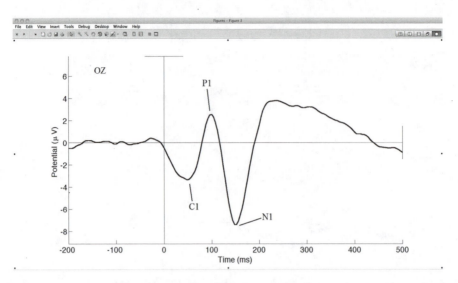

Figure 5.11   Individual plot of the experiment-wise grand-average ERP at channel Oz.

ms) are clearly visible in the first 200 ms following stimulus onset and the timing of each component can be estimated accurately from the enlarged figure. Taken together, the information garnered from Figures 5.10 and 5.11 can be used to determine the parameters that will be used to measure component amplitudes in individual subject ERPs. For example, one might determine from these figures that an appropriate measure of the N1 component would be to calculate the minimum (polarity) value of the ERP between 100 ms and 200 ms (timing) at channel Oz (topography).

A complementary visualization that can be very useful for characterizing the properties of an ERP component(s) is a plot of all channels overlaid on the same axis (sometimes called a 'butterfly plot'). Unfortunately, ERPlab does not currently contain a function for making such a plot. However, one can easily be implemented combining functions already available in EEGlab with some of Matlab's basic plotting tools. As an example of such a function, 'ERP_butterfly.m' is available on the companion website (www.sagepub.co.uk/dickter) and can be used to generate a butterfly plot from any ERP structure. To use the function, be sure you have placed a copy of the 'ERP_butterfly.m' file into Matlab's default directory (e.g., C:\My Documents\Matlab). Then type the following at the Matlab command line:

ERP_butterfly(ERP,9,[1:8],7:27,[-200 500])

Note that the function takes five inputs (in parentheses). The first, 'ERP' references the Matlab data structure created by ERPlab and containing the currently loaded erpset. The second input, '9', indicates that only data from the 9th bin should be plotted. The third, '[1:8]' indicates that topographical maps should be included for only the first eight bins. The fourth, '7:27' indicates that only

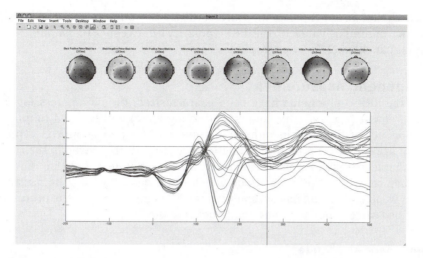

Figure 5.12 Butterfly plot showing topographical distribution of the N2 component across conditions.

channels seven through 27 should be plotted in the figure. Finally, the fifth input, '[−200 500]' indicates the time range (in ms) to plot.

When you press ENTER, a figure window will appear containing a butterfly plot of the GA_{EW} in the bottom panel and eight topographical maps (one for each condition) in the top panel (see Figure 5.12). By default, the topographical maps represent the voltage at the first time-point (-200 ms). Using the cross-hairs to navigate, clicking the left mouse button at points in the butterfly plot will cause the topographical maps to be updated to reflect the voltage topography at the selected time-point. The figure will continue to update the topographies with every click of the left mouse button until either the right mouse button is clicked, or a key is pressed on the keyboard.

Consider the N2 component occurring between 200 ms and 300 ms. Clicking at the most negative point in that window (about 258 ms) reveals a new set of topographical maps in the top panel. Notice that the predominant feature of many of the topographical maps is a positive voltage distributed over midline parietal electrodes. This may at first seem to contradict one's impression of the distribution of the N2 component given that the negative-going deflection is most clearly visible over midline frontal electrodes in Figure 5.12. In fact, this is illustrative of how volume conduction complicates the measurement of ERP components. That is, there appear to be (at least) two distinct voltage fluctuations with overlapping time-courses in the recorded ERP. One is a high-amplitude, low-frequency, positive-going potential that is maximal over posterior electrodes and the other is the lower-amplitude, higher-frequency, negative-going potential that is most negative over anterior electrodes. In this case, it is necessary to base judgments about the measurement parameters on several visualization methods as well as previous research. For example, one might determine based on an evaluation of Figures 5.11 and 5.12 and previous research that an appropriate measure of the N2 component would be to calculate the minimum value of the ERP (polarity) between 210 ms and 280 ms (timing) at channel Fz (topography).

Component Measurement

Once the ERP components have been characterized, the parameters for their measurement (e.g., polarity, timing, and topography) will be used to quantify components of the ERP in individual subjects. The two quantities typically sought are component amplitude and latency (e.g., timing). Even in the case of well-characterized components, there are a number of decisions that must still be made regarding the methods by which these quantities will be measured. Again, we focus here on measurement of the N2 component, but the procedures described can be applied to any components of the ERP.

Component Amplitude

Amplitude is the most commonly targeted measure of an ERP component. There are two commonly used methods for assessing component amplitude, both of which rely on the time window identified during component characterization. The first is referred to as the 'peak amplitude' method and is sometimes described as 'peak-picking'. In most cases, the peak amplitude method simply involves the selection of the most positive or negative (depending on the polarity of the component) point on the ERP waveform between the two points of the time window characterizing the component. Fraught with shortcomings (see Luck, 2005), the peak amplitude method is generally not recommended for conventional ERP analyses.

The second common method for quantifying component amplitude is to use the mean amplitude between the two points of the time window characterizing the component. There are a number of advantages of using mean amplitude over peak amplitude (see Luck, 2005). For example, mean amplitude is less susceptible to high-frequency noise, which can introduce artifactual peaks in the measurement window. Mean amplitude, unlike peak amplitude measures, is also more closely related to the amplitude of the component observed in the grand-average ERPs. This is important because statistics describing the experimental variance between conditions will thus be reflected in the grand average waveforms when using mean amplitude measures, but this may not be the case when using peak amplitude.

Component Latency

Characterizing the timing of an ERP component in the experiment-wise grand average constitutes the establishment of lower and upper boundaries for defining the latency of that ERP component observed in the grand-average waveforms of individual subjects. There are two common ways of defining the latency of an ERP component within that time window. The first, peak latency, involves a simple search within the time window for the point at which voltage is maximal (or minimal, depending on the polarity of the targeted ERP). The latency of that peak time-point is then used as a measure of the component's latency. Peak latency measures are, however, vulnerable to all of the same shortcomings as measures of peak amplitude. For example, it is highly susceptible to influence by high-frequency noise in the data, which can introduce 'peaks' anywhere along the waveform. Taking an average of the peak latencies across subjects may also lead to an estimate of the component latency that is not well-reflected in the experiment-wise grand average, making exposition of the results somewhat confusing (Luck, 2005). Methods for improving the validity of peak latency measures include the use of low-pass filters to reduce high-frequency noise, and peak definition specifications to ensure that the selected peak is a 'local' maximum/minimum (i.e., adjacent points are smaller in amplitude).

The second common measure of ERP latency is known as the 'fractional area latency' (FAL). Measuring the FAL involves computing the area under the ERP waveform between the boundaries of the time window and then, beginning at the lower bound of the window, finding the point at which some proportion of that total area is reached. If you assume that the voltages representing an ERP component are symmetric about their midpoint, then the point at which the area reaches 50% of its total seems like a reasonable definition of the component's latency and this is often the criterion used. FAL has some advantages over peak latency, but is not without problems of its own (Luck, 2005). It is worth mentioning that FAL can also be used to define onset and offset latencies. One might, for example, define the 10% FAL and 90% FAL as the onset and offset latencies of an ERP component respectively.

Measuring ERP Components with ERPlab

All of the amplitude and latency measures just described are available in ERPlab. In the interest of parsimony, we will describe the procedures for measuring mean amplitude; however, peak amplitude, peak latency, and FAL are all options available in the 'Measurements GUI' of ERPlab.

Open the ERP Measurement Tool

- ERPLAB>ERP Measurement Tool

  o Select the 'From ERPset files' option, and then click the button labeled 'Add ERP set'. A file browser will open in which you can select all of the individual erpset files saved during subject averaging.

  o Under the 'Measurement' heading, select 'Mean amplitude between two fixed latencies', then enter the start and end latencies for the N2 component (e.g., 210 and 280 ms) into the 'Between latencies' field.

  o Under the 'Bin(s) & Channels(s)' heading, select all eight of the bins (separately) using the drop-down menu and enter '7:27' into the 'Chan' text field (this indicates that amplitudes and latencies are desired only for the 7th through the 27th channel and thus ignores peri-ocular channels 1–6).

o   Designate an output file (e.g., 'N2_mean_amp') in the text field under the 'Save output file as' heading and select the 'One measurement per line (long format)' option.

When 'Run' is clicked, each of the selected erpsets will be loaded and measurements will be made based on the specified parameters. The progress of this process will be displayed in the Matlab command window. The results will be written to the specified output file in the following format:

ERPset	bin	chindex	chlabel	value
1001	1	1	FP1	-19.505
1001	1	2	FPZ	-17.617
.	.	.	.	.
.	.	.	.	.
.	.	.	.	.
1015	8	26	O2	−6.987
1015	8	27	OZ	−7.092

The 'ERPset' column contains the subject identifiers, the 'bin' column contains the bin (i.e., condition) identifier, the 'chindex' contains the index of each channel, the 'chlabel' column contains the labels associated with the corresponding channel indexes and finally, the 'value' column contains the mean amplitude (or other specified measurement). Note that the values obtained may be slightly different from those presented here given differences in the treatment of data during pre-processing stages.

Data Management

By now you likely appreciate that a fair amount of footwork is required before one can submit data from an ERP experiment to statistical analyses. While it is possible to selectively export measures from just a single channel using the Measurement GUI in ERPlab, this is not an option with some software. Moreover, it is often desirable to investigate experimental effects at more than just a single electrode. Thus, it is important to be able to efficiently organize the exported amplitudes and latencies so that the data are compatible with statistical analysis software.

Organizing Component Measurements with Pivot Tables

'Pivot table' is the term used to describe a data summarization tool commonly found in spreadsheet and data visualization programs. The pivot table is actually a secondary table used to cross-tabulate data in a primary table. The strength of the pivot table lies in its ability to quickly and easily organize large datasets into smaller summary tables. Pivot tables can be generated using spreadsheet software available in most office productivity suites (e.g., Microsoft Office© and OpenOffice). Although the steps vary slightly across programs and operating systems, the general steps are as follows:

Generate pivot tables

- Use 'File>Open' to import the ERP measurements generated earlier. Then:

  o Highlight the entire data range (including column labels).

  o Activate the pivot table organizer from the menu bar.

  o Using the organizer, move the 'value' label to the 'Data' or 'Values' field. Move the 'ERPset' label to the 'Rows' field. Move the 'bin' label to the 'Columns' field. Finally, move the 'chlabel' label to the 'Page' or 'Report Filter' field.

Following the above steps will organize the pivot table in such a way that the data can very easily be copied to most statistical analysis software (e.g., SPSS), with data from each condition organized in columns and subjects occupying rows. An attractive feature of organizing data in this way is that the pivot table can be modified with a single click to control which channel(s) are displayed or even to aggregate data over several channels at a time. This is important because a common approach to the analysis of ERPs is to include measurements from several electrodes and treat the different electrodes as levels of an 'electrode' factor in an ANOVA (Dien & Santuzzi, 2005; Luck, 2005).

For present purposes, the data have been filtered so as to isolate N2 amplitudes at channel Fz for each of the eight bins. Copying these data into your favorite statistical analysis software, one can perform the 2 (Prime Valence: positive/negative) × 2 (Prime Race: Black/White) × 2 (Target Race: Black/White) repeated measures ANOVA appropriate to the design. The data spreadsheet and our analysis of the data, revealing a significant effect of Target Race and an interaction between Target Race and Prime Valence, are illustrated in Figure 5.13.

In addition to results of the statistical test and a graphical display of the measures used, usually in the form of a bar-chart (see Figure 5.13) it is important to also provide a graphical depiction of the ERP waveforms. This can be accomplished in a number of ways. For example, ERPlab provides utilities (ERPLAB>Export ERP) for exporting the ERP waveforms to a text file that is readable by software other than Matlab (e.g., Excel™ or SigmaPlot™). However, plots of ERP waveforms can also be generated using the same visualization tools you have already used in this chapter. Because illustration of the interaction between Target Race and Prime Valence requires collapsing the ERP waveforms over the Prime Race factor, it is first necessary to create new ERP averages using the 'bin operations' GUI in ERPlab.

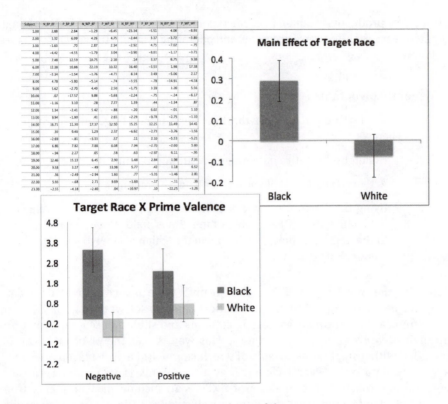

Figure 5.13 Data management and graphing of data.

Create new ERP waveforms by averaging over Prime Race

- ERPLAB>ERP Bin Operations
  - Enter the following equations into the top left field of the 'Bin Operation GUI' and click 'RUN':
  - b9=(b1+b3)/2 label Positive Prime – Black face
  - b10=(b2+b4)/2 label Negative Prime – Black face
  - b11=(b5+b7)/2 label Positive Prime – White face
  - b12=(b6+b8)/2 label Negative Prime – White face

Once the new bins 9–12 have been created, they can be visualized as before using ERPLAB>Plot ERP Waveforms.

REFERENCES

Bargh, J. A., Chen, M., & Burrows, L. (1996). Automaticity of social behavior: Direct effects of trait construct and stereotype activation on action. *Journal of Personality and Social Psychology, 71*, 230–244.

Bartholow, B. D., & Dickter, C. L. (2011). Person perception. In J. Decety & J. Cacioppo (Eds), *Handbook of Social Neuroscience.* New York: Oxford University Press.

Bartholow, B. D., Fabiana, M., Gratton, G., & Battencourt, B. A. (2001). A psycho-physiological examination of cognitive processing of and affective responses to social expectancy violations. *Psychological Science, 12*(3), 197–204. doi:10.1111/1467-9280.00336

Bodenhausen, G. V. (1990). Stereotypes as judgmental heuristics: Evidence of circa-dian variations in discrimination. *Psychological Science, 1,* 319–322.

Brewer, M. (1988). A dual process model of impression formation. In T. Srull & R. Wyer, Jr. (Eds), *Advances in social cognition* (Vol. 1, pp. 1–36). Hillsdale, NJ: Lawrence Erlbaum.

Cook, E. W., & Miller, G. A. (1992). Digital filtering: Background and tutorial for psy-chophysiologists. *Psychophysiology*, *29*(3), 350–362.

Correll, J., Park, B., Wittenbrink, B. & Judd, C. M. (2002). The police officer's dilemma: Using ethnicity to disambiguate potentially threatening individuals. *Journal of Personality and Social Psychology, 83,* 1314–1329.

Correll, J., Urland, G. R., & Ito, T. A. (2006). Event-related potentials and the decision to shoot: The role of threat perception and cognitive control. *Journal of Experi-mental Social Psychology*, *42*(1), 120–128.

Darley, J. M., & Gross, P. G. (1983). A hypothesis-confirming bias in labeling effects. *Journal of Personality and Social Psychology, 44,* 20–33.

Devine, P. G. (1989). Stereotypes and prejudice: Their automatic and controlled components. *Journal of Personality and Social Psychology, 56 (1),* 5–18.

Dickter, C. L., & Bartholow, B. D. (2007). Racial ingroup and outgroup attention biases revealed by event-related brain potentials. *Social Cognitive and Affective Neuroscience, 2,* 189–198.

Dickter, C. L., & Bartholow, B. D. (2010). Ingroup categorization and response con-flict: Interactive effects of target race, flanker compatibility and infrequency on N2 amplitude. *Psychophysiology, 47,* 596–601.

Dickter, C. L., & Gyurovski, I. I. (2012). The effects of expectancy violations on early attention to race in an impression formation paradigm. *Social Neuroscience, 7,* 240–251. doi:10.1080/17470919.2011.609906

Dien, J., & Santuzzi, A. M. (2005). Application of repeated measures ANOVA to high-density ERP datasets: A review and tutorial. In T. C. Handy (Ed.), *Event-related potentials: a methods handbook* (pp. 57–82). Cambridge, MA: The MIT Press.

Dovidio, J. F., Evans, N., & Tyler, R. B. (1986). Racial stereotypes: The contents of their cognitive representations. *Journal of Experimental Social Psychology, 22,* 22–37.

Eberhardt, J. L., Davies, P. G., Purdie-Vaughns, V., & Johnson, S. L. (2006). Looking deathworthy: Perceived stereotypicality of black defendants predicts capital-sentencing outcomes. *Psychological Science, 17*(5), 383–386. doi:10.1111/j.1467-9280.2006.01716.x

Fazio, R. H., Jackson, J. R., Dunton, B. C., & Williams, C. J. (1995). Variability in auto-matic activation as an unobtrusive measure of racial attitudes: A bona fide pipe-line? *Journal of Personality and Social Psychology, 69,* 1013–1027.

Fiske, S. T., & Neuberg, S. L. (1990). A continuum of impression formation, from category-based to individuating processes: Influences of information and motivation on attention and interpretation. In M. P. Zanna (Ed.), *Advances in experimental social psychology* (Vol. 23, pp. 1–74). New York: Academic Press.

Fiske, S. T., & Taylor, S. E. (1991). *Social cognition* (2nd ed.). New York: McGraw-Hill.

Galambos, R., & Sheatz, G. C. (n.d.). An electroencephalographic study of classical conditioning. *American Journal of Physiology*, *203*, 173–184.

Ito, T. A., & Bartholow, B. D. (2009). The neural correlates of race. *Trends in Cognitive Sciences*, *13*(12), 524–531.

Ito, T. A., & Urland, G. R. (2003). Race and gender on the brain: Electrocortical measures of attention to the race and gender of multiply categorizable individuals. *Journal of Personality and Social Psychology, 85,* 616–626.

Ito, T. A., & Urland, G. R. (2005). The influence of processing objectives on the perception of faces: An ERP study of race and gender perception. *Cognitive, Affective, & Behavioral Neuroscience*, *5*(1), 21–36.

Ito, T. A., Thompson, E., & Cacioppo, J. T. (2004). Tracking the timecourse of social perception: The effects of racial cues on event-related brain potentials. *Personality and Social Psychology Bulletin, 30,* 1267–1280.

Kubota, J. T., & Ito, T. A. (2007). Multiple cues in social perception: The time course of processing race and facial expression. *Journal of Experimental Social Psychology*, *43*(5), 738–752.

Jussim, L., Palumbo, P., Smith, A., & Madon, S. (2000). Stigma and self-fulfilling prophecies. In T. Heatherton, R. Kleck, M. R. Hebl, & J. G. Hull (Eds), *The Social Psychology of Stigma* (pp. 374–418). New York: Guilford Press.

Kornhuber, H. H., & Deecke, L. (n.d.). Cerebral potential changes in voluntary and passive movements in man: Readiness potential and reafferent potential. *Pflugers Archives Gesamte Physiologi*, *284*, 1–17.

Luck, S. J. (2005). An introduction to the event-related potential technique. Cambridge, MA: The MIT Press.

Luck, S. J., & Kappenman, E. S. (Eds.). (2011). *The Oxford handbook of event-related potential components*. Oxford: Oxford University Press.

Macrae, C. N., & Quadflieg, S. (2010). Perceiving people. *Handbook of social psychology*. Retrieved from http://onlinelibrary.wiley.com/doi/10.1002/9780470561119.socpsy001012/full

Osterhout, L., Bersick, M., & McLaughlin, J. (1997). Brain potentials reflect violations of gender stereotypes. *Memory & Cognition*, *25*(3), 273–285.

Payne, B. K. (2001). Prejudice and perception: The role of automatic and controlled processes in misperceiving a weapon. *Journal of Personality and Social Psychology, 81,* 181–192.

Picton, T., Bentin, S., Berg, P., Donchin, E., Hillyard, S., Johnson, R., Miller, G., et al. (2000). Guidelines for using human event-related potentials to study cognition: Recording standards and publication criteria. *Psychophysiology*, *37*, 127–152.

Sutton, S., Braren, M., Zubin, J., & John, E. R. (1965). Evoked-potential correlates of stimulus uncertainty. *Science (New York, N.Y.)*, *150*(3700), 1187–1188.

Van Duynslaeger, M., Van Overwalle, F., & Verstraeten, E. (2007). Electrophysiological time course and brain areas of spontaneous and intentional trait inferences. *Social Cognitive and Affective Neuroscience*, *2*(3), 174–188.

Walker, P. M., Silvert, L., Hewstone, M., & Nobre, A. C. (2008). Social contact and other-race face processing in the human brain. *Social Cognitive and Affective Neuroscience*, *3*(1), 16–25.

Walter, W. G., Cooper, R., Aldridge, V. J., McCallum, W. C., & Winter, A. L. (1964). Contingent negative variation: An electric sign of sensorimotor association and expectancy in the human brain. *Nature*, *203*(4943), 380–384.

Willadsen-Jensen, E. C., & Ito, T. A. (2006). Ambiguity and the timecourse of racial perception. *Social Cognition*, *24*(5), 580–606.

Willadsen-Jensen, E. C., & Ito, T. A. (2008). A foot in both worlds: Asian Americans' perceptions of Asian, White, and racially ambiguous faces. *Group Processes & Intergroup Relations*, *11*(2), 182–200.

Willis, J., & Todorov, A. (2006). First impressions making up your mind after a 100-ms exposure to a face. *Psychological Science*, *17*(7), 592–598.

6

FREQUENCY-DOMAIN ANALYSIS

Both EEG and ERPs can be analyzed in the frequency-domain. In fact, although the literature has historically been dominated by time-domain ERP analyses, the very first analysis of human EEG by Hans Berger (1929) was in the frequency-domain. Berger's seminal observation was the occurrence of dynamic oscillatory activity at about 10 Hz that was correlated with an individual's mental state. Over the years, Berger's 'Alpha' rhythm (now defined as 8–12 Hz) and convention for naming frequency bands that are observed to be related to cognitive processing has been expanded to include 'Delta' (0–4 Hz), 'Theta' (4–8 Hz),[1] 'Beta' (12–30 Hz), and 'Gamma' (30–80 Hz) oscillations. When observed in response to a stimulus, these event-related oscillations (EROs) are sometimes thought to reflect the coordinated activity of networks in large populations of neurons (Başar, Başar-Eroglu, Karakaş, & Schürmann, 2001). This is important in the context of social neuroscience research wherein the neural processes under study typically rely on the integration of a number of sensory, perceptual, and cognitive processes. In fact, appreciation for the importance of these EROs has grown rapidly over the past few decades in both the cognitive and social neurosciences and options for conducting analysis of EROs are now available in all commercially available software packages for EEG analysis.

THE SPECTRAL CONTENT OF EEG

To understand EROs and how they are measured, it is first necessary to review the frequency-domain representation of time-domain EEG signals. An assumption that is fundamental to both frequency and time-frequency domain analyses is that EEG waveforms consist of a number of oscillatory subcomponents. Decomposition of these component oscillations is believed to isolate, in some cases, the activity of localized neuronal populations recruited in the service of an experimental task. In most cases, each of these oscillatory components is described in

---

[1]Note that Theta rhythm is named for the hypothetical origin of oscillations in its range, the thalamus, rather than the chronological order in which it was discovered.

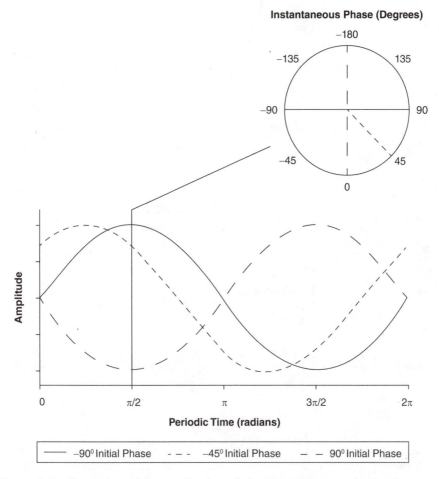

Instantaneous Phase (Degrees)

Figure 6.1   Illustration of the amplitude and phase components of a simple sinusoid.

terms of its (1) amplitude and (2) phase (see Figure 6.1). The amplitude of an oscillation refers to its magnitude and can be measured in units of signal amplitude (μV), power (μV^2), or in logarithmic decibel units ($20*\log10(\mu V)$ or $10*\log10(\mu V^2)$). The phase of an oscillation refers to the current position on a periodic wave and can be measured in radians or degrees (i.e., phase angle). The term phase can be used to describe either the initial phase of a sinusoidal wave or the instantaneous phase – the time-varying phase of an oscillation – and is commonly measured in degrees (see Figure 6.1).

Researchers in the field typically distinguish between three types of oscillatory activity in EEG, each of which varies in the extent to which it is time- and/or phase-locked to an exogenous stimulus (Galambos, 1992) (see Figure 6.2). 'Spontaneous' oscillations are those that occur completely independently of any experimental stimulus. Characterization of the stages of sleep is one example of the use

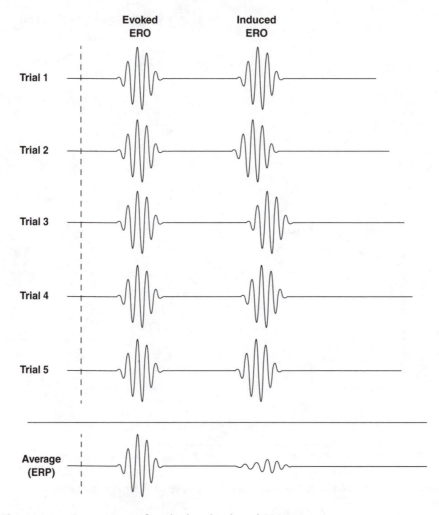

Figure 6.2   Comparison of evoked and induced EROs.

of spontaneous oscillations. 'Induced' oscillations are elicited by the onset of a stimulus and are thus correlated with experimental conditions, but the oscillatory activity is not necessarily phase-locked to the onset of the stimulus. Because of variability in the phase (i.e., timing) of an oscillation across occurrences (i.e., trials) of a stimulus, it can be distorted or even completely obscured when averages are taken across trials in the time-domain (see Figure 6.2). Finally, 'evoked' oscillations are those that are elicited by the onset of a stimulus and are phase-locked to stimulus onset, meaning that the phase of the oscillation is consistent across trials at a given time point. Because of this phase consistency, evoked oscillations will not be obscured by averaging in the time-domain. Evoked and induced EROs are illustrated in Figure 6.2. Notice that both types of oscillations appear to be related to stimulus onset (dotted line) in that they each reliably occur following the stimulus. However, even an apparently small degree of variability in the phase of the oscillation across trials leads to near cancellation of the signal in the time-domain average.

Figure 6.2 is also illustrative of the relationship between EROs (evoked in particular) and ERPs. That is, ERPs are closely related to the sum of the evoked EROs over all frequencies (at least those within the pass-band of any filters applied). In principle, EROs will be visible in the ERP, but this is generally true only for lower frequencies, which tend to have much larger amplitude. Because ERPs combine activity over all frequencies, those with lower amplitude (typically higher frequencies) can be difficult to see. However, recall that, according to Fourier theory, any stationary time-domain signal can be represented as the sum of a set of frequency components – sinusoidal waveforms, each with its own frequency, amplitude, and phase. Thus, application of the Fourier transform to the ERP waveform can be used to decompose the ERP into its constituent evoked EROs (a so-called 'spectral decomposition'), sometimes called the 'evoked band power' (EBP). Because the averaging process can seriously diminish the signal-to-noise ratio for induced EROs, performing a spectral decomposition of the ERP waveform is useful only when the signal of interest is more likely to be phase-locked to the eliciting stimulus. This may be the case for very early sensory/perceptual processes (e.g., those that occur <200 ms), but is less likely to be the case for later perceptual and high-order cognitive processes.

A more common approach to spectral decomposition is to compute the frequency-domain representation, or 'power spectral density' (PSD) of each single trial, then compute an average of the PSDs over trials. Because the average of the PSD across trials contains a mixture of the evoked and induced EROs, the result is sometimes referred to as the 'event-related band power' (ERBP). ERBP can be measured with respect to some pre-stimulus baseline but, unlike ERPs, is usually expressed as a proportion (e.g., % change). An increase in signal power (amplitude) relative to baseline, called event-related synchronization (ERS), is often interpreted to reflect an increase in the size of the neuronal assembly firing synchronously or an increase in the synchronicity with which a neuronal assembly is firing. Likewise, event-related de-synchronization (ERD) refers to decreases in the size/synchronization of a neuronal assembly with respect to a baseline period. In some cases, an experiment may be motivated by questions about only the induced band power (IBP). In order to distinguish IBP from the ERBP in which it is embedded, it is common to subtract from the ERBP that part which is attributable to evoked EROs (i.e., EBP). Although a number of methods have been proposed to accomplish this subtraction, one method that has been used is to simply subtract the PSD of the ERP, reflecting the evoked EROs, from the ERBP (Mørup, Hansen, & Arnfred, 2007). The process of computing EBP and IBP is illustrated in Figure 6.3.

Another use of spectral decomposition is to investigate the localized symmetry of neural activity across the two hemispheres of the brain. In this context, 'activity' is typically interpreted as the inverse of the observed power in the Alpha frequency band, with lower Alpha power indicating more neural activity (Lindsley & Wicke, 1974). By convention, asymmetry scores are typically calculated by computing the PSD or ERS/ERD values at a number of channels and then subtracting the values in

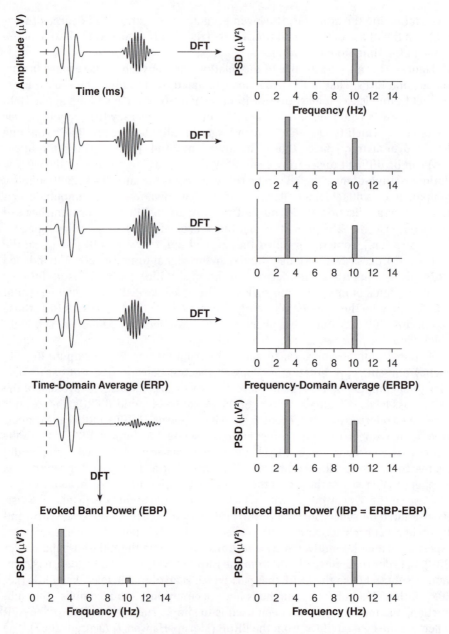

Figure 6.3   Illustration of the calculation of evoked, induced, and event-related band power.

channels over the left hemisphere from homologous channels over the right hemisphere, such that larger values of the difference indicate greater left hemisphere 'activation'. Such hemispheric asymmetry measures can be computed for resting-state EEG recordings (i.e., spontaneous oscillations) where they are sometimes interpreted to reflect the neural correlates of trait-like behavioral propensities or in response to eliciting events (i.e., EROs) where they are interpreted to reflect affective state and cognitive reactivity.

DOMAIN REVIEW

Hemispheric asymmetry has been shown to be important in several domains that social and personality psychologists study. In particular, because greater left fron-tal cortical activity has been linked with approach motivations and greater right frontal cortical activity has been associated with withdrawal motivations, meas-ures of hemispheric asymmetry have been used to study the processing of emotions (see Harmon-Jones, 2003 for a review). Much research has focused on individual differences in resting EEG asymmetry. During these studies, participants sit quietly while limiting muscle movements and eye blinks, alternating blocks with open and closed eyes. Results of these studies indicate that individual differences in trait positive and negative affect are related to hemispheric asymmetry (Tomarken, Davidson, Wheeler, & Doss, 1992), and that asymmetry in turn predicts self-reported affective responses to positive and negative film clips (Tomarken, Davidson, & Henriques, 1990; Wheeler, Davidson, & Tomarken, 1993). Furthermore, individuals with a relative right frontal baseline did not show changes in EEG asymmetry while viewing aversive slides from the IAPS, but individuals with a relative left frontal baseline showed greater left frontal activity in response to aversive pictures (Kline, Blackhart, & Williams, 2007).

More recently, researchers have demonstrated that approach and avoidance motivations and not affective responses *per se* are responsible for differences in hemispheric asymmetry. That is, resting frontal EEG asymmetry appears to be related to trait approach and withdrawal motivations more strongly than positive and negative affect (Harmon-Jones & Allen, 1997; Sutton & Davidson, 1997). For example, Harmon-Jones and Allen (1998) found that trait anger, an approach-related negative emotion, was positively correlated with left frontal cortical activ-ity but negatively correlated with right frontal activity. Indeed, work by McGregor, Nash, and Inzlicht (2009) demonstrated that compared to individuals with low self-esteem, those with high self-esteem showed heightened relative left frontal cortical activity following a threat manipulation, providing an account for the resil-ience of those with high self-esteem.

Further support for the idea that frontal asymmetry is related to motivation comes from work on psychopathology. Research has shown that trait indices of depres-sion are positively correlated with greater resting right frontal cortical activity (Allen, Iacono, Depue, & Arbisi, 1993; Henriques & Davidson, 1991; Schaffer, Davidson, & Saron, 1983). Because depression is associated with decreased positive affect and a lack of approach motivation, these findings support the role of asymmetry as a measurement of motivational tendencies. Thus, this work has demonstrated that hemispheric asymmetry can be used as a tool to examine relative differences in approach and avoidance motivations.

Researchers have also investigated hemispheric asymmetry in response to manipulations of affect. Harmon-Jones and Sigelman (2001) found that angering participants with an insult led to greater left frontal activation, which was corre-lated with subsequent self-reported anger and aggressive behavior. Another study found that inductions of approach-oriented positive affect caused greater left hem-ispheric asymmetry compared to a low-approach positive affect condition and a neutral condition (Harmon-Jones, Harmon-Jones, Fearn, Sigelman, & Johnson, 2008). Furthermore, participants showed differential frontal hemispheric asym-metry based on different facial expressions they made while EEG was recorded, with withdrawal-related emotions (i.e., fear) eliciting greater right frontal activity and approach-related emotions (i.e., happiness) eliciting greater left frontal activ-ity (Coan, Allen, & Harmon-Jones, 2001). Frontal asymmetry even appears to be sensitive to motivational manipulations in newborn infants, with researchers find-ing that interest and disgust facial expressions in response to different tastes were associated with increased left frontal activation and increased right frontal activa-tion, respectively (Fox & Davidson, 1986). Further research reported that female infants demonstrated more right frontal activation during maternal separation compared to when their mother was approaching (Fox & Davidson, 1987).

More recently, researchers have begun examining whether participants will show differential hemispheric asymmetry to specific visual stimuli. Balconi and Mazza (2010) found that participants viewing faces depicting negative emotions showed increased right frontal activation while faces depicting positive emotions yielded greater left frontal activation. These neural responses were also moderated by individual differences in behavioral activation (BAS) and behavioral inhibition (BIS), such that participants higher in BIS showed more right activation for nega-tive emotions and higher BAS participants showed more left activation to positive emotions. However, many additional studies have failed to find differences in hem-ispheric asymmetry to affective pictures, and this may be because the affective pic-tures on their own may not have elicited sufficient motivational tendencies to approach or avoid the stimuli. In support of this idea, Gable and Harmon-Jones (2008) presented participants with pictures of dessert items or neutral items and found that greater relative left frontal activation correlated with liking for desserts and time since last eaten. Other work has also shown that individual differences in attachment style affect EEG frontal asymmetry to video clips inducing different emotional responses, with avoidant and preoccupied individuals showing different patterns of self-reported arousal and EEG asymmetry in response to the videos (Rognoni, Galati, Costa, & Crini, 2008). Furthermore, Zinser, Fiore, Davidson, and Baker (1999) found increased left hemispheric activation in smokers shown smok-ing stimuli (i.e., physically present cigarettes), especially when they had withdrawn from smoking for 24 hours. Together, these studies suggest that motivation to approach stimuli can be measured by EEG asymmetry.

GUIDED ANALYSIS: MEASURING ERBP AND ALPHA ASYMMETRY IN EEGLAB/ERPLAB

In order to elucidate and illustrate the methods for spectral decomposition just described, we will consider the application of frequency-domain analyses to research questions regarding the modulation of Alpha power and frontal Alpha asymmetry by motivationally salient images. This guided analysis is based on Zinser and colleagues' (1999) research demonstrating that smokers show evidence of greater left hemispheric activation (e.g., higher Alpha asymmetry scores) in response to smoking-related stimuli (e.g., cigarettes). The Zinser et al. (1999) research was inspired by some of the literature reviewed above demonstrating that motivationally salient stimuli produce increased left hemispheric responses. In their study, habitual smokers viewed a lit cigarette placed in front of them for 60 seconds, during which time EEG activity was recorded. One group of participants was permitted to smoke immediately prior to the experiment and a second group was asked to refrain from smoking prior to the experiment. All participants were told that they would be allowed to smoke at a later time in an effort to encourage anticipatory cravings. The results confirmed expectations that hemispheric asymmetry would be largest for smokers who had not been allowed to smoke prior to the experiment. The authors interpreted these findings to indicate that smokers experiencing nicotine withdrawal showed increased approach motivation when presented with smoking cues.

In order to generate data for this guided analysis, a group of 20 participants completed an experimental protocol similar to that used by Zinser et al. (1999). Ten of the participants were habitual smokers and 10 were non-smokers. During the experimental procedure, all participants passively viewed a series of 40 images. Half of the images were smoking-related (i.e., containing cigarettes or smoking paraphernalia) and half were neutral images. Additionally, half of the images of each type were considered 'active' (e.g., a hand holding a lit cigarette) and the rest were 'inactive' (e.g., a cigarette lying on a table). The distinction between active and inactive image types is not relevant to the present analysis, but will be explored in Chapter 7. Each trial consisted of a single image, which remained on screen for 8000 ms. Images were separated by an inter-trial interval of 8000 ms. Consistent with the study by Zinser et al. (1999), smokers were instructed to refrain from smoking for at least three hours before their participation. Participants were also told that they would be asked to answer questions about the pictures at the conclusion of the experiment to ensure that they attended to the stimuli.

EEG data were recorded at a rate of 1000 Hz using a DBPA-1 Sensorium Bioamplifier (Sensorium Inc., Charlotte, VT) with an analog high-pass filter of 0.01 Hz and a low-pass filter of 500 Hz (four-pole Bessel). The EEG was recorded from 74 Ag-AgCl sintered electrodes in an electrode cap, placed using the expanded International 10–20 electrode placement system. All electrodes were referenced to the tip of the nose and the ground electrode was placed in the middle of the forehead, slightly above the eyebrows. Eye movement and blinking were recorded from peri-ocular electrodes placed on the lateral canthi and superior and inferior orbits, aligned with the pupils. Before data collection was initiated, all impedances were adjusted to within 0–20 kilohms. The raw data for this guided analysis can be found on the companion website (www.sagepub.co.uk/dickter). The data are in their original, raw format except that the sample rate was reduced to 250 Hz and the number of electrodes was reduced to 27 of the original channels corresponding with standard 10–20 positions. Participants 6001–6010 were smokers and participants 6011–6020 were non-smokers.

Data Pre-processing

Data for the guided analysis are available in their 'raw', unprocessed format. Thus, in preparation for measuring ERBP and Alpha asymmetry, each dataset should first be submitted to the pre-processing procedures described in Chapter 4. Once completed, load one of the pre-processed datasets (e.g., 6001_clean_oar.set) into EEGlab before beginning the remaining steps.

Segmentation

Just as the computation of ERPs requires the extraction of segments of data with respect to some time-locking event, so does the computation of EROs. Thus, the first required step is to segment the data with respect to the onset of the motivationally salient images. To segment the data, you will need to create a new bin descriptor file (BDF). In this case, the BDF is quite simple, consisting of only two bins – one for smoking-related images and one for neutral images. The onset of smoking-related images was marked by the codes 10 and 20 (the two codes reflect the conditions of an experimental manipulation unrelated to the present exposition) and neutral images were marked by the codes 30 and 40. Once the BDF file has been created (using any text editor) and saved to disk, the data segments can be extracted by the following procedures:

```
bin 1
Smoking-related Images
.{10;20}
bin 2
Neutral Images
.{30;40}
```

Modify the event list in EEGlab to be compatible with ERPlab

- ERPLAB>Eventlist>Create EEG Eventlist – Basic

   o When the dialog titled 'creabasiceventlistGUI' appears, click 'CREATE'.

   o If the 'Overwrite Confirmation' dialogue appears, click 'Overwrite them'.

   o When the dialog titled 'Dataset info – pop_newset()' appears, click the 'Overwrite it in memory' box and then click 'OK'.

Assign events in the current dataset to the bins in accordance with the criteria specified in the BDF file

- ERPLAB>Assign Bins (BINLISTER)

   o When the dialog titled 'BINLISTER GUI' appears, click the 'Browse' button under the heading 'Load Bin Descriptor File from'. Select the

'Chapter6_BDF.txt' file downloaded with the tutorial data (or the text file you created) and click 'RUN'

o   When the 'Dataset info – pop_newset()' dialog appears, select 'Overwrite it in memory' and click 'OK'.

Save the modified file

- File>Save current dataset as

  o   Choose a filename that reflects the application of the BDF, such as '6001_oar_BDF.set'.

Extract data segments from the continuous data

- ERPLAB>Extract Bin-based Epochs

  o   When the 'EXTRACT BINEPOCHS GUI' dialog appears, the user is asked to indicate the period of time around each event that should be extracted from the continuous data. For this dataset, because stimuli were presented to participants for 8000 ms, you can use the interval from −2000 to 8000. The pre-stimulus baseline is larger in this case than it was when we were computing the ERP in Chapter 5 because it is important to obtain a reliable estimate of the pre-stimulus oscillatory activity. Consider, for example, that one cycle of an 8 Hz oscillation takes 125 ms. A 200 ms pre-stimulus baseline, such as might be used for an ERP, would thus contain less than two full cycles of the oscillation.

  o   The parameters for baseline correction will also be specified in the 'EXTRACT BINEPOCHS GUI' dialog. Select the 'Pre' option to remove the average of the entire pre-stimulus (−2000 ms to 0 ms) interval from each of the segments and then click 'RUN'.

  o   When the 'Dataset info – pop_newset()' dialog appears, select 'Overwrite it in memory' and click 'OK'.

When the routine is completed, the fields of the EEGlab GUI will be re-populated to describe the segmented dataset. Notice that the 'Epochs' field now indicates the number of individual data segments that were extracted from the continuous recording.

Artifact Rejection

Although extreme artifacts in the data will have been removed during pre-processing (see Chapter 4), there may still be unwanted noise in the intervals of data selected during segmentation. The issue of artifact in the frequency-domain analysis is somewhat different than it was in Chapter 5 when computing time-domain ERPs. Recall that time-domain data are the sum (theoretically) of oscillations at all frequencies, meaning that high-frequency noise can obscure low-frequency signals. Thus, while the application of a low-pass (e.g., 0–20Hz) filter removes high frequencies from the time-domain data, improving the resolution of lower frequency ERP components, the same low-pass filter applied prior to spectral decomposition would have no impact on the resolution of lower frequencies inside the pass-band of the filter. This is because the process of decomposing the frequency content of EEG parses both signal and noise elements into a set of distinct frequency components. In other words, the high-frequency noise that obscured low-frequency ERP components in the time-domain will be, by virtue of the analysis, divorced from low-frequency components in the frequency domain.

Consequently, when artifacts are rejected from the data using conventional time-domain procedures such as simple voltage thresholds, it is not known which frequency components contained the unwanted noise. In fact, because common sources of large-amplitude fluctuations in EEG are skin potentials (<1 Hz), mains interference (50/60 Hz), and movement/muscle artifact (>60 Hz), artifacts rejected using a simple voltage threshold are likely either of very low or very high frequency. An ideal frequency-domain analog to the simple voltage threshold used in the time-domain would be to define a simple magnitude threshold for each frequency and reject trials based on the comparison of the PSD of each trial with the set of magnitude thresholds. In practice, however, such a procedure would be difficult to implement given that it would be computationally intensive and time-consuming, and it can be difficult to derive empirically justifiable thresholds for each frequency. Still, this may be a suitable approach to artifact rejection when a narrow frequency band of interest has been determined a priori or when the spectral properties of the noise are known.

That being said, artifact rejection by frequency-domain magnitude thresholding is not widely available and voltage thresholding in the time-domain remains the de facto procedure for artifact rejection in the field – even when the goal of an analysis is to characterize a narrow frequency band (e.g., Alpha). Thus, the guided analysis will proceed with conventional time-domain voltage thresholding for artifact rejection. However, given that the present analysis of Alpha asymmetry concerns frequencies well outside the range of frequencies most likely to be impacted by skin potentials and muscle artifact, a more liberal threshold will be used (−200 and 200 μV) than was the case in Chapter 5. Note that exploration and comparison of frequency-domain artifact rejection procedures is strongly encouraged and can be accessed directly from the EEGlab menus (Tools>Reject data epochs>Reject by spectra).

Detect segments containing artifacts with ERPlab

- ERPLAB>Artifact Detection>Simple voltage threshold

    o   When the 'Extreme Values' dialog appears, be sure the voltage limits are set to '−200 200'.

    o   The first six channels are the peri-ocular channels and should be excluded from the voltage threshold procedure. Set the Channel(s) field to '7:27' and click 'Accept'.

- o   When the procedure is finished, two new windows will appear. The first window titled 'Extreme Values detection view', permits a review of the segments that have been marked for rejection. It is *highly* recommended to review all of the selections carefully. Click 'Cancel' to close the window.

- o   The second window to appear, titled 'Dataset info – pop_newset()' is a prompt to let the user know that markers will be added to the file indicating which segments will be rejected from further analysis. Select 'Overwrite it in memory' and click 'OK'.

Save the modified file

- File>Save current dataset as

  - o   Choose a filename that reflects the segmentation (e.g., '6001_segmented_artrej.set').

Spectral Decomposition (PSD)

There are a number of ways to compute and visualize spectral decompositions in EEGlab. For example, the ERBP and EBP can be visualized over the 0 ms to 8000 ms epoch following image onset for all channels by selecting 'Plot>Channel spectra and maps'. When the 'Channel spectra and maps' dialog appears, enter '0 8000' for epoch time range over which to compute PSD, enter '100' in the 'Percent data to sample' field, select frequencies 8, 10, and 12 to plot as scalp maps, enter 'BOTH' in the 'Apply to...' field, and enter '2 25' in the 'Plotting frequency range' field. Click 'OK' to execute the transform and plot the results. The figure generated by EEGlab displays the PSD (logarithmically scaled) as a function of frequency for all channels in a way that is similar to the butterfly plot used to visualize ERPs in the previous chapter. The top panel displays the EBP (i.e., PSD of the ERP) and the bottom panel displays the ERBP (i.e., average PSD of each trial).

One of the first things you may have noticed about the resulting figure is that the plot of PSD as a function of frequency looks very different from the idealized spectra in Figure 6.3 where all of the power is localized to one or two frequencies. This is due partly to the fact that EEG waveforms are complex, consisting of oscillations at many frequencies but also partly to estimation error in the DFT. When signal power is spread out over neighboring frequencies, this error is referred to as spectral 'leakage'. While the mathematical details to which leakage can be attributed are beyond the scope of this book, it is important to understand (at least conceptually) the nature of spectral leakage as it will contribute to an improved understanding of the algorithmic options that are available for computing PSD. One source of leakage in the frequency spectrum is the discrete nature of the DFT attempting to ascribe signal power to a set of discrete frequency 'bins', none of which may be equal to the *true* frequency of the oscillatory activity contained in the EEG data. This is really a problem of frequency resolution, which can be improved by either sampling the time-domain signal at a higher rate or by submitting longer segments of time to the DFT.

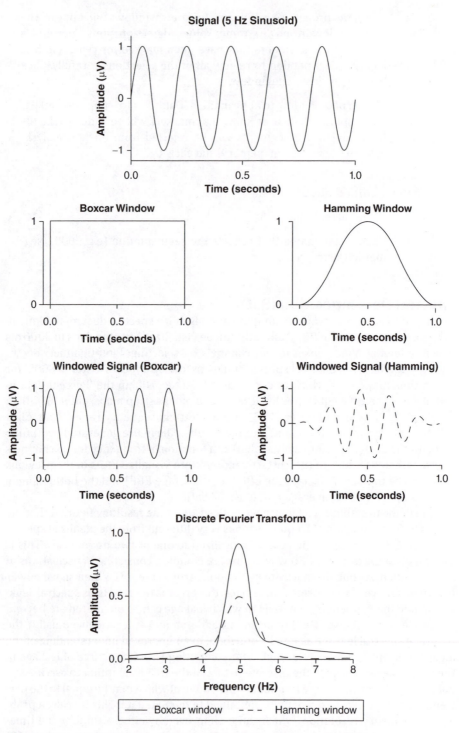

Figure 6.4   Illustration of windowing functions used with the DFT.

Another source of leakage is the windowing function that is applied to the data prior to the spectral decomposition. When a windowing function is combined with the time-domain signal, the spectral properties of the windowing function itself influence estimates of PSD obtained for the signal. Though you may not have realized it, a 'step' (AKA 'boxcar') function, was implicitly applied to the data when a finite segment (e.g., 0–8000 ms) was selected for analysis. The step function is equal to one for all points defined by the segment of interest and zero over all points outside the segment (see Figure 6.4). Although using a step function ensures high accuracy with respect to the amplitude (power) of the PSD estimates, that accuracy comes with the cost of spectral leakage. It is possible, however, to mitigate the effects of spectral leakage by using other windowing methods. There are many common window functions that can be used to reduce leakage in estimates of the PSD. The Hamming window is commonly an option in commercial software for EEG analysis and is used by EEGlab. Use of a Hamming window generally provides a good trade-off between amplitude accuracy and low spectral leakage (see Figure 6.4). Other common windows include Hanning and Blackman windows. The selection of a windowing function is a complex issue that should be motivated by the nature of the research question. For example, when it is important to discriminate between the PSD at two neighboring frequencies, a window should be selected that will provide the least spectral leakage, and when it is important to closely approximate the true amplitude of an oscillatory component, a window should be selected that provides the best amplitude accuracy.

You may have noticed that the figure produced by the 'Channel spectra and maps' command in EEGlab did not include any condition labels to identify the unique bins (e.g., 'Smoking-related Images' and 'Neutral Images'). In fact, this method for computing the PSD in EEGlab averages over all trials in the dataset without consideration of the bin labels. In order to compare the PSD between two or more conditions in EEGlab, it is necessary to separate the trials by condition into separate EEGlab datasets and create an EEGlab 'STUDY'. The STUDY functions in EEGlab permit organization of data from many subjects and experimental conditions and provide many analysis options. Though use of the STUDY functions in this context may be a more efficient approach to the frequency-domain analysis, the steps involved lack the transparency desired in order to elucidate the process of computing measures of PSD and ERBP. ERPlab also includes several functions for visualizing PSD; however, performing comparisons between experimental conditions as described in this guided analysis is not possible from the options currently available in the ERPlab GUI. Thus, in an effort to keep the frequency-domain processing stages completely transparent to you the reader and to maximize the use of the GUI interfaces of both EEGlab and ERPlab, the remaining steps of the guided analysis rely on a Matlab function written specifically for this book.

The 'DK_PSD.m' function will compute the PSD separately for each of the segments in a currently loaded EEGlab dataset, replacing the time-domain data for each channel with its frequency domain representation – amplitude as a function of frequency. A word of strong caution: The 'DK_PSD' function alters some of the core parameters of the EEG data structure. These changes essentially fool the

EEGlab GUI into treating the frequency-domain representation of the data as though it were time-domain. While this facilitates use of many of the visualization and analysis tools in EEGlab and ERPlab, neither were developed with the intention of conducting analyses in this way and it is generally not recommended that users modify the EEG data structure. To execute the PSD transform, enter the following command at the Matlab prompt and press ENTER:

[EEG ALLEEG CURRENTSET com]=DK_PSD(EEG,ALLEEG,CURRENTSET,'datawindow',[2000 8000])

Once the spectral decomposition is complete, enter the command, 'eeglab redraw' at the Matlab prompt and press Enter. This will perform an internal data consistency check and refresh the EEGlab GUI.

The EEGlab GUI will be updated to reflect the newly created dataset. Execution of the 'DK_PSD' function computes the PSD over the interval 2000 ms to 8000 ms post-stimulus. By default, the new EEG dataset will have the same name as the original dataset prepended with 'PX'. Like the frequency-domain analyses in EEGlab, the 'DK_PSD' function uses the 'pwelch' function in Matlab to compute the PSD. The 'pwelch' function is an implementation of Welch's method for computing the PSD. Briefly, Welch's method improves the reliability of the PSD estimate by dividing a discrete time signal into a subset of shorter segments, applying the DFT to each of the segments in the subset and then averaging the results. Because windowing of the sub-segments attenuates the signal at the two ends of the windowing function, overlapping sub-segments are often used to reduce data loss. The 'DK_PSD' function uses Matlab's default settings for the 'pwelch' function, dividing the signal from each channel/trial into eight sub-segments with 50% overlap between consecutive segments.

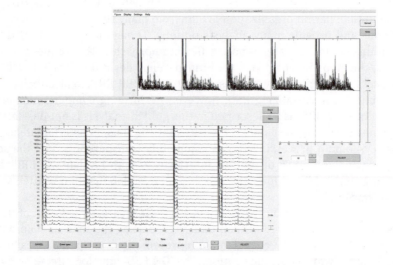

Figure 6.5   Visualization of the trial-by-trial power spectrum.

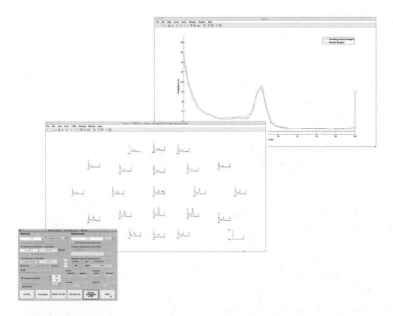

Figure 6.6   Visualizing the event-related band power.

Select 'Plot>Channel data (scroll)' to open an interactive plot of the single-trial PSD values (see Figure 6.5). The figure shows all trials consecutively with channels plotted as separate rows. Scrolling through the individual trials, one can observe the distribution of power over the frequency spectrum within each trial. Another useful visualization method is, again, the butterfly plot, which overlays all of the frequency traces from each channel. Use the 'Settings' menu in the figure window to limit the display to just one channel, then click the 'Stack' button at the upper right corner of the figure window. This will cause the figure window to display a butterfly plot of the PSD for each consecutive trial (see rear panel of Figure 6.5). Click 'Cancel' when you are done reviewing the data.

Averaging (ERBP)
Once the time-domain, single-trial data have been converted to the frequency domain, calculation of the ERBP is accomplished by averaging the single-trial PSD values over trials at each frequency. This is completely analogous to generating an ERP in the time-domain. Thus, ERBP can be calculated using ERPlab in the same way that ERPs were generated in the previous chapter using the following steps:

Compute ERBP by averaging over trials

- ERPLAB>Compute Averaged ERP

  - When the 'Averager GUI' appears, be sure that the 'Dataset(s)' field contains the index of the new 'PX...' dataset then click 'RUN'.

- ○ When the 'Save Erpset GUI' dialog appears, enter a name for the ERBP dataset, which will be saved as a new ERP structure in the workspace and click 'OK'.

When the averaging is complete, the details of the new ERP structure containing the ERBP values will be displayed in the Matlab Command Window. The ERPB values can be visualized in a number of ways using options available for visualizing ERPs in ERPlab. To view the ERBP for each channel in a topographic arrangement, select 'ERPLAB>Plot ERP Waveforms'. When the 'ERP Plotting GUI' appears, use the recommended parameter settings in Table 6.1 (also see Figure 6.6) then click 'Plot'. The resulting figure contains individual plots of the PSD as a function of frequency for each channel. Clicking on an individual channel will open a new figure, permitting closer inspection of that channel in isolation (see Figure 6.6). Visualizing the data in this way can help to identify frequency bands of interest for further analysis, channels with aberrant values, and experimental effects across frequencies. For example, inspection of Figure 6.6 reveals the presence of a peak in the PSD function over the Alpha frequency band. This peak is maximal centrally over parietal recording sites.

Just as with ERPs, it is essential to carefully review the ERBP data from each subject. Thus, it is important to visualize the data in several different ways. Again, the butterfly plot can be a useful way to evaluate data quality and identify noteworthy peaks in the PSD over a range of frequencies. The 'ERP_butterfly' function that was used to plot ERPs in Chapter 5 can also be used with the modified erpset containing ERBPs. Type the following (exactly as it appears):

ERP_butterfly(ERP,1,[1:2],7:27,[2 20]);

at the Matlab command line and press ENTER to generate the butterfly plot (see Figure 6.7). The bottom portion of the figure window contains the butterfly plot of ERBP values over the range 2 to 20 Hz. The top portion of the figure window contains the topographical maps of PSD for each of the two conditions. Click

Table 6.1   ERP Plotting GUI – recommended parameter settings.

Parameter Name	Setting	Notes
Bins to plot	1 2	Bins 1 & 2 refer to the 'Smoking-related Images' and 'Neutral Images' respectively
Channels to plot	7:27	This will plot EEG channels 7 through 27, ignoring peri-ocular channels 1 through 6
Time range (ms) to plot (start end)	2 20	Note that this refers to frequencies in the modified ERPset
Baseline correction	None	
Topographic arrangement (radio button)	Checked	Indicates to plot each channel in a topographic arrangement

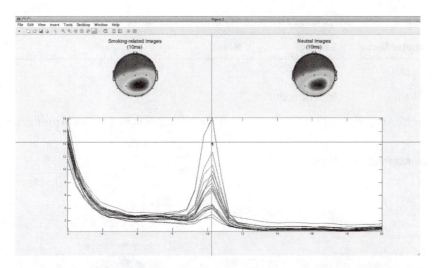

Figure 6.7 Butterfly plot of the power spectra with topographical maps for each condition.

anywhere in the butterfly plot to update the topographical maps to reflect the ERBP at a specific frequency defined by the location of the cursor. For example, clicking at the peak of the ERBP at ~9 Hz reveals that PSD is similarly distributed over the scalp at that frequency between the smoking-related and neutral image conditions for this subject.

While the previous examples illustrate useful methods for reviewing the ERBP at each channel/frequency over a wide frequency range (e.g., 2–20 Hz), it is also possible to review the distribution of the ERBP averaged over a range of frequencies. Because the goal of the present analysis is to characterize ERBP in the Alpha (8–12 Hz) range, it may be informative to plot the mean Alpha power topographically. To do this, select 'ERPLAB>Plot ERP Scalp Maps', and use the recommended parameter settings in Table 6.2 when the 'Scalp Mapping GUI' appears. Click the 'Plot' button to generate the topographical maps (see Figure 6.8). Unsurprisingly, the distribution of the mean Alpha-band ERBP is similar to the topographical maps observed in Figure 6.7. By default, ERPlab will scale the colormaps of each scalp plot individually, based on the range of values within the corresponding bin, obscuring significant differences between conditions in some cases. If this is the case, try repeating the scalp plot procedure but specifying a range to be used for *both* plots in the 'Custom (µV)' field of the 'Color bar scale' section of the 'Scalp Mapping GUI'. Moreover, while it is useful to visualize the experimental effects in individual subjects, it is also important to remember that any conclusions will be based on the statistical properties of the ERBP measured over many subjects.

Subtract Homologous Electrode Pairs (Asymmetry)
Once the data have been reviewed, asymmetry scores can be computed by subtraction of the ERBP from homologous electrodes over the left and right hemispheres.

Table 6.2   Scalp Mapping GUI – recommended parameter settings.

Parameter Name	Setting	Notes
Bins to plot	1 2	
Measurement	Mean amplitude	
Latency(ies) to plot	8 12	Note that this refers to frequencies in the modified ERPset
Baseline correction	None	

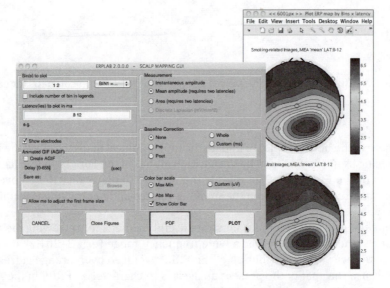

Figure 6.8   Visualizing the topography of ERBP averaged over a range of frequencies in the Alpha band.

It is common, however, to first convert PSD into decibel (dB) units by taking the base 10 logarithm of the ERBP. This first step can be accomplished by selecting 'ERPLAB>ERP Bin Operations'. When the 'Bin Operation GUI' appears, enter the following equations into the empty field at the top left of the GUI then click 'RUN':

b3 = 10*log10(b1) label Smoking-related Images (dB)

b4 = 10*log10(b2) label Neutral Images (dB)

This will create two new bins, 'b3' and 'b4', that are equal to the common logarithm of 'Smoking-related Images' and 'Neutral Images' bins respectively.

The next step is to compute the asymmetry scores by subtracting homologous electrodes. By convention, asymmetry is calculated by subtracting channels in the left hemisphere from their homologs in the right hemisphere. Gable and Harmon-Jones (2008) also identified a small region of interest over the anterior scalp using electrodes AF3/4, F3/4, F5/6, and F7/8 and then generated a composite frontal asymmetry index by averaging over those scores. The data included for this guided analysis have only two of these four electrode pairs. Thus, the present analysis will be based on measurements computed only from F3/4 and F7/8. Both channel subtraction and regional averaging are accomplished by selecting 'ERPLAB>ERP Channel Operations' and entering the following equations in the field at the top left of the GUI:

ch28 = ch13-ch11 label F4-3

ch29 = ch14-ch10 label F8-7

ch30= (ch28+ch29)/2 label Regional Asymmetry

Click 'RUN' to execute the operations. The operation is applied to each of the bins in the ERPset. The first two equations will generate two new channels, each the result of the subtraction of homologous pairs of electrodes. The third equation generates the composite scores, by computing the mean of the two new channels.

The composite asymmetry scores can be visualized over the Alpha frequency band by selecting 'ERPLAB>Plot ERP Waveforms' to open the 'ERP Plotting GUI'. Use the recommended parameters in Table 6.3 and click 'Plot'. The resulting figure plots the composite asymmetry measure as a function of frequency over the 8–12 Hz Alpha band (see Figure 6.9). Because Alpha power is considered to be inversely related to brain 'activity', Figure 6.9 indicates that there was more (numerically at least) left hemisphere activity following smoking-related images by comparison with neutral images. Since this first participant was a smoker, these data are in line with Zinser et al.'s (1999) findings that withdrawn smokers show more of an approach motivation to smoking-related cues than to neutral cues. Be sure to save the ERPset using 'ERPlab>Save current ERPset' before continuing.

Table 6.3 ERP Plotting GUI – recommended parameter settings.

Parameter Name	Setting	Notes
Bins to plot	3 4	Bins 3 & 4 refer to the dB-scaled (i.e., log-transformed) versions of bins 1 & 2
Channels to plot	30	This is the channel created by averaging over F3/4 and F7/8
Time range (ms) to plot	8 12	Note that this refers to frequencies in the modified ERPset
Baseline correction	None	

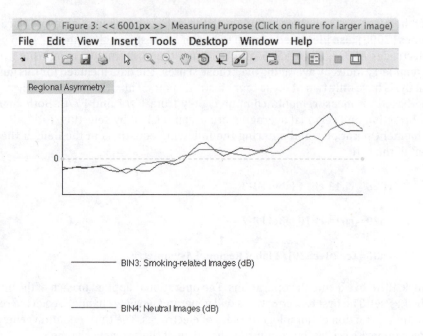

Figure 3: << 6001px >> Measuring Purpose (Click on figure for larger image)

File   Edit   View   Insert   Tools   Desktop   Window   Help

Regional Asymmetry

0

———— BIN3: Smoking-related Images (dB)

———— BIN4: Neutral Images (dB)

Figure 6.9   Visualization of regional asymmetry at each condition.

Table 6.4   ERP Measurements GUI – recommended parameter settings.

Parameter Name	Setting	Notes
From ERPset files (radio button)	Checked	Use the 'Add ERP set' button to select ERPset files
Measurement	Mean amplitude between two latencies	
Between latencies	8 12	Note that this refers to frequencies in the modified ERPset
Baseline period	None	
Bin	3 4	These are the bins that have been converted to dB units
Chan	30	This is the channel created by averaging over AF3/4, F3/4, F4/6, and F7/8
Save output file as	One measurement per line (long)	Use the 'Browse' button to designate the name and location of the to-be-saved output file

Data Management

Having completed all previous steps for each subject, the composite asymmetry scores can be compiled and exported using the same methods that were used to export mean amplitudes of ERP waveforms in Chapter 5. Select 'ERPlab>ERP Measurement Tool' to open the 'ERP Measurements GUI' and use the recommended parameters in Table 6.4.

After clicking 'RUN', each of the selected ERPsets will be loaded and measurements will be made based on the specified parameters. The progress of this process will be displayed in the Matlab command window. The results will be written to the specified text file with the following format:

ERPset	bin	chindex	chlabel	value
6001PX	3	30	RegionalAsymmetry	0.660
6001PX	4	30	RegionalAsymmetry	0.578
.	.	.	.	.
.	.	.	.	.
.			.	
6020PX	4	30	RegionalAsymmetry	0.586

The 'ERPset' column contains the subject identifiers (a 'PX' is appended to the subject number by the DK_PSD program), the 'bin' column contains the bin (i.e., condition) identifier, the 'chindex' contains the index of each channel, the 'chlabel' column contains the labels associated with the corresponding channel indexes and finally, the 'value' column contains the composite asymmetry index for that participant and condition. Note that the values obtained may be different from those presented here given differences in the treatment of data during preprocessing stages. The text file exported by the 'ERP Measurements GUI' can be easily organized using a pivot table (see Chapter 5).

Having organized the data with a pivot table, it can be readily copied to your favorite statistical analysis software. A bar chart can be used to group the data by smoking status (e.g., smoker/non-smoker) and evaluate whether smoking-related images are associated with an appetitive affective response reflected in larger asymmetry index scores in those participants who smoke (see Figure 6.10). An appropriate analysis is a mixed measures ANOVA with Image Type (smoking-related/neutral) as a repeated measure and Smoker (Yes/No) as a between-subjects measure. In light of prior research, the prediction is that smokers but not non-smokers will evidence an exaggerated approach response to smoking-related images. Although the qualitative pattern (see Figure 6.10) conforms with prior research suggesting an appetitive approach response by smokers to smoking-related images, neither differences between groups nor the interaction between Smoker and Image Type was statistically significant in this small sample. Nonetheless, these data nicely illustrate the application of measures of hemispheric asymmetry to study individual differences in motivational tendencies and affective reactivity (e.g., Gable & Harmon-Jones, 2008; Zinser et al., 1999).

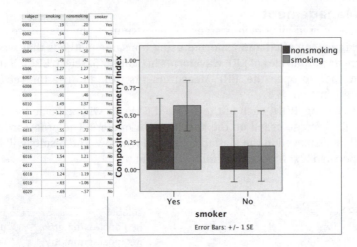

Figure 6.10   Regional asymmetry annalysis and plot.

REFERENCES

Allen, J. J., Iacono, W. G., Depue, R. A., & Arbisi, P. (1993). Regional electroencephalographic asymmetries in bipolar seasonal affective disorder before and after exposure to bright light. *Biological Psychiatry*, *33*(8–9), 642–646.

Balconi, M., & Mazza, G. (2010). Lateralisation effect in comprehension of emotional facial expression: a comparison between EEG alpha band power and behavioural inhibition (BIS) and activation (BAS) systems. *Laterality: Asymmetries of Body, Brain and Cognition*, *15*(3), 361–384.

Başar, E., Başar-Eroglu, C., Karakaş, S., & Schürmann, M. (2001). Gamma, alpha, delta, and theta oscillations govern cognitive processes. *International Journal of Psychophysiology*, *39*(2–3), 241–248.

Berger, H. (1929). Über das Elektrenkephalogramm des Menschen. *European Archives of Psychiatry and Clinical Neuroscience*, *87*(1), 527–570.

Coan, J. A., Allen, J. J. B., & Harmon-Jones, E. (2001). Voluntary facial expression and hemispheric asymmetry over the frontal cortex. *Psychophysiology*, *38*(6), 912–925.

Fox, N. A., & Davidson, R. J. (1986). Taste-elicited changes in facial signs of emotion and the asymmetry of brain electrical activity in human newborns. *Neuropsychologia*, *24*, 417–422.

Fox, N. A., & Davidson, R. J. (1987). Electroencephalogram asymmetry in response to the approach of a stranger and maternal separation in 10 month old infants. *Developmental Psychology*, *23*, 233–240.

Gable, P. A., & Harmon-Jones, E. (2008). Approach-motivated positive affect reduces breadth of attention. *Psychological Science*, *19*(5), 476–482.

Galambos, R. (1992). A comparison of certain gamma band (40-Hz) brain rhythms in cat and man. In E. Başar & T. Bullock (Eds), *Induced Rhythms in the Brain*. Boston, MA: Birkhäuser.

Harmon-Jones, E. (2003). Clarifying the emotive functions of asymmetrical frontal cortical activity. *Psychophysiology*, *40*(6), 838–848.

Harmon-Jones, E., & Allen, J. (1997). Behavioral activation sensitivity and resting frontal EEG asymmetry: Covariation of putative indicators related to risk for mood disorders. *Journal of Abnormal Psychology*, *106*(1), 159–163.

Harmon-Jones, E., & Allen, J. (1998). Anger and frontal brain activity: EEG asymmetry consistent with approach motivation despite negative affective valence. *Journal of Personality and Social Psychology*, *74*(5), 1310–1316.

Harmon-Jones, E., Harmon-Jones, C., Fearn, M., Sigelman, J. D., & Johnson, P. (2008). Left frontal cortical activation and spreading of alternatives: Tests of the action-based model of dissonance. *Journal of Personality and Social Psychology*, *94*(1), 1–15.

Harmon-Jones, E., & Sigelman, J. (2001). State anger and prefrontal brain activity: Evidence that insult-related relative left-prefrontal activation is associated with experienced anger and aggression. *Journal of Personality and Social Psychology*, *80*(5), 797–803.

Henriques, J. B., & Davidson, R. J. (1991). Left frontal hypoactivation in depression. *Journal of Abnormal Psychology*, *100*(4), 535–545.

Kline, J. P., Blackhart, G. C., & Williams, W. C. (2007). Anterior EEG asymmetries and opponent process theory. *International Journal of Psychophysiology*, *63*(3), 302–307.

Lindsley, D. B., & Wicke, J. D. (1974). The electroencephalogram: Autonomous electrical activity in man and animals. In R. F. Thompson & M. M. Patterson (Eds), *Bioelectric Recording Techniques (Part B)*. New York: Academic Press.

McGregor, I., Nash, K. A., & Inzlicht, M. (2009). Threat, high self-esteem, and reactive approach-motivation: Electroencephalographic evidence. *Journal of Experimental Social Psychology*, *45*(4), 1003–1007.

Mørup, M., Hansen, L. K., & Arnfred, S. M. (2007). ERPWAVELAB: A toolbox for multi-channel analysis of time–frequency transformed event related potentials. *Journal of Neuroscience Methods*, *161*(2), 361–368.

Rognoni, E., Galati, D., Costa, T., & Crini, M. (2008). Relationship between adult attachment patterns, emotional experience and EEG frontal asymmetry. *Personality and Individual Differences*, *44*(4), 909–920.

Schaffer, C. E., Davidson, R. J., & Saron, C. (1983). Frontal and parietal electroencephalogram asymmetry in depressed and nondepressed subjects. *Biological Psychiatry*, *18*(7), 753–762.

Sutton, S. K., & Davidson, R. J. (1997). Prefrontal brain asymmetry: A biological substrate of the behavioral approach and inhibition systems. *Psychological Science*, *8*(3), 204–210.

Tomarken, A. J., Davidson, R. J., & Henriques, J. B. (1990). Resting frontal brain asymmetry predicts affective responses to films. *Journal of Personality and Social Psychology*, *59*(4), 791–801.

Tomarken, A. J., Davidson, R. J., Wheeler, R. E., & Doss, R. C. (1992). Individual differences in anterior brain asymmetry and fundamental dimensions of emotion. *Journal of Personality and Social Psychology*, *62*(4), 676–687.

Wheeler, R. E., Davidson, R. J., & Tomarken, A. J. (1993). Frontal brain asymmetry and emotional reactivity: A biological substrate of affective style. *Psychophysiology*, *30*(1), 82–89.

Zinser, M. C., Fiore, M. C., Davidson, R. J., & Baker, T. B. (1999). Manipulating smoking motivation: Impact on an electrophysiological index of approach motivation. *Journal of Abnormal Psychology*, *108*(2), 240–254.

7

TIME-FREQUENCY ANALYSIS

INTRODUCTION TO TIME-FREQUENCY ANALYSIS

In the previous chapter, we explored the transformation of time-domain EEG signals to the frequency-domain via the Fourier transform. You may have noticed that in the process of decomposing the frequency components, all information about timing (i.e., latency) was lost. That is, despite the fact that the PSD analysis included data recorded over several seconds following the onset of target images, transformation to the frequency-domain revealed only the amplitude (and phase) of the oscillatory activity in that window and did not reveal anything about when those oscillations may have occurred. This is because the very basis of the Fourier transform is that it re-represents time-domain waveforms as a set of *sinusoidal* component waveforms. An important property of sinusoids is that they are perfectly repetitive, meaning that their amplitude is constant over time. Thus, one could reasonably plot the time-course of the frequency components derived from the Fourier transform, but the results would simply be a collection of time-invariant amplitudes (see top panel Figure 7.1). This is sometimes referred to as the 'time frequency trade-off' because resolution in the frequency-domain always comes at the cost of resolution in the time-domain. To make the inverse nature of the relationship between temporal and frequency resolution clear, consider the highest temporal resolution achievable in a sampled signal – a single point. This single point yields the most accurate information about the amplitude of the signal at a given point in time, but with just one sample nothing can be known about the oscillatory nature of the signal. There are, however, methods offering a compromise between resolution in the time and frequency domains. Two popular methods are the 'short time' Fourier transform (STFT) and the discrete wavelet transform (DWT). These 'time-frequency analyses' provide information about the time-varying nature of the oscillatory components of a signal.

The STFT is a relatively straightforward extension of the DFT described earlier. Using the STFT, a Fourier transform is applied to a series of consecutive (sometimes overlapping) temporal windows within a larger time period of interest. As a result of this windowing of the signal, estimates of the amplitude (and phase) of the frequency

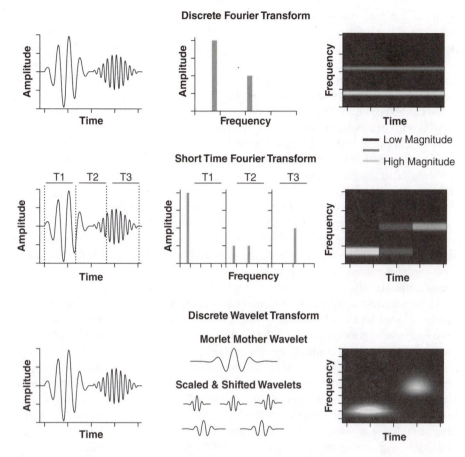

Figure 7.1   Illustration of DFT, STFT, and DWT methods for analysis of EEG in the frequency and time-frequency domains.

components can be determined with a temporal precision defined by the width of the window. Selection of an appropriate window size for the STFT is complicated by the fact that the frequency resolution of the Fourier transform is inversely proportional to the length (i.e., number of points) of the input signal. Thus, short windows yield good temporal resolution in exchange for poor frequency resolution and long windows yield good frequency resolution in exchange for poor temporal resolution (remember the time frequency trade-off!). Another limitation of the STFT is that once a window size is selected, that same window is used at all times and frequencies. In other words, both time and frequency resolution is constant over the time-frequency spectrum (see middle panel of Figure 7.1). This can be problematic when a signal contains both low frequency oscillations extending over long windows and high frequency oscillations in short windows, as is often the case in EEG.

The second popular method for time-frequency analysis, the DWT, addresses some of the limitations of the STFT (see Allen & MacKinnon, 2010; Handy, 2005 for technical reviews). Whereas the Fourier transform describes the original signal in terms of a set of sinusoidal waves localized in frequency but constant over the duration of the input signal (see Figure 7.1), the DWT describes the original signal in terms of its similarity to a set of 'scaled' and 'shifted' wavelets that are localized in *both* frequency and time. All of the scaled and shifted wavelets used with any given DWT are derived from a single 'mother' wavelet. There are an infinite number of mother wavelets to choose from. The most commonly used mother wavelet in the context of EEG is the Morlet wavelet – a sinusoidal wavelet that offers a desirable balance of resolution in the time and frequency domains. The scale of a wavelet refers to the extent to which the wavelet is expanded or compressed. At a low scale, wavelets are highly compressed and thus possess shorter temporal duration (i.e., length) and higher frequencies. Keeping in mind the time-frequency trade-off, this means that the DWT will have better temporal resolution but poorer frequency resolution at lower scales (i.e., higher frequencies) and better frequency resolution but poorer temporal resolution at higher scales (see Figure 7.2).

The values returned by a DWT analysis, called wavelet coefficients, represent the similarity between the scaled/shifted wavelets and the original data. When the wavelet is complex-valued, containing both amplitude and phase information, the wavelet coefficients are also complex-valued, yielding information about both the time-varying amplitude and phase of oscillatory activity at each frequency. While emphasis is often placed on the magnitude of the spectral content in frequency-domain and time-frequency transformations, information about the time-varying phase of EROs can and has been used fruitfully to measure intracortical coupling, addressing exciting questions about the nature of both local and long-distance communication in the brain as it may relate to cognitive functioning (Lachaux, Rodriguez, Martinerie, & Varela, 1999). In the guided analysis below, we will see how phase can also be used to make inferences about the extent to which EROs are evoked or induced by an eliciting stimulus. The wavelet coefficients are most commonly displayed using a two-dimensional spectrogram with a conventional Cartesian coordinate system for time and frequency axes and the magnitude corresponding to each time-frequency point represented by intensity or color (right column of Figure 7.1).

Figure 7.1 also illustrates the benefits of time-frequency analyses with regard to their capacity to discern the time-varying nature of EROs. Like the frequency-domain analysis, time-frequency transformations can also be used to discriminate between evoked and induced EROs. In fact, the procedure for discriminating these two classes of EROs is completely analogous to the procedure described in Chapter 6.

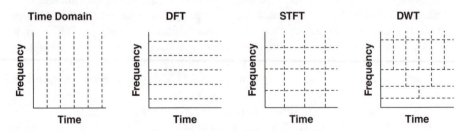

Figure 7.2   Illustration of the time and frequency resolutions for data in the time, frequency, and time-frequency domains.

Briefly, time-frequency transformation of the ERP yields estimates of the evoked EROs, while the average of the time-frequency transformations of each individual trial provides estimates of the ERBP (ERBP = evoked + induced EROs). Thus, estimates of the induced EROs are typically obtained by subtracting the evoked activity from the ERBP.

DOMAIN REVIEW: MU/MIRROR NEURONS

While recording single-cell activity in a macaque, di Pellegrino, Fadiga, Fogassi, Gallese, and Rizzolatti (1992) discovered a subset of neurons in the premotor cortex with unique properties. They found that a subset of motor neurons not only fired when the macaque performed an action, but also when the macaque observed the same action being performed by the experimenter. Furthermore, these neurons only discharged when observing or performing goal-directed actions such as grasping an object, and did not exhibit firing patterns consistent with a motor preparation, or 'priming', hypothesis (Rizzolatti, Fadiga, Gallese, & Fogassi, 1996). These neurons were thus termed mirror neurons and are typically thought of as visuo-motor neurons. In a review of the mirror neuron literature, Uddin, Iacoboni, Lange, and Keenan (2007) explained that, in the macaque, mirror neurons are sensitive to the precise grip being used in the goal-directed action. That is, mirror neurons discharge when the macaque sees a peanut being cracked but not when someone mimics the action without the peanut present (Gallese, Fadiga, Fogassi, & Rizzolatti, 1996; Umiltà et al., 2001). Interestingly, mirror neurons also respond to the sound of actions being executed (Keysers et al., 2003). In humans, single cell recordings of mirror neurons are rarely possible, but non-invasive neurophysiological evidence suggests that there is a human mirror neuron system that is similar to that in monkeys (Uddin et al., 2007).

The presence of a mirror neuron system in humans has been established through the measurement of EEG frequency oscillations in the brain. The Mu rhythm is typically described as an 8–12 Hz frequency oscillation occurring over the sensorimotor cortex. The Mu rhythm typically is more active when participants are at rest and becomes desynchronized or disrupted when an action is performed. Thus, the suppression of the Mu rhythm occurs when an individual makes a motor movement *and* when an individual perceives a motor movement (see Pineda, 2005 for a review). The desynchronization of the Mu rhythm has been induced during finger movement observation (Babiloni et al., 2002; Cochin, Barthelemy, Roux, & Martineau, 1999), by performing and observing precision grasps (Muthukumaraswamy & Johnson, 2004), and by viewing images of others in pain (Yang, Decety, Lee, Chen, & Cheng, 2009). Evidence with subdural electrodes has revealed that Mu rhythm desynchronization corresponds to specific somatosensory regions within the cortex (i.e., face and hand areas; Arroyo et al., 1993).

Imitation/Empathy

Imitation is an extremely important part of human behavior, in that it can help with the synchronization of body postures, gestures, voices, and facial expressions. Newborns can successfully imitate facial expressions within hours of being born and hand movements in the first few months after birth (Meltzoff & Moore, 1989, 1997). In addition, imitation seems to increase liking between individuals. Chartrand and

Bargh (1999) found that individuals who imitated participants' body movements such as rubbing the face were liked better than those who did not imitate; indeed, the social interaction was also judged more positively when imitation occurred (for a review, see Dijksterhuis, 2005). Using the Mu rhythm to examine the activation of the mirror neuron system in response to the execution and observation of goal-directed action is important in our understanding of imitation. For example, McFarland, Miner, Vaughan, and Wolpaw (2000) found that both performing and imagining performing bilateral hand movements desynchronized the Mu rhythm. Future research may seek to explore how more complicated goal-directed actions are processed in the mirror neuron system.

In addition to studying imitation, social psychologists have also deemed it important to understand how empathy affects social interactions. Our ability to understand others and to put ourselves in the shoes of others is exceedingly important to functioning well in society. Social neuroscience studies using EEG have begun to shed some light on how empathy plays out in the brain through the mirror neuron system. Muthukumaraswamy, Johnson, and McNair (2004) found evidence for Mu rhythm desynchronization when participants viewed individuals reaching towards objects but not when they were reaching towards nothing, providing support for the idea that the mirror neuron system reflects goal-directed actions *per se* rather than simply responding to movement. Oberman, Pineda, and Ramachandran (2007) showed participants video clips of three individuals (1) tossing a ball in the air to themselves, or (2) tossing a ball to each other, or (3) tossing a ball to each other *and* towards the camera as if to include the participant. The researchers found that as the level of social interaction increased, the participants' Mu rhythm became more desynchronized. In addition, Pineda and Hecht (2009) found that Mu rhythm desynchronization positively correlated with the accuracy on an emotion matching task and a person–object interaction matching task. Thus, these studies suggest that Mu suppression is linked to higher social information processing, which could be indicative of social skills. Accordingly, groups who typically are associated with high or low levels of empathy should also show differences in Mu suppression while viewing others' behavior. Indeed, Yang and colleagues (2009) discovered that female participants had significantly more Mu desynchronization than male participants. Their finding provides neural evidence for the generally acknowledged gender differences often found in behavioral research on empathic processing. In addition, researchers have investigated the Mu rhythm in individuals with Autism Spectrum Disorder (ASD), who have been identified as experiencing social impairments such as a lack of empathy. Oberman, Hubbard, McCleery, Altschuler, Ramachandran, and Pineda (2005) showed healthy adults and adults with ASD a video of a hand performing a series of gestures. The participants watched the videos and then performed those actions later as EEG was recorded. Results indicated that although there were no differences in the Mu rhythm desynchronization between healthy and ASD participants during the performance trials, there was significantly more Mu rhythm desynchronization for the healthy adults while perceiving others' motor movements compared to those with ASD.

Much work examining the experience of empathy has focused on participants viewing others in painful situations. For example, Yang and colleagues (2009) recorded the Mu rhythm of individuals as they viewed images of hands in potentially painful and non-painful situations (e.g., scissor blades near one's fingers). As hypothesized, there was significantly more Mu desynchronization while participants viewed the painful images than non-painful images. Further work demonstrated that Mu suppression is related to identification with the person being viewed. That is, Perry, Bentin, Bartal, Lamm, and Decety (2010) showed participants pictures of patients' hands being pricked by a needle or touched by a Q-tip. The patients were described as either similar to the participants (i.e., healthy patient who responded normally to pain) or dissimilar (i.e., diseased patient who responded abnormally to pain). Results indicated that although Mu suppression was greater when participants viewed the needle touching the patients' hands compared to the Q-tip, participants experienced greater Mu suppression to the similar patients than the dissimilar patients in the pain condition, suggesting that empathy can be moderated by identification with the target. Other work has also demonstrated that empathy can be moderated by simple group membership. That is, Gutsell and Inzlicht (2010) found that participants displayed Mu suppression when observing racial ingroup members engaging in a goal-directed action, but not when observing racial outgroup members; this was especially pronounced in individuals high in prejudice.

Desynchronization of the Mu rhythm has also been demonstrated to be sensitive to 'implied' motion wherein goal-directed actions are inferred from static images (Urgesi, Moro, Candidi, & Aglioti, 2006). Recently, Moore, Gorodnitsky, and Pineda (2012) demonstrated findings consistent with face mimicry of implied action during the perception of static emotional faces. Significant event-related desynchronization of the Mu rhythm was observed for both happy and disgust emotional expressions regardless of whether the task instructions encouraged empathy with the target faces. The fact that event-related Mu desynchronization has been observed in response to both animated and static images makes it broadly useful as a tool for addressing questions regarding empathy, social competency, affective reactivity, and many others relevant to social and personality psychology.

GUIDED ANALYSIS: TIME-FREQUENCY ANALYSIS WITH EEGLAB

In order to demonstrate the application of time-frequency analysis to the study of vicarious activation of motor cortex as indicated by suppression of the Mu rhythm, we will use the same set of 20 datasets that were used to investigate hemispheric asymmetry in Chapter 6. Recall that participants viewed a series of 40 images. Half of the images were smoking-related (i.e., containing cigarettes or smoking paraphernalia) and half were neutral images (e.g., pencil, barbeque lighter, etc.). Additionally, half of the images of each type were considered 'active' (e.g., a hand holding a lit cigarette, hand holding a pencil, etc.) and the rest were 'inactive' (e.g., a cigarette or pencil lying on a table). Whereas the distinction between smoking-relevant and neutral images was of foremost interest in Chapter 6, the present analysis is primarily concerned with the distinction between active and inactive image types irrespective of image content. The primary hypothesis was that actions would be inferred from the active images, leading to vicarious activation of the mirror neuron system.

Twenty college-aged participants viewed the series of images. Each trial consisted of a single image that remained on a computer screen for 8000 ms. Images were separated by an inter-trial interval of 8000 ms. The raw data for this guided analysis can be found on the companion website (www.sagepub.co.uk/dickter).

Whereas the frequency-domain analysis in Chapter 6 was structured so as to maintain a high level of transparency with respect to the various processing stages, the complexities inherent to time-frequency analysis make a similar approach difficult to accomplish without heavy reliance on familiarity with Matlab programming. Thus, the following guided analysis will make use of EEGlab's STUDY functions, permitting both group-wise analysis of the data as well as built-in routines for making statistical comparisons between conditions. In fact, the STUDY functions in EEGlab can be used to perform analyses similar to those described in Chapters 5 and 6.

Data Pre-processing

Data for the guided analysis are the same as were used to demonstrate the frequency-domain analysis in Chapter 6 and are available on the companion website (www.sagepub.co.uk/dickter) in their 'raw', unprocessed format. Thus, in preparation for the time-frequency analysis, each dataset should first be submitted to the pre-processing procedures described in Chapter 4. Once completed, load one of the pre-processed datasets into EEGlab. If you have already completed the pre-processing for these data in the course of following the guided analysis of Chapter 6, simply load one of those pre-processed datasets (e.g., 6001_clean_oar.set).

Segmentation

Just as in previous chapters, one of the first steps of the time-frequency analysis is to extract segments of data with respect to some time-locking event – in this case, the onset of the target pictures. To segment the data, you will again need to create a bin descriptor file (BDF). As in Chapter 6, the BDF will consist of just two bins. Image onset was marked by one of four codes: (1) 10 = active/smoking-related, (2) 20 = inactive/smoking-related, (3) 30 = active/neutral, (4) 40 = inactive/neutral. Thus, the BDF file should specify one bin labeled 'Active', containing trials marked by 10s and 30s and one bin labeled 'Inactive', containing trials marked by 20s and 40s. Once the BDF file has been created (using any text editor) and saved to disk, the data segments can be extracted by the following procedures:

```
bin 1
Active
.{10;30}
bin 2
Inactive
.{20;40}
```

Modify the event list in EEGlab to be compatible with ERPlab

- ERPLAB>Eventlist>Create EEG Eventlist

  o When the dialog titled 'CREATE BASIC EVENTLIST GUI' appears, click 'CREATE'.

  o If the 'Overwrite Confirmation' dialogue appears, click 'Overwrite them'.

  o When the dialog titled 'Dataset info – pop_newset()' appears, click the 'Overwrite it in memory' box and then click 'OK'.

Assign events in the current dataset to the bins in accordance with the criteria specified in the BDF file

- ERPLAB>Assign Bins (BINLISTER)

  o When the dialog titled 'BINLISTER GUI' appears, click the 'Browse' button under the heading 'Load Bin Descriptor File from'. Select the 'Chapter7_BDF.txt' file downloaded with the tutorial data (or the text file you created) and click 'RUN'.

  o When the 'Dataset info – pop_newset()' dialog appears, select 'Overwrite it in memory' and click 'OK'.

Extract data segments from the continuous data

- ERPLAB>Extract Bin-based Epochs

  o When the 'EXTRACT BINEPOCHS GUI' dialog appears, the user is asked to indicate the period of time around each event that should be extracted from the continuous data. For this dataset, because stimuli were presented to participants for 8000 ms, you can use the interval from –2000 to 8000. Again, the pre-stimulus baseline is larger in this case than it was when we were computing the ERP in Chapter 5 because it is important to obtain a reliable estimate of the pre-stimulus oscillatory activity. Consider, for example, that one cycle of an 8 Hz oscillation takes 125 ms. A 200 ms pre-stimulus baseline, such as might be used for an ERP, would thus contain less than two full cycles of the 8 Hz oscillation.

  o The parameters for baseline correction will also be specified in the 'EXTRACT BINEPOCHS GUI' dialog. Baseline correction will not have any effect on the spectral estimates, but is important for the artifact rejection process and can be useful for visualizing data prior to time-frequency decomposition. Select the 'Pre' option to remove the average of the entire pre-stimulus (–2000 ms to 0 ms) interval from each of the segments and then click 'RUN'.

  o When the 'Dataset info – pop_newset()' dialog appears, select 'Overwrite it in memory' and click 'OK'.

When the routine is completed, the fields of the EEGlab GUI will be re-populated to describe the segmented dataset. Notice that the 'Epochs' field now indicates the number of individual data segments that were extracted from the continuous recording.

Artifact Rejection

Although extreme artifacts in the data will have been removed during pre-processing (see Chapter 4), there may still be unwanted noise in the intervals of data selected during segmentation. Considerations with respect to artifact rejection are the same for time-frequency analyses as they are with the frequency-domain analysis (see discussion in Chapter 6). However, simple time-domain voltage thresholds remain the de facto standard.

Detect segments containing artifacts with ERPlab

- ERPLAB>Artifact detection in epoched data>Simple voltage threshold

  o When the 'Extreme Values' dialog appears, be sure the voltage limits are set to '−200 200'.

  o The first six channels are the peri-ocular channels and should be excluded from the voltage threshold procedure. Set the Channel(s) field to '7:27' and click 'Accept'.

  o When the procedure is finished, two new windows will appear. The first window, titled 'Extreme Values detection view', permits a review of the segments that have been marked for rejection. It is *highly* recommended to review all of the selections carefully. Click 'Cancel' to close the window.

  o The second window to appear, titled 'Dataset info – pop_newset()' is a prompt to let the user know that markers will be added to the file indicating which segments will be rejected from further analysis. Select 'Overwrite it in memory' and click 'OK'.

Save the modified file

- File>Save current dataset as

  o Choose a filename that reflects the segmentation (e.g., '7001_segmented_artrej.set').

In order to use the STUDY functions in EEGlab, it is necessary to save the segments of data corresponding with each bin into a separate file.

Separate the segments into separate files by condition

- Edit>Select epochs or events

- o When the 'Select events' dialog appears, enter 'B1(10) B1(30)' into the 'type' field or click the ellipsis button next to the 'type' field and select those entries from the list. These two trial types refer to all of the segments included in bin 1 (i.e., B1) containing the 'active' image types. Click 'OK' to extract those segments.

- o A confirmation dialog will appear, indicating the number of trials that will be deleted in order to isolate the selected trial types. Click 'OK'.

- o When the 'Dataset info' dialog appears, give an appropriate name to the subset of segments (e.g., 7001_Active) and select 'Save it as file', providing a similar name for the file that will be saved to disk. Click 'OK'.

- o When EEGlab has finished creating the new dataset, the EEGlab GUI will be refreshed with the contents of the new dataset (i.e., 7001_Active). Thus, it is necessary to re-load the original set of all data segments in order to proceed with the extraction of bin 2 containing the inactive images. To do this, click 'Datasets' and then select the original dataset (e.g., 7001_segmented_artrej) from the list.

- o Repeat these steps for bin 2, using a similar nomenclature (e.g., 7001_Inactive) when saving files.

Create EEGlab STUDY

Once the previous steps have been completed for all participants you should have a collection of 40 new EEGlab datasets, each containing the segments of one of the two bins for a single participant (e.g., 7001_Active.set, 7001_Inactive.set ... 7020_Active. set, 7020_Inactive.set). The STUDY structure in EEGlab is, like the EEG data structure, a Matlab variable that represents a collection of related variables. The STUDY structure contains a collection of information about multiple datasets, plus information relevant to the experimental design such as group membership (e.g., smoker/non-smoker), condition (e.g., Active/Inactive), and session. When a STUDY has been loaded into EEGlab, a number of STUDY-specific functions become available for performing group-wise analyses and statistical testing (among other things).

   NOTE: Before creating the STUDY structure, it is a good idea to change the memory options in EEGlab so that no more than one dataset is loaded at a time. To configure this memory option, select 'File>Memory and other options'. When the 'Memory options' dialog appears, check that the 'If set, keep at most one dataset in memory' option is selected then click 'OK'.

Create an EEGlab STUDY structure

- File>Create study>Browse for datasets

  - o When the 'Create a new STUDY set' appears, use the ellipsis buttons in the 'Browse' column to locate and add each of the individual data subsets (e.g., 7001_Active) to the STUDY structure. For each dataset that is added, enter the corresponding subject number, session (all 1 in this case), condition (Active/Inactive), and group (smoker/non-smoker) information. Use the right arrow button to add more files once the first 10 fields have been used. Enter a name for the STUDY set (e.g., Time-Frequency) and, if desired, a name describing the task (e.g., Active–Inactive). When all participants and conditions have been added, click 'OK' to create the STUDY.

When the STUDY has been created, the EEGlab GUI will be updated to reflect the contents of the STUDY set, including the study name, number of subjects, numbers of conditions and groups, etc. Notice that the 'STUDY' menu item, previously greyed out, is also now available for user interaction. Once the STUDY has been created, the STUDY's 'design' can be specified, instructing EEGlab about the nature of the comparisons that will be made between conditions, groups, etc.

- STUDY>Select/Edit study design(s)
  - When the 'Edit STUDY design' dialog appears, ensure that all subjects are selected for analysis. Designs can be specified with up to two independent variables. The variable names (e.g., condition, group, etc.) are listed under the headings 'Independent variable 1' and 'Independent variable 2'. Selecting one of the listed variable names will cause the values associated with that variable to be listed in fields below (e.g., 'Ind. Var. 1 values'). For the present purpose of making comparisons between the active and inactive image types, select the 'condition' variable in the 'Independent variable 1' list. The values, 'active' and 'inactive', should appear below. Select 'None' in the list of 'Independent variable 2' variable names. Select the box next to 'Save the STUDY' and click 'OK'.

Time-Frequency Analysis

Having created the STUDY structure and designated the design parameters, the time-frequency analysis can be implemented for every participant, condition, and channel in just one step.

Perform the time-frequency analysis

- STUDY>Pre-compute channel measures
  - When the 'Select and compute component measures for later clustering' dialog appears, specify the options and parameters indicated in Table 7.1 and then click 'OK' to begin the analysis.
  - **NOTE:** The analysis will likely take several hours to complete

There are a number of options that can be specified when pre-computing channel measures in an EEGlab STUDY. Several of the options recommended in Table 7.1 are

Table 7.1 Pre-compute channel measures GUI – recommended parameter settings.

Parameter Name	Setting	Notes
ERPs	Checked	Compute time-domain ERPs for each channel
Baseline ([min max] in ms)	−200 0	Specify baseline correction interval for ERPs
Power Spectrum	Checked	Compute power spectrum (FFT) for each channel
Spectopo parameters	'specmode', 'fft','freqrange',[1 75]	Use FFT to compute power spectrum and limit output to frequencies between 1 and 75 Hz
ERSPs	Checked	Compute the event-related spectral perturbation (ERSP)
ITCs	Checked	Compute the inter-trial coherence (ITC)
Time/freq parameters	'cycles', [3 0.5], 'freqs',[4 75]	Uses the default 'cycles' option for the time-frequency analysis and limits the output to 100 linearly spaced frequencies between 1 and 75 Hz

suggested in order to illustrate some of those functions that approximate the ERP and frequency-domain analyses described in Chapters 5 and 6 respectively. For example, selecting the 'ERP' option will perform both single subject and grand averaging of the time-domain data. A 'baseline' can optionally be specified for the ERP analysis. Specifying start and end points for the baseline window (e.g., −200 0) instructs ERPlab to compute the average amplitude within the window and subtract that value from the entire data segment (done separately for each subject, condition, trial, and channel). Likewise, selecting the 'Power spectrum' option will apply a Fourier transform to each subject, condition, channel, and trial. The resulting power spectra will be averaged over trials, yielding a measure of ERBP for each channel, condition, and participant similar to that done in Chapter 6. The power spectrum analysis uses the 'spectopo' function in EEGlab to perform the frequency-domain analysis. There are many options that can be specified to this function (type 'help spectopo' at the Matlab command line to see them all) such as the size of the FFT windows and amount of overlap between successive windows (see discussion of FFT windowing in Chapter 6) in order to tailor the analysis to specific research questions. For present purposes, we suggest only the addition of the '"freqs", [1 75]' option, which limits the analysis to the range of frequencies between 1 and 75 Hz.

The time-frequency options include event-related spectral perturbation (ERSP) and inter-trial coherence (ITC). These analyses are performed using the 'newtimef' function in EEGlab and are therefore highly configurable. Type 'help newtimef' at the Matlab command line to see a complete list (and brief description) of the available options. ERSP, a generalization of ERS and ERD described in Chapter 6, is a measure of event-related changes in the amplitude of EEG frequency spectra as a function of time. ERSP is computed by the following steps: (1) compute baseline time-frequency spectra over the pre-stimulus interval, (2) compute the trial time-frequency spectra over the post-stimulus interval, (3) normalize the trial time-frequency spectra by dividing by their respective mean baseline spectra, (4) compute the average of the normalized trial spectra for many trials. Notice that because the frequency spectra are computed for individual trials before averaging, ERSP in the time-frequency domain is analogous to baseline normalized ERBP (i.e., ERS & ERD) in the frequency domain (see Figure 7.3). Thus, ERSP is a measure of both induced and evoked amplitude dynamics across the frequency spectrum.

Whereas ERSP measures amplitude dynamics irrespective of the phases of the EROs, ITC is a measure of phase dynamics irrespective of amplitude. Specifically, ITC

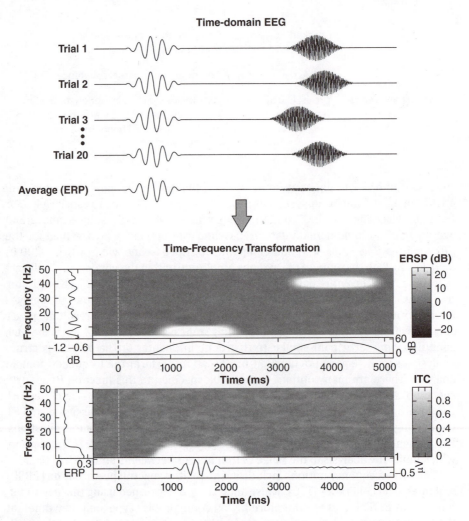

Figure 7.3   Illustration of the time-frequency analysis and the relationship between measures of ERSP and ITC in EEGlab.

is a measure of the consistency of the instantaneous phase across trials at each frequency and time-point. ITC ranges between zero and one, with a value of zero indicating random phase across trials and value of one indicating perfectly consistent phase across trials. Recall that the instantaneous phase of a sinusoid describes the current position of the oscillation and that a collection of sinusoidal waveforms of the same amplitude, but variable phase, will tend to cancel each other out when averaged in the time-domain (see Figure 6.3). Thus, evoked oscillatory dynamics (i.e., EBP) will be represented as localized changes in amplitude in the ERSP *and* higher ITC (i.e., phase locking) at corresponding times and frequencies. Induced oscillations (i.e., IBP), by contrast, may have similar amplitude dynamics reflected in measures of ERSP, but will be associated with lower values of ITC at corresponding times and frequencies. Together with ERSP, ITC can therefore be considered to reflect the extent to which ERSP is driven by evoked or induced oscillatory activity (see Figure 7.3).

The relationship between evoked/induced EROs and measures of ERSP and ITC as computed by the 'newtimef' function in EEGlab is illustrated in Figure 7.3. The top panel of Figure 7.3 shows the time-domain EEG for a collection of individual trials. An evoked 8 Hz oscillation, with highly consistent phase across trials, can be seen to occur early in the data segments. Later in the segments, a 40 Hz oscillation with the same magnitude can be seen in each trial, but with little phase consistency across trials. The bottom panel of Figure 7.3 illustrates the results of the time-frequency analysis in EEGlab. The upper spectrogram is a representation of the ERSP magnitude at each time and frequency. Both evoked and induced oscillations are clearly visible as 'hot-spots' in the time-frequency plane. The narrow plot at the leftmost end of the ERSP spectrogram shows the mean baseline power spectrum (e.g., PSD) and the narrow plot at the bottom shows the 'envelope' (highest magnitudes (dark line) and lowest magnitudes (gray line)) of the spectral estimates over time.

The lower spectrogram is a representation of the ITC at each time and frequency. The evoked nature of the 8 Hz oscillation is clearly discernable in the ITC, with values near one indicating near perfect consistency of the phase of the 8 Hz signal across trials. Likewise, the induced nature of the 40 Hz oscillatory activity is also clearly visible, with ITC values near zero reflecting the phase inconsistency of the 40 Hz signal across trials. The narrow plot to the left of the ITC shows the mean ITC over time and the plot at the bottom of ITC shows the time-domain ERP.

Several approaches to the computation of ERSP and ITC are optionally available in EEGlab. For example, the time-frequency spectra can be estimated using either the STFT or Wavelet-based analyses. For present purposes, we will employ EEGlab's default procedure for estimation of ERSP and ITC using Morlet wavelets. Two optional input arguments were specified to the 'Precompute channel measures' dialog that determined the nature of the ERSP/ITC decomposition (as indicated in Table 7.1). The 'nfreqs' argument simply directed EEGlab to restrict the range of frequencies to be analyzed to a small subset of frequencies (e.g., 1–75 Hz) more typically of interest in cognitive psychophysiology research. The value(s) setting for the 'cycles' argument determines the selection of STFT or wavelet-based decomposition and also can be used to determine the specific shape of the time-frequency windows. When set to a value of zero, EEGlab will use the STFT method with a constant window length across all frequencies. An integer value, $n>0$, directs EEGlab to use the Morlet wavelet-based analysis with n cycles per wavelet. Recall that the cycles of a wavelet is directly related to the width of the wavelet at each frequency. For example, if the number of cycles is set to 3, then the width of the wavelet will be about 600 ms at 5 Hz (3 * 1/5) and about 75 ms at 40 Hz (3 * 1/40). Thus, using wavelets with more cycles will lead to better frequency resolution because the wavelet will be wider (i.e., extend over more time) whereas using a smaller number of cycles will have the opposite effect, improving temporal resolution at the expense of frequency resolution.

When the 'cycles' argument is supplied with two values (e.g., [3 0.5]), the second value is used as a scaling factor to increase the number of cycles in the wavelets as the frequency increases. A scaling factor of 0.5 instructs EEGlab to slowly increase the number of cycles in the wavelets used for higher frequencies until the corresponding width of the wavelet reaches half (0.5) the width of the wavelet at the lowest frequency. For example, if a time-frequency analysis is requested for frequencies between 5 and 75 Hz and EEGlab is provided with the values [3 0.5] for the 'cycles' argument, then the wavelet will have 3 cycles at the lowest frequency of 5 Hz, having a width of about 600 ms (.6 s), and about 23 cycles at 75 Hz ((.6/2)/(1/75)). While increasing the number of cycles at higher frequencies negates some of the temporal resolution that is gained by using wavelets, doing so preserves more of the frequency resolution, reducing the 'blurring' that can occur over higher frequencies in conventional wavelet-based time-frequency decompositions.

Once all channel measures have been pre-computed, the results can be visualized using options in the STUDY menu.

Visualize the time-frequency analysis

- STUDY>Plot channel measures

    o   When the 'View and edit current channels' dialog appears, you will have the option to display any of the pre-computed measures (e.g., ERP, PSD, and time-frequency). The dialog makes available both group-level and single subject-level visualization of the results. Group-level analyses are accessible from the buttons on the left side of the dialog window and single subject-level analyses are accessible from buttons on the right.

    o   Given their proximity to the sensory-motor cortex, electrodes C3 and C4 are most commonly used to measure desynchronization of the Mu rhythm. Begin by selecting one of these channels from the list of channels on the left of the dialog window.

    o   Click the 'Plot ERSPs' button on the left and, once the figure has rendered, click the 'Plot ITCs' button on the left. These actions will produce visualizations of the group-level ERSP and ITC analyses for each of the active and inactive image types (see Figure 7.4).

There are several noteworthy features of these visualizations that can be used to garner information about the results. First, notice that there is an increase in ERSP between about 100 and 700 ms over the 2–6 Hz frequency range. Oscillations in this time-frequency window are consistent with voltage fluctuations typically observed in an ERP waveform. The fact that there is a corresponding increase in ITC over the same time-frequency window and that both ERSP and ITC dynamics are similar in active and inactive conditions suggests that the corresponding ERSP is due to evoked rather than induced oscillatory activity, which is also consistent with the assertion that this region of the time-frequency plot reflects the ERP to the onset of the image.

The second noteworthy feature is the transient increase in ERSP between about 300 and 400 ms over the 25–70 Hz (i.e., Gamma) frequency range. The increase in ERSP appears to be larger in the active condition, indicating that this region of oscillatory activity may be related to experimental manipulation. Additionally, there does not appear to be a corresponding increase in ITC over this time-frequency window, suggesting that the Gamma-band ERSP is a function of induced oscillatory activity.

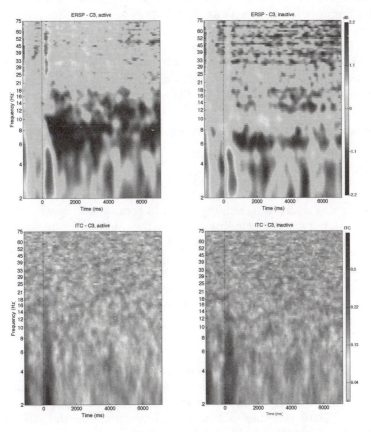

Figure 7.4   ERSP and ITC plotted for each condition at channel C3.

The third noteworthy feature regards the specific hypothesis outlined for this guided analysis. Recall that vicarious activation of motor cortex by the perception of implied movement is thought to be reflected in a desynchronization of the mirror neuron system oscillating at about 8–13 Hz (i.e., Mu). The visualization clearly shows a decrease in ERSP over the Mu frequency range that is larger in magnitude for active images, depicting human interaction with an object, than for inactive images. This Mu desynchronization appears to reach an early peak at about 1000 ms but maintain at a lower level over the course of the 8-second image presentation. The lack of any qualitative changes in ITC over the Mu frequency range suggests that the desynchronization is an induced oscillatory phenomenon.

The next step is to consider making formal (i.e., statistical) comparisons between the two conditions. There are two common approaches to making statistical comparisons between conditions in the time-frequency domain – 'massive univariate analysis' (MUA) and 'region of interest' (ROI) analysis. As the name implies, MUA involves the submission of each of the hundreds to thousands of unique points in the time-frequency plane to an independent test of statistical significance. There are several analytic approaches within this general framework including parametric and non-parametric tests as well as methods for addressing inflation of the Type I error rate that comes with making many simultaneous comparisons. Coverage of these methods is beyond the scope of this book but can be found elsewhere (Blair & Karniski, 1993; Lage-Castellanos, Martinez-Montes, Hernandez-Cabrera, & Galan, 2009; Suckling & Bullmore, 2004). Several varieties of the MUA analyses are available in EEGlab.

Performing the MUA Analysis with EEGlab

- STUDY>Plot channel measures

  - Click the 'Params' button that is adjacent to the 'Plot ERSPs' and 'Plot ITCs' buttons. This will open the 'Set ERSP|ITC plotting parameters' dialog in which the user can control parameters of the displayed results, including scaling of the time and frequency axes and the addition of topographical plots. In order to address the specific hypothesis outlined for this guided analysis, we will restrict the visualization and testing to the Mu frequency range in channel C3 and request conventional parametric tests with correction for multiple comparisons using the false discovery rate (Benjamini, Krieger, & Yekutieli, 2006; Lage-Castellanos et al., 2009). First, select channel C3 from in the 'Select channel(s) to plot' field and select 'All subjects' in the 'Select subject(s) to plot' field. Next, enter '8 13' in the 'Freq. range in Hz [Low High]' field and click 'OK'. Next, click the 'STATS' button Select and select the option to 'Compute 1st independent variable statistics.' Next, select the option to 'Use EEGLAB statistics', select 'use parametric statistics' and set the 'Statistical threshold (P-value)' to '.05'.

o Once the visualization parameters have been set, click the 'Plot ERSPs' button on the left to perform the analysis and plot the results (see Figure 7.5). Restriction of the range of frequencies plotted makes even more clear the qualitative differences between conditions, with active images eliciting a reduction in the amplitude of oscillatory activity in the Mu frequency range. Additionally, a third plot (on the right) shows the results of the MUA analysis, marking only those points in the time-frequency plane where the result of the corresponding statistical test was less than the criterion *P*-value of .05.

ROI analyses are the second common approach to statistical testing in the time-frequency domain. As the name implies, ROI analyses involve the designation of a specific region of the time-frequency plane for which statistical comparisons will be made. In many cases, ROIs are simply defined by subjective 'islands' of increased/decreased ERSP in the time-frequency spectrogram or guided either by an MUA analysis. Once the ROI has been designated, composite ERSP/ITC scores are generated by averaging over the times and frequencies included in the ROI. EEGlab possesses a convenient tool for performing ROI analysis of time-frequency data.

In this case both the frequency range (e.g., Mu) and scalp topography (e.g., C3/C4) were established a priori. It is important to note that this is often not the case and care must be taken to evaluate the ERSP/ITC plots over a collection of channels in order to determine those frequencies, times, and channels that are most appropriate. Plotting the topography of an ROI can also be a useful way of visualizing experimental effects even in cases like the present where an electrode or group of electrodes were targeted a priori. Inspection of the time-course of experimental effects revealed by the MUA analysis in Figure 7.5, combined with the a priori hypotheses regarding the Mu frequency range suggests that a reasonable ROI for the current analysis might include ERSP over 500–5000 ms and over 8–13 Hz. Analyses and topographical maps for this ROI analysis can be accomplished using the following steps.

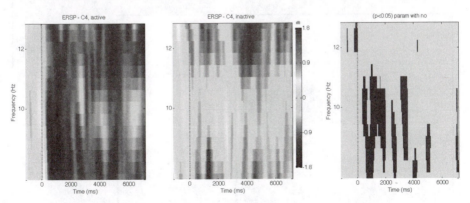

Figure 7.5   Applying parametric tests to the time-frequency data.

Perform the ROI Analysis

- STUDY>Plot channel measures

  o Select all but the peri-ocular channels (use Shift+click to select multiple channels) in the 'Select channels to plot' field.

  o Select the 'All subjects' option in the 'Subjects to plot' field.

  o Click the 'Params' button that is adjacent to the 'Plot ERSPs' and 'Plot ITCs' buttons. In the dialog box that opens, enter '500 5000' in the 'Plot scalp map at time [ms]' field to define the temporal window of the ROI and enter '8 13' in the 'Plot scalp map at freq. [Hz]' field to define the frequency range of the ROI. Click OK to close the dialog box.

  o Click the 'STATS' button and select the 'Compute 1st independent variable statistics', 'Use EEGLAB statistics', 'use parametric statistics', and 'Use FDR correction' options. Finally, enter '.05' into the 'Statistical threshold (p-value)' field. Click 'OK' to continue.

  o Click 'Plot ERSPs' on the left side of the 'View and edit current channels' dialog to plot the topographical maps of the ROI (see Figure 7.6).

Examination of Figure 7.6 reveals that there were broadly distributed perturbations of oscillatory activity over the times and frequencies of the ROI.

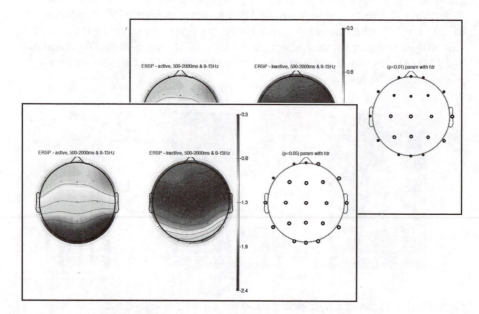

Figure 7.6   Illustration of the definition of a region of interest.

Channels at which there are significant differences across conditions for the ERSP ROI composite scores are indicated with a small red dot in the panel on the right (indicated by open circles in Figure 7.6). In the present example, differences were significant at most electrodes using the critical value of $p < .05$ (even with false discovery rate correction!). In an effort to gain some clarity about how the effects were localized on the scalp, try re-computing the statistical tests using a more conservative threshold of $p < .01$ (see rear panel of Figure 7.6). As can be seen in the figure, channels surviving the more conservative significance tests are localized to the central-parietal scalp, consistent with the hypothesis that differences in Mu desynchronization would be concentrated over the motor and sensory-motor cortices. Taken together, the MUA analysis at channels C3 and C4 combined with the ROI analysis indicate that motor imagery associated with implied movement is reflected in suppression of the Mu rhythm.

REFERENCES

Allen, D. P., & MacKinnon, C. D. (2010). Time-frequency analysis of movement-related spectral power in EEG during repetitive movements: A comparison of methods. *Journal of neuroscience methods*, *186*(1), 107. doi:10.1016/j.jneumeth.2009.10.022

Arroyo, S., Lesser, R. P., Gordon, B., Uematsu, S., Jackson, D., & Webber, R. (1993). Functional significance of the Mu rhythm of human cortex: An electrophysiologic study with subdural electrodes. *Electroencephalography and Clinical Neurophysiology*, *87*(3), 76–87.

Babiloni, C., Babiloni, F., Carducci, F., Cincotti, F., Cocozza, G., Del Percio, C., Moretti, D. V., et al. (2002). Human cortical electroencephalography (EEG) rhythms during the observation of simple aimless movements: a high-resolution EEG study. *Neuroimage*, *17*(2), 559–572.

Benjamini, Y., Krieger, A. M., & Yekutieli, D. (2006). Adaptive linear step-up procedures that control the false discovery rate. *Biometrika*, *93*(3), 491–507.

Blair, R. C., & Karniski, W. (1993). An alternative method for significance testing of waveform difference potentials. *Psychophysiology*, *30*(5), 518–524.

Chartrand, T. L., & Bargh, J. A. (1999). The chameleon effect: The perception–behavior link and social interaction. *Journal of Personality and Social Psychology*, *76*(6), 893–910.

Cochin, S., Barthelemy, C., Roux, S., & Martineau, J. (1999). Observation and execution of movement: Similarities demonstrated by quantified electroencephalography. *European Journal of Neuroscience*, *11*(5), 1839–1842.

di Pellegrino, G., Fadiga, L., Fogassi, L., Gallese, V., & Rizzolatti, G. (1992). Understanding motor events: A neurophysiological study. *Experimental Brain Research. Experimentelle Hirnforschung. Expérimentation Cérébrale*, *91*(1), 176–180.

Dijksterhuis, A. (2005). Why we are social animals: The high road to imitation as social glue. *Perspectives on Imitation: From Neuroscience to Social Science*, *2*, 207–220.

Gallese, V., Fadiga, L., Fogassi, L., & Rizzolatti, G. (1996). Action recognition in the premotor cortex. *Brain, 119*(2), 593–609.

Gutsell, J. N., & Inzlicht, M. (2010). Empathy constrained: Prejudice predicts reduced mental simulation of actions during observation of outgroups. *Journal of Experimental Social Psychology, 46*(5), 841–845.

Handy, T. C. (2005). *Event-related potentials: A methods handbook*. Cambridge, MA: MIT Press.

Keysers, C., Kohler, E., Umiltà, M. A., Nanetti, L., Fogassi, L., & Gallese, V. (2003). Audiovisual mirror neurons and action recognition. *Experimental Brain Research, 153*(4), 628–636.

Lachaux, J., Rodriguez, E., Martinerie, J., & Varela, F. (1999). Measuring phase synchrony in brain signals. *Human Brain Mapping, 8*, 194–208.

Lage-Castellanos, A., Martinez-Montes, E., Hernandez-Cabrera, J. A., & Galan, L. (2009). False discovery rate and permutation test: An evaluation in ERP data analysis. *Statistics in Medicine, 29*, 63–74.

McFarland, D., Miner, L., Vaughan, T., & Wolpaw, J. (2000). Mu and Beta rhythm topographies during motor imagery and actual movements. *Brain Topography, 12*(3), 177–186.

Meltzoff, A. N., & Moore, M. K. (1989). Imitation in newborn infants: Exploring the range of gestures imitated and the underlying mechanisms. *Developmental Psychology, 25*(6), 954.

Meltzoff, A. N., & Moore, M. K. (1997). Explaining facial imitation: A theoretical model. *Early Development and Parenting, 6*(34), 179–192.

Moore, A., Gorodnitsky, I., & Pineda, J. (2012). EEG Mu component responses to viewing emotional faces. *Behavioural Brain Research, 226*(1), 309–316.

Muthukumaraswamy, S. D., & Johnson, B. W. (2004). Primary motor cortex activation during action observation revealed by wavelet analysis of the EEG. *Clinical Neurophysiology, 115*(8), 1760–1766.

Muthukumaraswamy, S. D., Johnson, B. W., & McNair, N. A. (2004). Mu rhythm modulation during observation of an object-directed grasp. *Cognitive Brain Research, 19*(2), 195–201.

Oberman, L. M., Hubbard, E. M., McCleery, J. P., Altschuler, E. L., Ramachandran, V. S., & Pineda, J. A. (2005). EEG evidence for mirror neuron dysfunction in autism spectrum disorders. *Cognitive Brain Research, 24*(2), 190–198.

Oberman, L. M., Pineda, J. A., & Ramachandran, V. S. (2007). The human mirror neuron system: A link between action observation and social skills. *Social Cognitive and Affective Neuroscience, 2*(1), 62–66.

Perry, A., Bentin, S., Bartal, I. B.-A., Lamm, C., & Decety, J. (2010). 'Feeling' the pain of those who are different from us: Modulation of EEG in the Mu/alpha range. *Cognitive, Affective & Behavioral Neuroscience, 10*(4), 493–504.

Pineda, J. A. (2005). The functional significance of Mu rhythms: Translating. *Brain Research Reviews, 50*(1), 57–68.

Pineda, J. A., & Hecht, E. (2009). Mirroring and Mu rhythm involvement in social cognition: Are there dissociable subcomponents of theory of mind? *Biological Psychology, 80*(3), 306–314.

Rizzolatti, G., Fadiga, L., Gallese, V., & Fogassi, L. (1996). Premotor cortex and the recognition of motor actions. *Cognitive Brain Research, 3*(2), 131–141.

Suckling, J., & Bullmore, E. (2004). Permutation tests for factorially designed neuroimaging experiments. *Human Brain Mapping, 22*(3), 193–205.

Uddin, L. Q., Iacoboni, M., Lange, C., & Keenan, J. P. (2007). The self and social cognition: The role of cortical midline structures and mirror neurons. *Trends in Cognitive Sciences, 11*(4), 153–157.

Umiltà, M. A., Kohler, E., Gallese, V., Fogassi, L., Fadiga, L., Keysers, C., & Rizzolatti, G. (2001). I know what you are doing: A neurophysiological study. *Neuron, 31*(1), 155–165.

Urgesi, C., Moro, V., Candidi, M., & Aglioti, S. M. (2006). Mapping implied body actions in the human motor system. *Journal of Neuroscience, 26*(30), 7942–7949.

Yang, C.-Y., Decety, J., Lee, S., Chen, C., & Cheng, Y. (2009). Gender differences in the Mu rhythm during empathy for pain: An electroencephalographic study. *Brain Research, 1251*(0), 176–184.

8

CURRENT DOMAINS AND FUTURE DIRECTIONS

Research using EEG measures has extended behavioral work in the fields of social and personality psychology by providing measures that can be used to address important distinctions between competing theoretical perspectives that have been historically difficult to study with behavioral and/or explicit measures alone. Here, we review several other areas of research not covered in previous chapters but in which EEG studies have made important theoretical contributions. In each of these topic areas, we suggest some future directions for using this social neuroscience technique to study additional social and personality psychological research questions.

SELF-REGULATION

Self-regulation refers to the process of inhibiting a particular behavior, thought, or emotion, such as a dieter refraining from grabbing a delicious-looking cookie in the interest of maintaining a weight loss program. Because self-control is thought to be supported by an executive control system in the brain (Ellis, Rothbart, & Posner, 2004), EEG methods are well-suited for personality and social psychological investigations of these processes. Indeed, work by Amodio, Jost, Master, and Yee (2007) found that individual differences in the error-related negativity (ERN) component of the ERP, which is thought to reflect self-regulation, are related to political orientation such that stronger conservatism was associated with lower amplitude ERNs. This study extended previous self-report and behavioral work demonstrating that conservatives have a higher need for structure and closure than liberals (Jost, Glaser, Kruglanski, & Sulloway, 2003), by showing that this difference is associated with differences in self-regulation mechanisms. Studies such as this one show how EEG measures can extend our knowledge of individual differences. In addition, EEG evidence has corroborated behavioral social psychological work demonstrating that self-control is a limited resource (e.g., Baumeister & Heatherton, 1996; Muraven & Baumeister, 2000). Specifically, studies have shown that larger ERN waveforms occurred during a Stroop task following the viewing of an emotional movie in which participants suppressed their emotions compared to participants who did not suppress their emotions (Inzlicht & Gutsell, 2007). This research provided neural evidence in support of the theory that the processes involved in self-regulation are limited, and provided an ideal demonstration of how EEG measures can be used to extend current behavioral work and support social and personality psychological theories.

One area of interest among researchers interested in self-regulation is emotion regulation, which involves regulating the extrinsic and intrinsic processes involved in emotion generation, such as inhibiting facial expressions resulting from the emotional response to a particular stimulus. Because emotion regulation can involve regulating physiological and neurological activation, cognitive appraisal, and attentional processes (Thompson, 1994), EEG measures can help investigate this phenomenon. Research investigating emotion regulation processes in the brain has used EEG hemispheric asymmetry (see Chapter 6). Kim & Bell (2006) demonstrated that left frontal asymmetry was associated with greater emotional regulation skills in children. Individuals who demonstrated greater right frontal asymmetry, on the other hand, were more likely to show behavioral inhibition (Fox, Henderson, Rubin, Calkins, & Schmidt, 2001). Furthermore, a longitudinal study demonstrated that greater right frontal asymmetry was associated with more physiological arousal during an anxiety-provoking task (i.e., giving a speech) and poorer aptitude at emotion regulation (Hannesdóttir, Doxie, Bell, Ollendick, & Wolfe, 2010). Future research can aid in the understanding of how individual differences in self-regulation are related to the role that the frontal lobes play during emotion regulation in response to emotionally arousing events.

THE SELF

Social psychologists acknowledge that stimuli that have to do with the self tend to be attention-grabbing and important in the perceiver, as demonstrated by much behavioral work in the field. Social neuroscience researchers have begun to examine how the neural processing of information related to the self compares to the neural processing of information related to others. This work has shown that self-related information yields more attention than other-related information, by demonstrating that P3 amplitude is larger for participants' own name compared to others (Berlad & Pratt, 1995; Folmer & Yingling, 1997; Tacikowski & Nowicka, 2010), even among unconscious individuals (Fischer, Dailler, & Morlet, 2008). Taken together, these findings provide neural evidence for the cocktail party effect previously identified by social psychologists (Moray, 1959; Wolford & Morrison, 1980; Wood & Cowan, 1995). More recent work has examined how the processing of one's own face differs from the processing of others' faces. Although some findings suggest that hemispheric differences occur between processing faces of the self and the other, face recognition studies using fMRI and PET have found conflicting results. Because we are fast and efficient when it comes to identifying our own faces (Tong & Nakayama, 1999), EEG's ability to provide excellent temporal resolution during cognition can provide benefits over neuroimaging methods in that it can help elucidate the stages of facial recognition and provide the temporal basis for facial processing. The N170, a negative deflection occurring 140–200 ms after stimulus onset over occipito-temporal sites, has been identified as being associated with face processing, with larger amplitudes to faces relative to other stimuli (Bentin, Allison, Puce, Perez, & McCarthy, 1996; Rossion & Jacques, 2008). Keyes, Brady, Reilly, and Foxe (2010) found that larger N170 amplitudes occur following self faces compared to other faces. Research also suggests that the P3 is sensitive to this distinction, in that a larger amplitude P3 occurs to self compared to other faces (Ninomiya, Onitsuka, Chen, Sato, & Tashiro, 1998). Other work suggests that self faces induce an increased positivity compared to other faces between 220 and 700 ms at fronto-central sites (Sui, Zhu, & Han, 2006). Together, this work suggests that self faces are processed differently than other faces but it is clear that more research needs to investigate exactly at which temporal stages these differences emerge. In addition, the degree to which this processing is related to behavior and whether individual differences exist are fruitful avenues for future work.

ATTRACTION AND INTERPERSONAL RELATIONSHIPS

Research on attractiveness has found that attractiveness-related information about a face is processed within 300 ms post-stimulus and as early as 150 ms in frontal and posterior sites (Schacht, Werheid, & Sommer, 2008; Werheid, Schacht, & Sommer, 2007). Researchers have also demonstrated a correlation between LPP amplitude and the perceived beauty of faces (Johnston & Oliver-Rodriguez, 1997), which is consistent with biological models suggesting that the dopaminergic reward system is activated when individuals view attractive faces and when individuals who are infatuated with their romantic partner view pictures of their significant other (e.g., Aron et al., 2005). In support of this model, Langeslag, Jansma, Franken, and Strien (2007) found that participants who reported being in love demonstrated larger LPP amplitudes to the face of their romantic partner than the face of a friend or an unknown attractive individual, suggesting that the experience of love increases attention for the face of a significant other. Furthermore, an EEG study examining human sexual desire demonstrated that, in support of previous behavioral work showing that participants rated pictures of non-desired people more quickly than pictures of desired individuals, N2 amplitudes were able to distinguish between undesired and desired individuals of the opposite sex (Ortigue & Bianchi-Demicheli, 2008). This work revealed that the cognitive processing of sexual desire occurs earlier than previously thought and sheds some light on the neural processes involved in attraction to potential opposite-sex partners.

Researchers have also examined issues related to attachment using EEG methods. For example, Proverbio, Brignone, Matarazzo, Del Zotto, and Zani (2006) found that parents showed larger P3 amplitudes to unfamiliar infant faces than non-parents; additionally, fathers demonstrated a larger N170 amplitude to infant faces than mothers. Birth and adoptive mothers also displayed larger P3 amplitudes towards pictures of their own children compared to other children (Grasso, Moser, Dozier, & Simons, 2009). Together, these findings suggest that parental status may affect the neural processing of the P3.

As this work on attraction and interpersonal relationships has just begun, the possibilities for future research on these topics are endless, and psychologists will be able to unravel the neural processes involved in romantic attraction, friendship, and various stages of loving relationships.

THEORY OF MIND

One important area of social psychology that has recently received a lot of empirical attention is that of theory of mind, which involves an individual's ability to infer the mental states of others. This skill is clearly important in social interactions with others and can be instrumental in helping people read social situations and predict others' behaviors. To investigate the neural networks involved during theory of mind tasks, Sabbagh and Taylor (2000) measured EEG activity in college students who were thinking about another individual's belief regarding the location of objects (i.e., theory of mind task) compared with when they were thinking about another individual who took a picture of objects (i.e., control task). Results demonstrated that the theory of mind task elicited more positive ERPs over left frontal sites as well as more negative ERPs over left parietal sites compared to the matched control task from 300–840 ms post-stimulus. The authors postulated that these results identify an additional step that perceivers take when engaging in theory of mind activities. Furthermore, these findings extended previous fMRI work identifying the localization of theory of mind tasks in the brain to suggest that based on the late onset of the processing differences between the two tasks, mental representation during theory of mind is not as automatic as was previously thought. In a follow-up study to this experiment, Liu, Sabbagh, Gehring, and Wellman (2009) had normal adults engage in a task in which they reasoned about what a character was thinking (i.e., theory of mind) compared to where a character was located (i.e., control). Results demonstrated that ERP components occurring approximately 800 ms into this task diverged in the left frontal regions, consistent with processing in the left orbitofrontal cortex. More recent ERP work has further suggested that theory of mind processing is located in the left middle frontal gyrus (Zhang, Sha, Zheng, Ouyang, & Li, 2009). Together, these studies help researchers understand the neural and temporal processes involved in theory of mind judgments and help clarify the regions of the brain in which these judgments occur. Because most of the tasks in these studies involve mentalizing about a fictional character (e.g., a puppet or cartoon character), an important future direction for this research will be to examine the processing of theory of mind regarding another human individual.

PERSONALITY

Recent work has also investigated personality differences using EEG. Studies have ranged from examining personality differences in basic ERP responses to differences in the processing of various types of stimuli. This research can help illuminate the neural underpinnings of the cognitive processing differences that exist between individuals with different personality traits. For example, personality psychologists interested in subjective well-being typically identify positive affect, negative affect, and life satisfaction as three separable components (e.g., Andrews & Withey, 1976). As reviewed in Chapter 6, EEG work has contributed to our understanding of subjective well-being by demonstrating that individual differences in trait positive and negative affect are related to differences in hemispheric asymmetry (Tomarken, Davidson, Wheeler, & Doss, 1992). In addition, research by Larson, Good, and Fair (2010) found that increased satisfaction with life was associated with decreased ERN responses on trials containing errors, suggesting that errors may be less meaningful for those with higher life satisfaction. Together, these findings can add to the behavioral personality literature by revealing the underlying neural processing differences for important individual difference variables.

Researchers have also been interested in examining individual differences in anxiety sensitivity and trait anxiety. Because individuals high in anxiety are thought to have impaired cognitive control, ERP responses in a paradigm that requires cognitive control are particularly well-suited to examine cognitive processing during this task. Sehlmeyer, Konrad, Zwitserlood, Arolt, Falkenstein, & Beste (2010) presented participants with differences in anxiety sensitivity with a paradigm in which participants had to inhibit their responses on some trials. Results revealed that P3 amplitude to the trials in which participants had to inhibit their responses were significantly associated with anxiety sensitivity, suggesting that anxious individuals maintain a higher level of cognitive control than less anxious individuals. These findings can help researchers understand the ways in which individuals with differing levels of anxiety process prepare and monitor their responses that involve cognitive control.

Although only a handful of studies examining EEG processing patterns in personality variables have been conducted, these results are provocative and provide evidence that using EEG to study individual difference variables can provide interesting insight into an ever-growing field. There are many more personality traits that have yet to be examined.

CONCLUSION

As you can see from the research described in this chapter and the previous chapters in this book, EEG techniques have improved our understanding of a number of phenomena relevant to social and personality psychology. Although EEG has been used by researchers since the 1990s to study topics related to social and personality, most of this work is in its infancy and still other topics in these fields are yet to be explored. As EEG equipment and analysis software become increasingly available and accessible, the use of EEG techniques in social and personality psychology will certainly continue its rapid growth. Our hope is that, in reading this book, you are as inspired as we are to take advantage of the unique insight that EEG can provide into your own research and that you will become a part of the exciting field of social neuroscience.

REFERENCES

Amodio, D. M., Jost, J. T., Master, S. L., & Yee, C. M. (2007). Neurocognitive correlates of liberalism and conservatism. *Nature Neuroscience*, *10*(10), 1246–1247.

Andrews, F. M., & Withey, S. B. (1976). Social indicators of well-being: Americans' perceptions of life quality. New York: Plenum Press.

Aron, A., Fisher, H., Mashek, D. J., Strong, G., Li, H., & Brown, L. L. (2005). Reward, motivation, and emotion systems associated with early-stage intense romantic love. *Journal of Neurophysiology*, *94*(1), 327–337.

Baumeister, R. F., & Heatherton, T. F. (1996). Self-regulation failure: An overview. *Psychological inquiry*, *7*(1), 1–15.

Bentin, S., Allison, T., Puce, A., Perez, E., & McCarthy, G. (1996). Electrophysiological studies of face perception in humans. *Journal of Cognitive Neuroscience*, *8*(6), 551–565.

Berlad, I., & Pratt, H. (1995). P300 in response to the subject's own name. *Electro-encephalography and Clinical Neurophysiology/Evoked Potentials Section*, *96*(5), 472–474.

Ellis, L. K., Rothbart, M. K., & Posner, M. I. (2004). Individual differences in executive attention predict self-regulation and adolescent psychosocial behaviors. *Annals of the New York Academy of Sciences*, *1021*(1), 337–340.

Fischer, C., Dailler, F., & Morlet, D. (2008). Novelty P3 elicited by the subject's own name in comatose patients. *Clinical Neurophysiology*, *119*(10), 2224–2230.

Folmer, R. L., & Yingling, C. D. (1997). Auditory P3 responses to name stimuli. *Brain and Language*, *56*(2), 306–311.

Fox, N. A., Henderson, H. A., Rubin, K. H., et al. (2001). Continuity and discontinuity of behavioral inhibition and exuberance: psychophysiological and behavioral influences across the first four years of life. *Child Development*, *72*(1), 1–21.

Grasso, D. J., Moser, J. S., Dozier, M., & Simons, R. (2009). ERP correlates of attention allocation in mothers processing faces of their children. *Biological Psychology*, *81*(2), 95–102.

Hannesdóttir, D. K., Doxie, J., Bell, M. A., Ollendick, T. H., & Wolfe, C. D. (2010). A longitudinal study of emotion regulation and anxiety in middle childhood: Associations with frontal EEG asymmetry in early childhood. *Developmental Psychobiology*, *52*(2), 197–204.

Inzlicht, M., & Gutsell, J. N. (2007). Running on empty neural signals for self-control failure. *Psychological Science*, *18*(11), 933–937.

Jeong Kim, K., & Ann Bell, M. (2006). Frontal EEG asymmetry and regulation during childhood. *Annals of the New York Academy of Sciences*, *1094*(1), 308–312.

Johnston, V. S., & Oliver-Rodriguez, J. C. (1997). Facial beauty and the late positive component of event-related potentials. *Journal of Sex Research*, *34*(2), 188–198.

Jost, J. T., Glaser, J., Kruglanski, A. W., & Sulloway, F. J. (2003). Political conservatism as motivated social cognition. *Psychological Bulletin*, *129*(3), 339.

Keyes, H., Brady, N., Reilly, R. B., & Foxe, J. J. (2010). My face or yours? Event-related potential correlates of self-face processing. *Brain and Cognition*, *72*(2), 244–254.

Langeslag, S. J. E., Jansma, B. M., Franken, I. H. A., & Van Strien, J. W. (2007). Event-related potential responses to love-related facial stimuli. *Biological Psychology*, *76*(1–2), 109–115.

Larson, M. J., Good, D. A., & Fair, J. E. (2010). The relationship between performance monitoring, satisfaction with life, and positive personality traits. *Biological Psychology*, *83*(3), 222–228.

Liu, D., Sabbagh, M. A., Gehring, W. J., & Wellman, H. M. (2009). Neural correlates of children's theory of mind development. *Child Development*, *80*(2), 318–326.

Moray, N. (1959). Attention in dichotic listening: Affective cues and the influence of instructions. *Quarterly Journal of Experimental Psychology*, *11*(1), 56–60.

Muraven, M., & Baumeister, R. F. (2000). Self-regulation and depletion of limited resources: Does self-control resemble a muscle? *Psychological Bulletin*, *126*(2), 247–259.

Ninomiya, H., Onitsuka, T., Chen, C.-H., Sato, E., & Tashiro, N. (1998). P300 in response to the subject's own face. *Psychiatry and Clinical Neurosciences*, *52*(5), 519–522.

Ortigue, S., & Bianchi-Demicheli, F. (2008). The chronoarchitecture of human sexual desire: A high-density electrical mapping study. *NeuroImage*, *43*(2), 337–345.

Proverbio, A. M., Brignone, V., Matarazzo, S., Zotto, M. D., & Zani, A. (2006). Gender differences in hemispheric asymmetry for face processing. *BMC Neuroscience*, *7*(1), 44.

Rossion, B., & Jacques, C. (2008). Does physical interstimulus variance account for early electrophysiological face sensitive responses in the human brain? Ten lessons on the N170. *NeuroImage*, *39*(4), 1959–1979.

Sabbagh, M. A., & Taylor, M. (2000). Neural correlates of theory-of-mind reasoning: An event-related potential study. *Psychological Science*, *11*(1), 46–50.

Schacht, A., Werheid, K., & Sommer, W. (2008). The appraisal of facial beauty is rapid but not mandatory. *Cognitive, Affective, & Behavioral Neuroscience*, *8*(2), 132–142.

Sehlmeyer, C., Konrad, C., Zwitserlood, P., Arolt, V., Falkenstein, M., & Beste, C. (2010). ERP indices for response inhibition are related to anxiety-related personality traits. *Neuropsychologia*, *48*(9), 2488–2495.

Sui, J., Zhu, Y., & Han, S. (2006). Self-face recognition in attended and unattended conditions: an event-related brain potential study. *NeuroReport*, *17*(4), 423–427.

Tacikowski, P., & Nowicka, A. (2010). Allocation of attention to self-name and self-face: an ERP study. *Biological Psychology*, *84*(2), 318–324.

Thompson, R. A. (1994). Emotion regulation: A theme in search of definition. *Monographs of the Society for Research in Child Development*, *50*(2–3), 25–52.

Tomarken, A. J., Davidson, R. J., Wheeler, R. E., & Doss, R. C. (1992). Individual differences in anterior brain asymmetry and fundamental dimensions of emotion. *Journal of Personality and Social Psychology*, *62*(4), 676–687.

Tong, F., & Nakayama, K. (1999). Robust representations for faces: Evidence from visual search. *Journal of Experimental Psychology: Human Perception and Performance*, *25*(4), 1016.

Werheid, K., Schacht, A., & Sommer, W. (2007). Facial attractiveness modulates early and late event-related brain potentials. *Biological Psychology*, *76*(1–2), 100–108.

Wolford, G., & Morrison, F. (1980). Processing of unattended visual information. *Memory & Cognition*, *8*(6), 521–527.

Wood, N. L., & Cowan, N. (1995). The cocktail party phenomenon revisited: Attention and memory in the classic selective listening procedure of Cherry (1953). *Journal of Experimental Psychology: General*, *124*(3), 243–262.

Zhang, T., Sha, W., Zheng, X., Ouyang, H., & Li, H. (2009). Inhibiting one's own knowledge in false belief reasoning: An ERP study. *Neuroscience Letters*, *467*(3), 194–198.

Appendix

GENERATING A SIMPLE EXPERIMENT WITH PSYCHOPY

INTRODUCTION TO PSYCHOPY

PsychoPy (Peirce, 2009) is an open-source application for the design and presentation of experimental protocols for a wide range of neuroscience, psychology, and psychophysics research. PsychoPy is a free, powerful alternative to Presentation™ or E-Prime™ and is written in Python, a free alternative to Matlab™. To begin programming an experiment, you must first download and follow the installation instructions for PsychoPy (www.psychopy.org/). The following tutorial was generated using version 1.76.00. However, because PsychoPy is under perpetual development, you may notice subtle changes to the user interface. All screen captures of the PsychoPy interface were reproduced with permission.

One advantage of PsychoPy is that it offers the full flexibility of the Python programming language but additionally includes a user-friendly GUI, obviating knowledge of the Python programming language. In fact, there are three ways to generate experiments with PsychoPy. The GUI, called the 'Builder view', provides a simple user interface for anyone with or without knowledge of programming in Python. The 'Coder view' permits basic interaction with the Python code underlying the experiment generation in the Builder view and is best for individuals with some knowledge of programming, but who are less experienced with Python. Finally, the application programming interface (API) provides a complete interface between Python and PsychoPy for experienced Python programmers. In the demonstration that follows, we will provide an introduction to generating a simple experiment in the Builder view with a simple example of how to insert time-locking triggers for an EEG-based experiment.

Begin by opening the stand-alone PsychoPy application. You will notice that there are several frames internal to the GUI. The central frame displays the current timeline. This frame will be used to visualize the component timing for each routine. The components that can be part of each routine include stimulus events such as the presentation of text, images, and videos and/or response events such as key

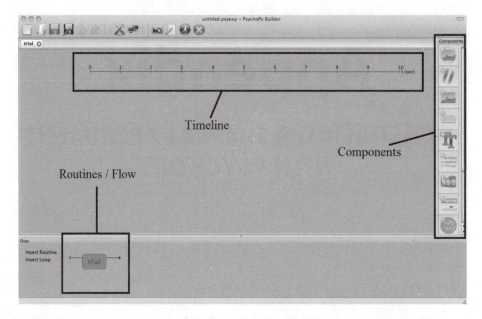

Figure A1

presses and verbal responses. Routines in PsychoPy describe the major elements of the experimental procedure. For example a 'trial' routine might contain all of the events (e.g., stimulus, response, and feedback) that constitute a single trial of the experiment. The flow of the various routines over the course of the experiment is displayed as a flowchart in the 'Flow' frame at the bottom of the GUI. Finally, the 'Components' frame on the right of the GUI provides an interactive list the various components (i.e., events) available (see Figure A1).

COMPONENTS OF THE PROTOCOL

Before beginning to build an experiment, it is important to have a clear idea about the major components of the protocol and how they will be compiled into routines and ultimately constitute the flow of the experiment. For present purposes, we will develop an experiment that is similar to that used by Dickter and Gyurovski (2012) which was used to generate the data for the guided analysis in Chapter 5. Briefly, the protocol involved an impression-formation procedure wherein participants' expectations regarding the race of a subsequent target were persuaded by a descriptive sentence read by participants immediately prior to seeing a target image consisting of a Black or White male. The sentences could be positive or negative in valence and consistent with stereotypes associated with either Black or White Americans. Target stimuli consisted of headshot photographs of Black and White males. Each trial consisted of a fixation cross which appeared for 500 ms, followed by the impression-formation sentence (which remained on the screen until participants indicated by button press that they had finished reading),

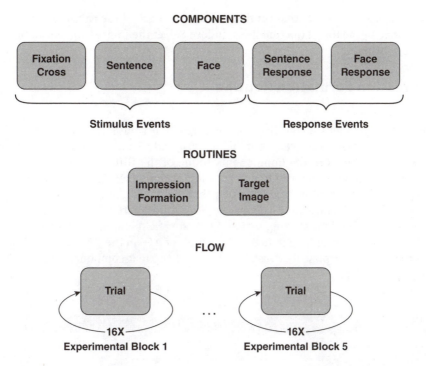

Figure A2

followed by the target face, which remained on the screen for 500 ms. Participants were asked to indicate whether the target could be the person described in the preceding sentence by pressing one of two keys on the keyboard. The inter-trial interval (ITI) varied randomly between 2000 and 4000 ms. The experimental task included five blocks of 16 trials each. EEG data were time-locked to the onset of the target faces. From this description, the major elements of the protocol can be distilled in terms of components, routines, and flow. These elements are depicted in Figure A2.

As is illustrated in Figure A2, the procedure can be conceptualized as consisting of two primary routines. The first is the Impression Formation Routine, which begins with a fixation cross and ends when the participant responds to indicate he/she is finished reading the impression formation sentence. The second is the Target Image routine, which presents the target image and then collects the participant's response regarding the perceived association between the content of the sentence and the individual pictured in the target image. Thus, the first step is to create placeholders for these two routines. Click 'Insert Routine' button on the left side of the 'Flow' frame at the bottom of the GUI and select '(new)'. Enter a name for the first routine (e.g., 'Impression Formation') and click 'OK'. Then click on a position to the right of the default 'Trial' routine in the flowchart in order to place the new routine. Repeat this process to create a Target Image routine to the left of the Impression Formation routine. Finally, right-click the default 'Trial' routine and select 'Remove' to delete that routine. Notice that each of the routines has its own tab labeled at the top of the timeline window. Select the Impression Formation tab before continuing.

Impression Formation Routine

Fixation Cross

The first component of the Impression Formation routine is the fixation cross, which is presented to the center of the monitor and remains on screen for 500 ms. Click the 'Text' icon in the Components frame of the GUI. This will open a 'Text Properties' dialog with various presentation options (see Figure A3). There are many parameters that can be set using this dialog. For present purposes, enter 'Fixation' in the 'Name $' field, change the 'Stop' duration to 0.5 seconds, change the color to black by right-clicking inside the 'Color' field and using the color-picker, and change the 'Letter height' to 0.1. Finally, enter a '+' in the 'Text' field (this is the text that will be displayed). Press 'OK' to insert the text component into the Trial routine's timeline.

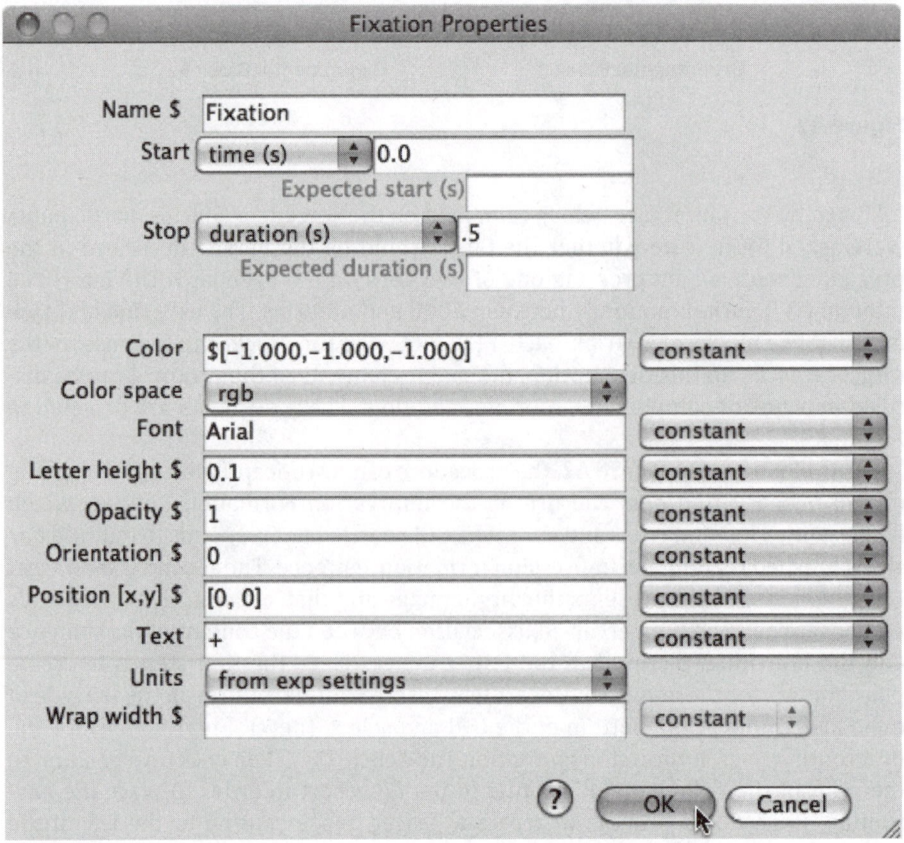

Figure A3

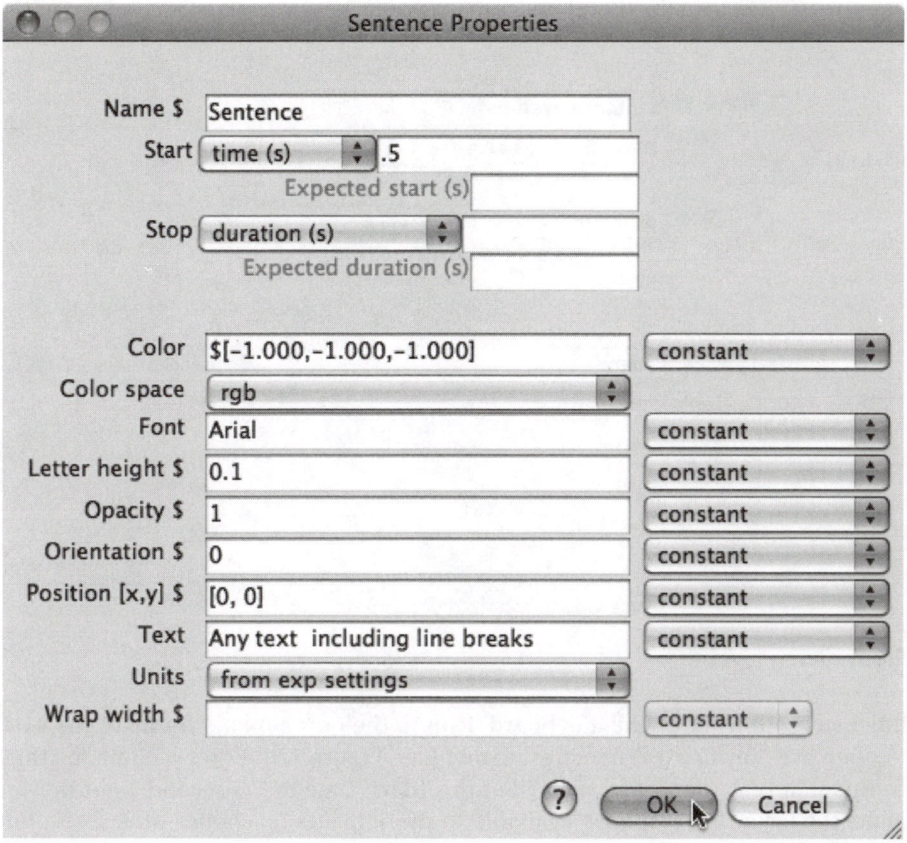

Figure A4

Sentence

The next component of each trial is the impression-formation sentence, which is displayed to the screen until the participant presses a key to indicate that he/she has finished reading. Again, click the 'Text' icon in the Components frame of the GUI to open a new 'Text Properties' dialog (see Figure A4). This time, enter 'Sentence' for the name, set the 'Start time (s)' to 0.5 so that the sentence appears immediately following the fixation cross. Next, set the stop duration to infinite by leaving the field blank, and set the color to black. Entering the literal text of each sentence into the 'Text' field (like we did with the fixation cross) would require the creation of as many separate text displays as there were sentences to be presented. Instead, we will take advantage of PsychoPy's ability to load information from external files and use the information in those lists to automatically populate the 'Text' field on each trial. For now, simply leave the default value of the 'Text' field. Press 'OK' to insert the Sentence component into the timeline.

Sentence Response

Recall that we set the duration of the Sentence component to be infinite. Thus, we need a way to terminate the display of the sentence once the participant has

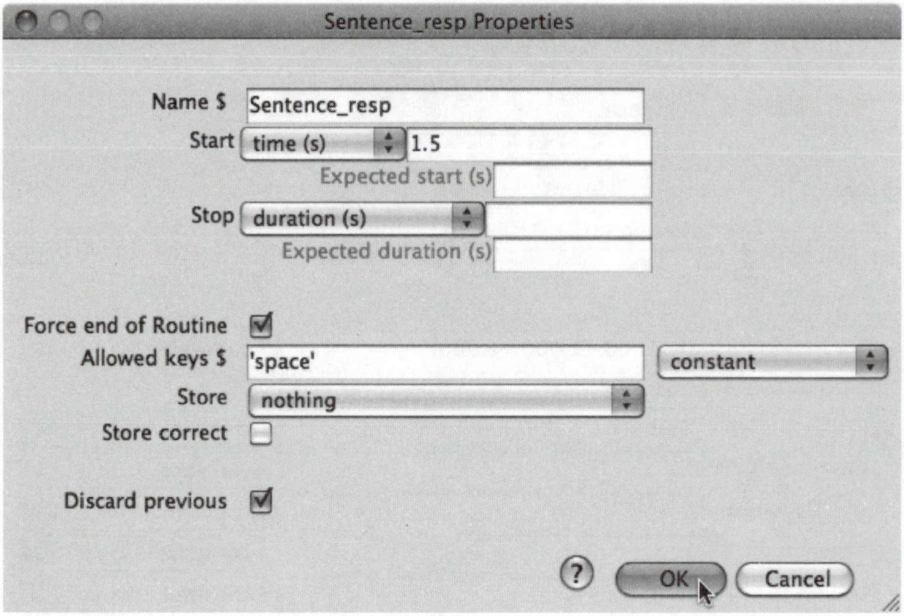

Figure A5

finished reading. Click the 'Keyboard' icon in the Components frame of the GUI to open the 'Keyboard Properties' dialog (see Figure A5). Enter a name for this component (e.g., 'Sentence_resp'). Set the 'Start' time to 1.5 seconds in order to make the keyboard response available to participants no sooner than 1 second following the onset of the sentence (recall that the first 0.5 seconds of the routine consists only of the fixation cross). Next, set the 'Stop' duration to be infinite (by leaving the field blank). This will cause the experiment to pause indefinitely until a response is pressed. Check the box next to 'Force end of Routine'. Enter the word 'space' (including quotation marks) into the 'Allowed keys $' field so that the only legal response to the sentence is the spacebar. Finally, use the drop-down menu to set the value of the 'Store' parameter to 'nothing' since we are not interested in logging response data here.

Target Image Routine
Before continuing to construct the Target Image routine, be sure to select the 'Target Image' tab at the top of the timeline window. Notice that the timeline associated with the Target Image routine is empty.

Target Image
The first component of the Target Image routine is the image itself. Click the 'Image' component in the Components frame on the right to open the 'Image Properties' dialog (see Figure A6). Enter a name for the image component (e.g., 'TargetImage') and set the Start time and duration to 0.0 and 0.5 seconds

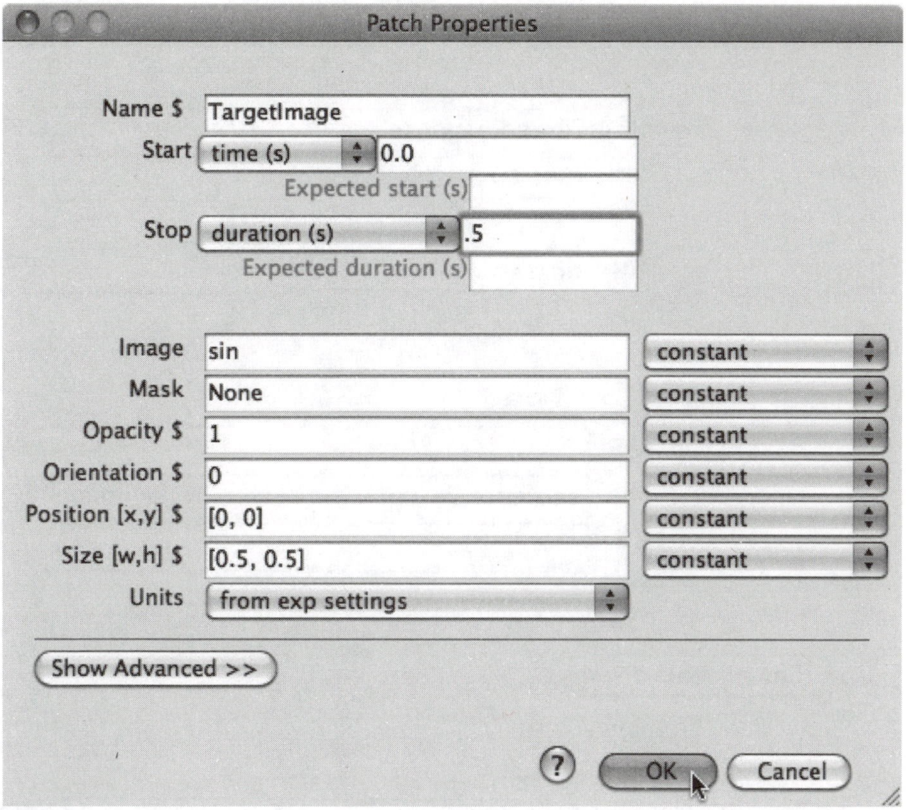

Figure A6

respectively. Leave the 'Image' field at its default value. Similar to the Sentence component above, we will later use PsychoPy's ability to import trial information from an external file so that it is not necessary to create a separate image component for each of the faces we wish to show. Click 'OK' to place the TargetImage component in the timeline.

Target Response
The second component of the Target Image routine is the response by the participant, indicating whether they believe that the sentence described the person in the target image. This can be accomplished in the same way that responses were required following presentation of the sentence in the Impression Formation routine. In short, we will present a text message following the target image and then place a keyboard component to collect the response. In the TargetImage routine, click the 'Text' component to add the message text and open the 'Text Properties' dialog (see Figure A7). Enter a name for the component in the 'Name' field (e.g., 'TargetResponseText'). Enter 0.5 for the 'Start' time so that it immediately follows the target image. Set the 'Stop' time to be infinite (i.e., leave field

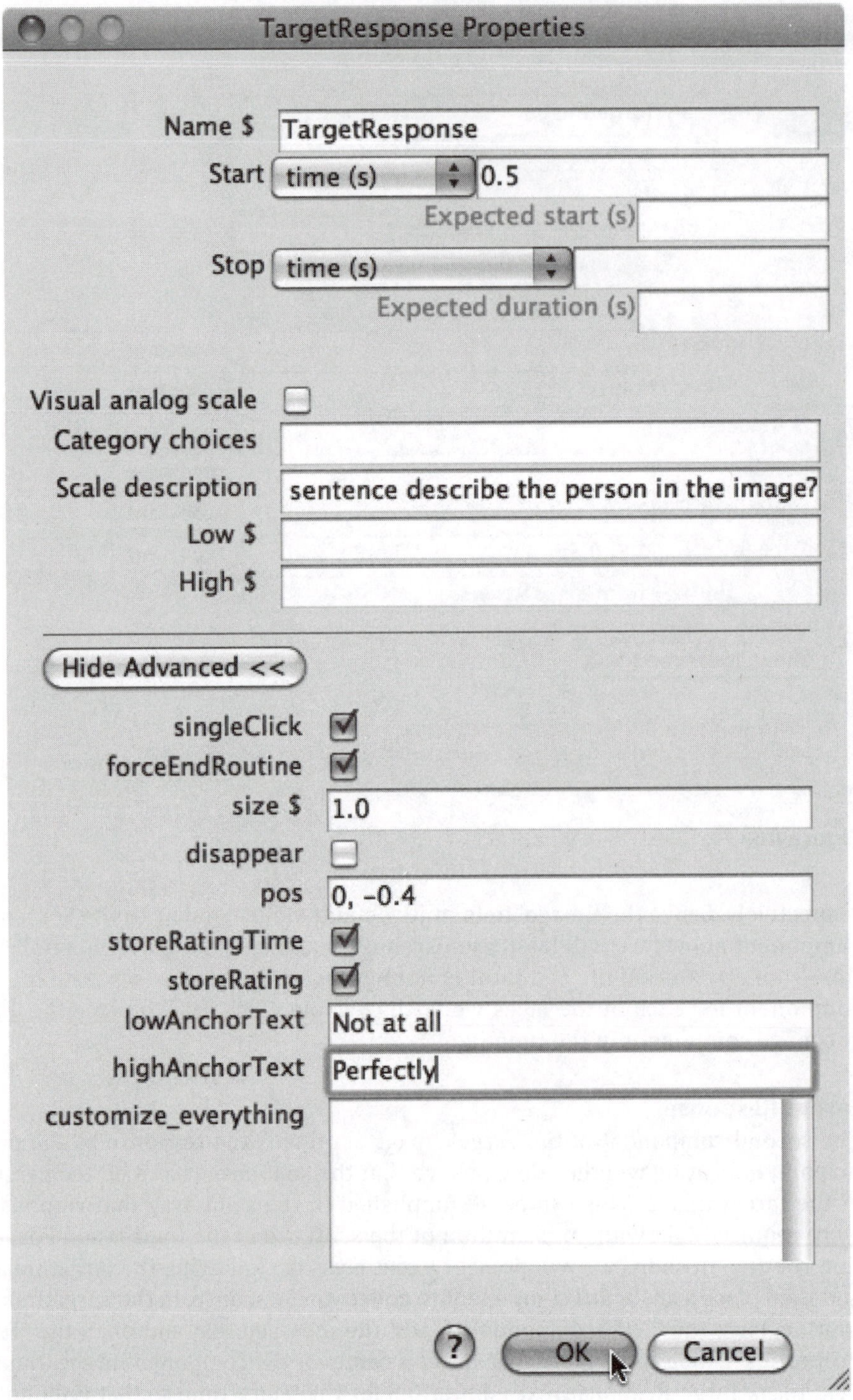
TargetResponse Properties
Name $
TargetResponse
Start
time (s)
0.5
Expected start (s)
Stop
time (s)
Expected duration (s)
Visual analog scale
Category choices
Scale description
sentence describe the person in the image?
Low $
High $
Hide Advanced <<
singleClick
forceEndRoutine
size $
1.0
disappear
pos
0, -0.4
storeRatingTime
storeRating
lowAnchorText
Not at all
highAnchorText
Perfectly
customize_everything
?
OK
Cancel

Figure A7

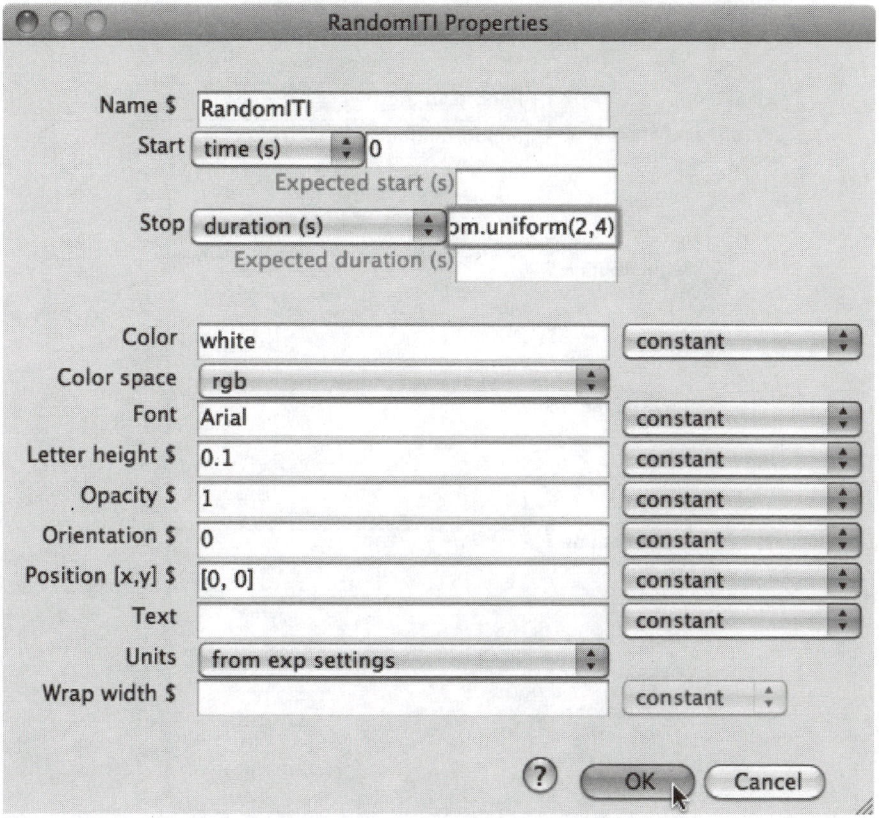

Figure A8

blank) so that the component remains on screen indefinitely or until a response is made. Set the color to black. Enter the text message for participants in the 'Text' field (e.g., 'Does the sentence describe the person in the image? ... Enter Y for YES or N for NO'). Click 'OK' to insert the text component into the timeline. Next, click to add a 'Keyboard' component. Enter a name (e.g., 'TargetResponse') for the component. Set the start time to 0.5 so that response collection becomes available at the offset of the target image and set the duration to be infinite (i.e., leave the 'Stop' field empty). Next, enter 'y','n' in the 'Allowed keys $' field. Finally, ensure that the 'Force end of Routine' option is selected and that 'last key' is selected for the 'Store' option (this tells PsychoPy to record the response made by participants).

Having created the two primary routines for the experiment, the next step is to consider the flow of the experiment. For example, Dickter and Gyurovski (2012) separated each trial by an inter-trial interval that varied randomly between 2 and 4 seconds. One simple way to place an interval between trials is to add a routine with a blank Text component that follows Target Image routine. Click the 'Insert Routine' button on the bottom left of the GUI and select '(new)'. Type a name for the

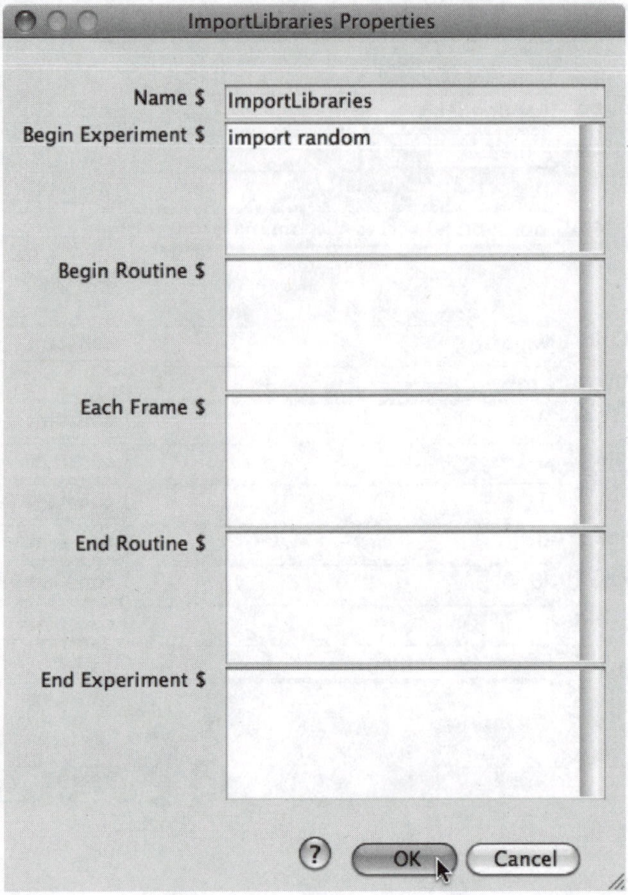

Figure A9

new routine (e.g., 'ITI') and press 'OK'. Click on the icon for the new ITI routine in the flowchart and then click to add a Text component (see Figure A8). Give the component a name (e.g., 'RandomITI'), leave the 'Start' time at 0 seconds and set the 'Stop' duration to 'random.uniform(2,4)', which is a python function that will return a random number drawn from a uniform distribution over the interval 2 to 4 seconds. Then delete any text in the 'Text' field and press 'OK'.

Because the RandomITI component uses the 'random.uniform' function, which is not available by default in PsychoPy, it is necessary to import the 'random' library (a collection of functions) when the experiment is executed. To do this, click the 'Code' component in the Components frame to open the 'Code Properties' dialog. Code components permit the insertion of Python code into an experiment, providing a great deal of additional flexibility. Enter a name for the component (e.g., 'ImportLibraries') and enter the text 'import random' to the 'Begin Experiment' field, then click 'OK' (see Figure A9).

USING LOOPS TO CREATE BLOCKS OF TRIALS

At this point all of the components necessary to generate a block of trials are now in place. Each trial will begin with the Impression Formation routine, followed by the Target Image and ITI routines. Trial blocks can be created in PsychoPy using a 'loop' that will repeat the presentation of these routines a number of times. Click the 'Insert Loop' button at the bottom left corner of the GUI. Then click at a point just to the left of the Impression Formation routine and then again at a point just to the right of the ITI routine to indicate the start and end points in the loop. When the 'Loop Properties' dialog appears (see Figure A10), enter a name for the loop (e.g., 'BlockLoop') and set the 'nReps' field to 1 (this will make sense soon). The experiment now consists of a single trial, as described by Dickter and Gyurovski (2012), and should appear similar to Figure A11. You may want to save your experiment at this point by selecting 'File>Save as' and entering a name for the experiment (e.g., 'MyExperiment.psyexp').

The purpose of this loop added in the previous step is to repeat the series of components that make up each trial. Setting the 'nReps' field of the BlockLoop properties dialog to 16 would yield a full block of 16 trial repetitions, but the text of the sentence presented by the Sentence component and the image presented by the TargetImage component would be the same on each cycle of the loop. Recall that we earlier left the 'Text' field of the Impression Formation component and the 'Image' field of the Target Image component at their default values because we would later add functions to automatically populate the fields using a list of trial parameters. In order to automatically populate those fields on each cycle of the loop, we will attach a list of values to the BlockLoop loop. This list can be conveniently stored in either a comma-delimited (i.e., CSV) text file or a Microsoft™ Excel spreadsheet (XLSX format only!). The list must be formatted such that the values of each variable are listed in a separate column and the first row of the list contains

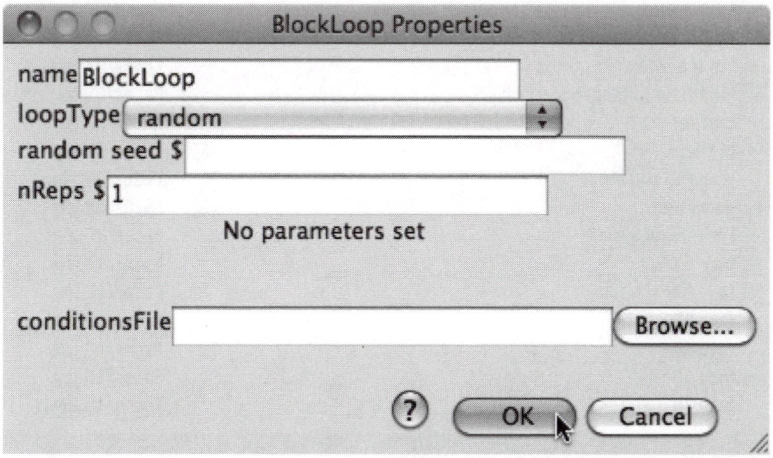

Figure A10

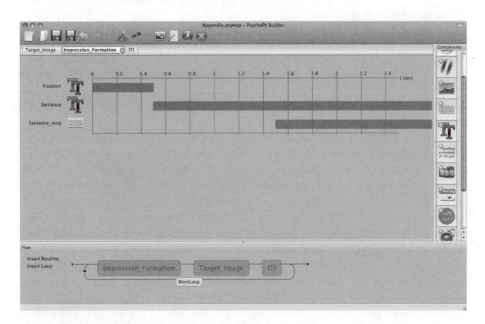

Figure A11

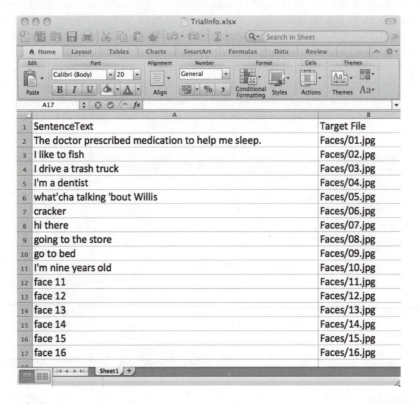

Figure A12

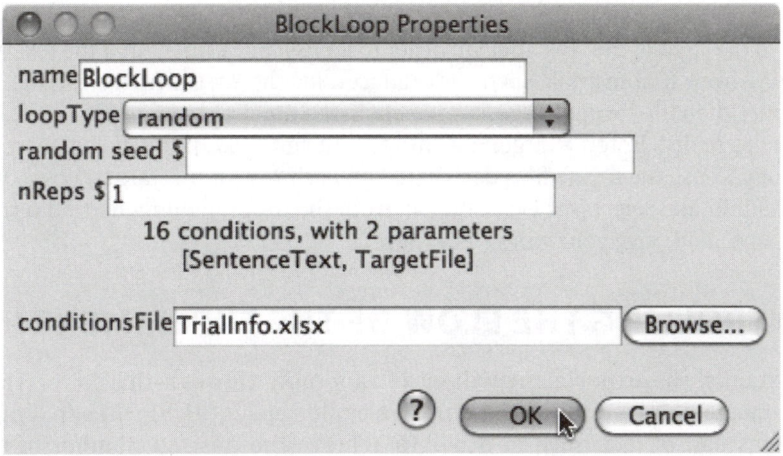

Figure A13

variable labels. For example, in order to provide PsychoPy with a unique sentence for each cycle of the Impression Formation component and a unique image for each cycle of the Target Image component, we will generate a list with two columns, one labeled 'SentenceText' and the other labeled 'TargetFile'. Each row of the Sentence-Text column contains a complete sentence to be used by the Impression Formation component. Each row of the TargetFile column contains the complete file path of an image file. Images for this sample experiment were generated using the FaceGen Modeler software (Toronto, ON; www.facegen.com) and can be found in the 'Faces' folder on the companion website (www. sagepub.co.uk/dickter). Be sure to place a copy of the 'Faces' folder in the same directory as your PsychoPy experiment. Finally, create a comma-delimited list using your favorite text editor (see Figure A12) or MS™ Excel and save the file to the same directory as your experiment (e.g., 'TrialInfo.csv').

Once the list has been created, it is necessary to attach the list to the BlockLoop loop. Click once on the 'BlockLoop' label in the flowchart inside the 'Flow' frame to open the 'BlockLoop Properties' dialog. Click the 'Browse' button next to the 'conditionsFile' field and then select the 'TrialInfo.xlsx' file created in the previous step. If the file loads without any errors, the number of conditions (i.e., trials; 16) and parameters (i.e., columns; 2) will be displayed inside the 'BlockLoop Properties' window (see Figure A13).

Notice that because the list has 16 conditions, a single cycle of the BlockLoop loop is interpreted as one cycle of the list of 16 trials. Next, it is necessary to instruct the Sentence component about which column of the list contains the sentences and instruct the Target Image component about which column contains the image file-names we wish to display. Click the icon for the Impression Formation routine in the flowchart, then click on the Sentence component (anywhere in the timeline) to open the Sentence properties. Type '$SentenceText' into the 'Text' field of the properties dialog and click 'OK'. The dollar symbol instructs PsychoPy that what follows is the name of a variable (i.e., parameter) rather than the literal text we wish to display. In this case, the variable 'SentenceText' refers to that column of the 'TrialInfo' file attached to the loop. It is also necessary to select 'set every repeat' in the drop-down menu to the right of the 'Text' field in order to let PsychoPy know that the text will be changing from trial to trial. Next, click the icon for the Target Image routine in the flowchart, then the Target Image component in the timeline to open the Target Image properties dialog. Enter '$TargetFile' into the 'Image' field of the dialog, instructing PsychoPy to use the image files designated on each row of the TargetFile column in the TrialInfo file. Select 'set every repeat' from the drop-down menu to the right of the 'Image' field. Save your work ('File>Save').

CONTROLLING THE FLOW OF THE EXPERIMENT

As it stands, the experiment will cycle randomly through the list of 16 sentence-image pairs a total of one time. We could repeat the BlockLoop loop four times instead of just once in order to achieve the desired number of trials; however, doing so would simply repeat the trials seamlessly in one block of 64 trials. The purpose of dividing the trials into blocks of 16 is usually to provide participants with a chance to rest periodically throughout the experiment. Thus, it is necessary to provide an occasional respite from the experiment, by placing a break routine to follow the BlockLoop loop. Click 'Insert Routine' in the Flow frame of the GUI and select '(new)'. Type a name (e.g., 'Break') for the break routine, press 'OK', and place the Break to the right of the BlockLoop loop (see Figure A14). Now select the Break routine and add two components to the timeline. Add a Text component that includes a brief text message to the participants, such as, 'Take a break and press any key when you are ready to

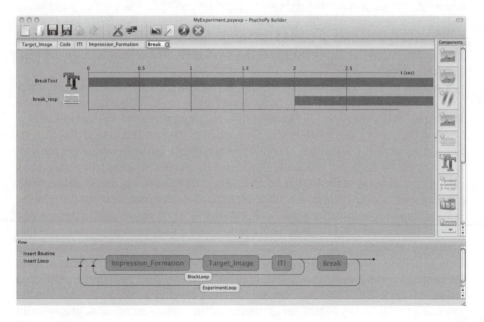

Figure A14

continue'. Set the start time of the Text component to zero and set its duration to infinite (i.e., leave the 'Duration' field blank). Next, add the 'Keyboard' component. Set the start time of the keyboard component to 1 and the duration to be infinite. Leave the 'Allowed keys' field empty (this will permit any response) and select the check-box for 'Force end of routine', which will force termination of the Break routine as soon as a key is pressed and allow the experiment to proceed.

Notice that the Break routine, combined with the components of the Block-Loop loop, constitutes all of the elements needed for the experimental procedure – that is, a block of 16 trials followed by a brief break. All that is needed is to instruct PsychoPy to repeat these routines a total of four times using a routine loop. Click 'Insert Loop' and then click on the left side of Impression Formation routine in the flowchart to indicate where the loop will start and then click to the right of the Break routine to indicate where the loop will stop. Enter a name for the loop (e.g., 'ExperimentLoop') and set the 'nReps' field to 4. The ExperimentLoop loop will repeat the BlockLoop and Break routines a total of four times (see Figure A14), yielding the desired total number of 64 trials separated into blocks of 16.

If you were to run the experiment at this point, the program would immediately begin with the first trial. Although verbal instructions can be provided to the participant prior to execution of the task, it is common to present task instructions to the computer screen. To add an instructions screen at the beginning of the experiment, click the 'Insert Routine' button in the Flow frame and select '(new)'. Provide a name for the new routine (e.g., 'Instructions') and place it at the very beginning of the flow chart. Next, click the new Instructions icon in the flowchart to view its timeline. Add a Text component to the timeline and name it 'InstructionsText'. Set 'Duration' to be infinite (leave it blank), change the 'Color' property of the InstructionsText component to black and enter the text of the instructions into the 'Text' field. Next, add a keyboard component and give it a name (e.g., 'Inst_resp'). Set the duration to be infinite and leave the 'Allowed keys' field blank (i.e., any response is allowed). Be sure the 'Force end of Routine' option is selected and click 'OK'. The Instructions routine will now display the InstructionsText component and wait (indefinitely) for a keypress. Once a key is pressed, the routine will terminate and PsychoPy will move on to the ExperimentLoop routine. The experiment is now ready to run. Save your work!

ADDING TRIGGERS FOR TIME-LOCKING ERPS

At this point, the experiment is complete. However, if one wishes to use the experiment in conjunction with EEG recordings, it is necessary to add a little Python code for sending event triggers over the parallel port to an EEG acquisition system. In fact, there are a number of ways to accomplish this task of interacting with the parallel port and not all solutions will work with all systems. Solutions will sometimes also vary by operating system (e.g., Windows, Mac, Linux), making it difficult to provide a complete guide for setting up EEG triggers. Here, we provide an outline of just one solution that worked in our lab on both Windows XP (32-bit) and Windows 7 (32-bit) computers. There are two prerequisite steps that must be completed prior to modifying the PsychoPy experiment to send event triggers. The first requirement is that a 'driver' must be installed that permits communication between Python and the parallel port. The present method of event triggering will make use of the 'DLPOR-TIO' (short for DriverLINX Port I/O) driver, which is widely used and freely available on the Web (a self-installing executable is available from http://real. kiev.ua/2010/11/29/dlportio-and-32-bit-windows/). The second prerequisite is that one must know the physical 'address' of the parallel port on the computer. This can most easily be obtained in Windows by the following steps: (1) click the 'Start' button, (2) right-click 'Computer' (or 'My Computer' if using Windows XP), (3) select 'Manage', (4) click 'Device Manager' in the left frame of the Computer Management window, (5) click the '+' symbol next to 'Ports (COM & LTP)', (6) right-click the label referring to your parallel port in the list of devices and select 'Properties', (7) click the 'Resources' tab in the Properties window. The port's address will be listed in hexadecimal format next to the label 'I/O Range'. The hexadecimal address (e.g., D050) can be converted to decimal format (e.g., 53328), which is the address of the port that will be provided to PsychoPy.

The primary aim of this experiment is to measure ERPs to the onset of the face stimuli. Thus, the goal is to send event triggers that are synchronized to the onset of the Target Image component of the Target_Image routine. To insert the event triggers, select the Target_Image routine to view its associated timeline. Next, click the 'Code' component in the Components frame to open the 'Code Properties' dialog. Give the Code component a name (e.g., 'Trigger') and fill in the fields of the 'Code Properties' dialog as specified in Figure A15, replacing '53328' with the parallel port address retrieved in the previous step. Note that you should check the resolution of the digital input on your EEG amplifier. Digital inputs commonly have a resolution of 8 bits, meaning that they can only resolve 256 (2^8) unique values, meaning that you will only be able to use event trigger values ranging from 1 to 256.

Table A1

Field Name	Value	Explanation
Begin Experiment	from psychopy import parallel	Import the 'parallel' module
	parallel.setPortAddress(#)	Set the 'address' of the parallel port to #
Begin Routine	parallel.setData(VALUE)	Send a trigger value to the port
Each Frame		
End Routine	parallel.setData(0)	Close the port by sending a value of 0
End Experiment		

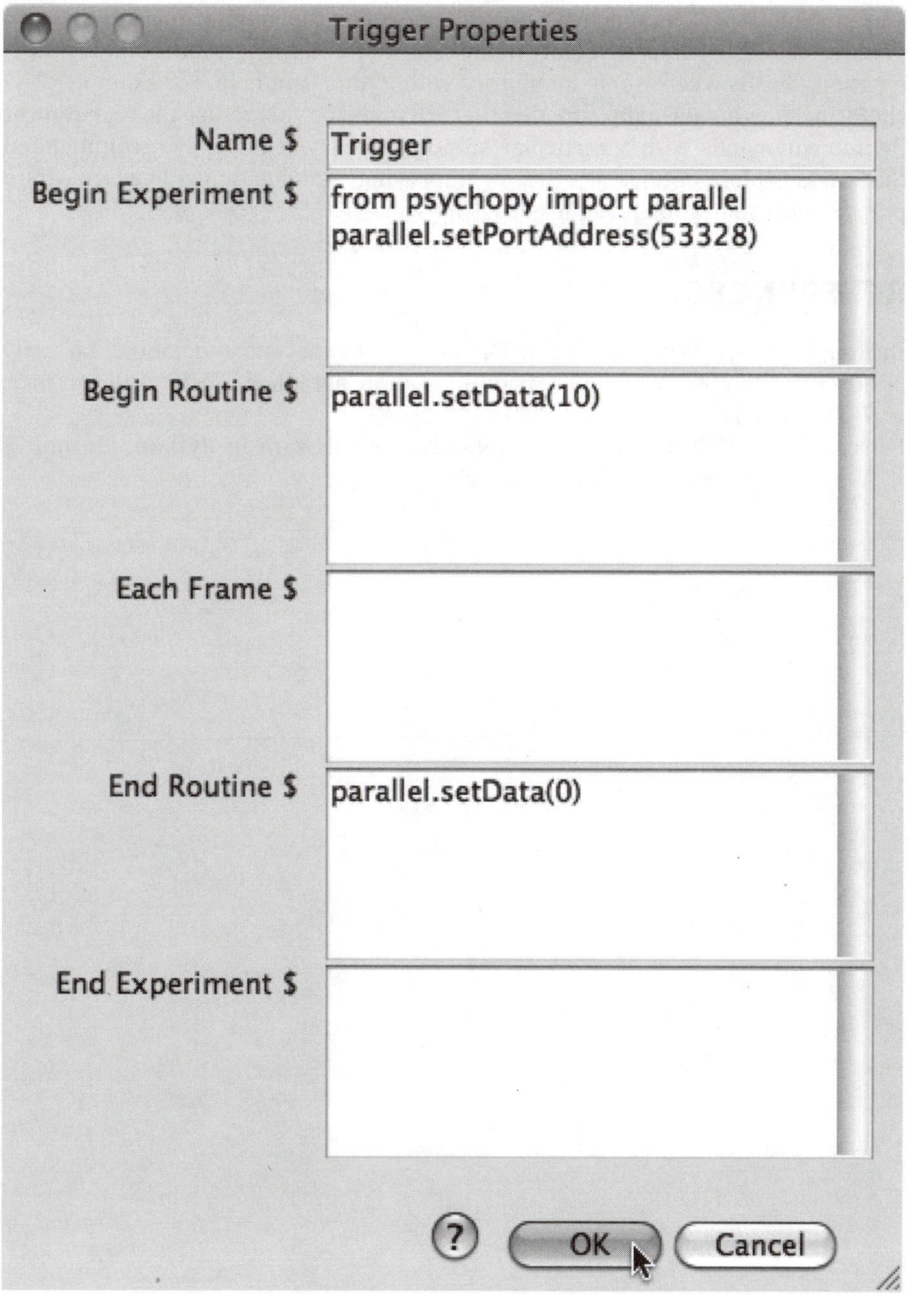

Figure A15

These instructions describe EEG trigger synchronization in its most elementary form. That is, the program was instructed to send a trigger at the same time that it began the Target Image routine. In practice, however, the start time of a Routine and the time at which an image actually appears on the monitor may not be very precise, leading to some variability in the timing of EEG triggers and stimulus presentation. This is where some familiarity with Python can help. For example, PsychoPy includes a 'callOnFlip' function that attempts to synchronize the execution of Python commands with a particular stimulus display. It is highly recommended that users explore options like this for improving stimulus timing in cases where precise synchronization is required.

REFERENCES

Dickter, C., & Gyurovski, I. (2012). The effects of expectancy violations on early attention to race in an impression-formation paradigm. *Social Neuroscience*, *7*(3), 240–251.

Peirce, J.W. (2007). PsychoPy - Psychophysics software in Python. *Journal of Neuroscience Methods*, 162(1–2), 8–13.

INDEX